I0442167

NDIC PRESS
NATIONAL DEFENSE INTELLIGENCE COLLEGE

Imperial Secrets
Remapping the
Mind of Empire

Patrick A. Kelley
Major, U.S. Army
Director of National Intelligence
and
National Defense Intelligence College
Research Fellow

NATIONAL DEFENSE INTELLIGENCE COLLEGE
WASHINGTON, DC
October 2008

The views expressed in this work are those of the author and do not reflect the policy or position of the Department of Defense or the U.S. Government

NDIC PRESS

The National Defense Intelligence College supports and encourages research that distills lessons and improves Intelligence Community capabilities for policy-level and operational consumers

Imperial Secrets: Remapping the Mind of Empire—Major Patrick A. Kelley, U.S. Army.

In this work, Patrick Kelley interprets the intelligence environment of political, military and information empires. His contribution sheds light on the cause of enduring intelligence collection deficits that afflict the center of such empires, and that can coincide with their ebb and flow. Alert intelligence practitioners, present and future, can note here just how useful a fresh interpretation of the intelligence enterprise can be to a coherent understanding of the global stream of worrisome issues. The long-term value of this work will be realized as readers entertain the implications of Churchill's comment that "The empires of the future are the empires of the mind."

The manuscript for this book was reviewed by scholars and intelligence practitioners, and was approved for public release by the Department of Defense's Office of Security Review.

Russell.Swenson@dia.mil,
Editor and Director
Center for Strategic Intelligence Research
and NDIC Press

CONTENTS

CONTENTS (continued)

CONTENTS (continued)

ACKNOWLEDGMENTS

In the past, I have tended to skip over "Acknowledgements" pages in my rush to get to the substance of a given work. After completing this project, it is a mistake I will not make in the future. I realize now the spare list of names on pages like this may well reflect collective time and effort equal to, if not exceeding, that of the primary author—this is certainly so in my case.

First and foremost, my thanks go out to Russell Swenson and his associates at the National Defense Intelligence College. Readers who dip even a few pages into the text at hand will quickly realize this project represents something of an intellectual experiment, and consequently a risk. Dr. Swenson's willingness to take that chance, and his fortitude in managing the risk as we went along, has proven decisive in bringing this work to print.

Other risks were taken by my military chain of command, for which I am equally grateful. In order to support this program, my superiors at the U.S. Pacific Command Joint Intelligence Operations Center essentially sacrificed a key Joint, by-name nomination billet without backfill during the course of my research. Nevertheless, they unstintingly provided workspace, travel and administrative support—and most importantly time, free of distraction.

The work at hand is not necessarily the work I wanted to create when these ideas first came to mind. To compose that ideal text would have required three or four PhDs in the Classics, European and Ottoman history, along with a supporting MA or two in linguistics, anthropology and philosophy. To even attempt this project with my rather more modest background was ambitious, to say the least, although foolhardy also comes to mind. By extraordinary good fortune, however (far more than I deserve), I enjoyed the counsel, wisdom and guidance provided by a host of first-rate academic minds. Mentors from my years at graduate school—chief among them Carla Sinopoli and Barbara and Thomas Metcalf—provided initial inspiration, guidance and personal introductions to scholars otherwise far out of my league. Even more critically, real yeoman's work was done by Dane Kennedy, Thomas McGinn, James Der Derian, and Nayanjot Lahiri. Along with Dr. Swenson, each of them contributed enormously through sharing their ideas, prompting avenues for further research, and—perhaps most arduously—through multiple readings of the maturing draft text. The wide variety of backgrounds, institutions, academic disciplines and philosophical perspectives represented by these names suggests how fruitful more interchange between academia and the security establishment can be for those willing to plow beyond the more traditional political-military fields.

Last but not least, my wife, Kori, should certainly be considered a candidate for beatitude, if not outright sainthood, for her shared labor in this project. She read draft after draft (cumulatively, she has probably read more of it than I have), put up with the weird hours and extended travel, and managed gracefully the careful balance between pointed criticism and unfailing support.

I am honored to be associated in any capacity with all those named above, although it is perhaps worth emphasizing strongly here at the outset that any and all flaws in the text that follows are entirely my own.

COMMENTARIES

Good intelligence, in both senses of the word, has been notably missing in U.S. foreign policy over the past several years. Skillfully moving from the Roman to the Ottoman to the British empires, adeptly applying ideas from a wide range of Eastern and Western philosophies, Patrick Kelley has produced a remarkable set of lessons-yet-to-be-learned for the United States. Full of trans-historical and cross-cultural insights, this is the perfect supplement and essential sequel to the U.S. Army and Marine Corps Counter-Insurgency Field Manual. Francis Bacon said knowledge is power: Kelley makes it so.

James Der Derian, Director,
Global Security Program, Watson Institute for
International Studies, Brown University

******

Patrick Kelley is that rare scholar-soldier who has dared to be self-reflexive. His monograph on "Imperial Intelligence" is carefully researched and lucidly written. Considering how crucial the question of intelligence gathering is, an understanding of its history should be of great interest to scholars, to statesmen, to intelligence gathering departments, and to interested non-specialist readers as well.

Nayanjot Lahiri, Professor,
Department of History,
University of Delhi, India

******

As Patrick Kelley observes near the close of this book, "all intelligence is fundamentally historicized." One of the main reasons we study history is to escape the insularity of the present, to overcome the unwarranted exceptionalism that so often afflicts our sense of ourselves, to remind us that the problems we face can be found to echo those of our predecessors. Kelley brings an historical perspective brilliantly to bear on contemporary America's intelligence capabilities and limitations, identifying its "way of knowing" as a distinctively imperial one and demonstrating that it shares much in common with the intelligence challenges of the Roman, the Ottoman, and the British empires.

Kelley identifies two interrelated dimensions to the problem of imperial intelligence. The first concerns the cultural and structural constraints that limit empires' efforts to gather intelligence. Challenging the view that empires' military and technological superiority gives them an intelligence advantage over their enemies, he argues instead that empires "are always at an information deficit." The problem isn't the dearth of information per se, but the failure to discern what elements of that information are important. This is rooted in turn in empires' distrust of difference and difficulties in cultivating the cross-cultural agents and institutions that are capable of making sense of the unfamiliar. This brings us to the second dimension of his analysis, which stresses the need to recognize that imperial intelligence operates within the confines of its own epistemological frame of reference. Its way of knowing the world is often profoundly at odds with those of its enemies, thereby constraining its ability to acquire meaningful intelligence about them. Kelley makes sophisticated use of postmodernist theories of knowledge to show that the sheer accumulation of "objective" information will never overcome this information deficit; we must instead acquire a more sophisticated appreciation of our own subjectivity and extend that appreciation to others if we are to make sense of their motives and intentions.

Imperial Secrets, then, is a challenging but hugely rewarding book. It is challenging in its deliberate disruption of conventional narrative patterns, its restless movement across the boundaries of time and space, and its frequent reference to the insights of recondite postmodernist theorists. But it is rewarding for the remarkable range of its historical examples, the relentless rigor of its comparative analysis, and, above all, the compelling way it obliges us to rethink the epistemological premises that inform our approach to the problem of intelligence. Others are far more qualified than I to speak to this book's value to specialists in military intelligence, but I can declare with confidence that this work will be welcomed and admired by historians and other scholars who study empires. It is an important and exciting contribution to our understanding of empires and their regimes of knowledge.

Dane Kennedy
Elmer Louis Kayser Professor of History and International Affairs
George Washington University, Washington, DC

******

I found this monograph interesting, as readers who take the time to tackle this complex work will agree. The author's central thesis is that the post 9/11 problems which the U.S. Intelligence Community faces are those "which have not been faced by traditional nation-states, but by 'historical imperial formations.'" He posits that in confronting these challenges the American IC needs to "[remap] the mind of empire" in order to find and understand the information flowing from its targets.

Major Kelley chooses three empires with which to at least implicitly compare our current intelligence circumstances. Each of these in turn faced challenges in understanding their empire's peoples; Rome in the first and second centuries of the Common Era, Ottoman Turkey in the sixteenth to eighteenth, and Britain in India in the eighteenth to early twentieth. He feels these warrant examination in light of our need to deal with peoples not subject to the U.S. in the traditional imperial sense, but whom we may seek to influence, principally to stop them from objecting to our "lawful" actions in our commercial and social interactions with their societies.

The author poses a key question: "If power shapes knowledge, does knowledge also shape power?" He notes that the ancient Indian strategist Kautilya "argued that state power rests fundamentally upon near-omniscient state knowledge." He then juxtaposes Kautilya's declaration with English jurist and reformer Jeremy Bentham's concept of Panopticism, in that "where Kautilya established a surveillance system through social networks, Bentham… [would have achieved] this end architecturally." In seeking to help us understand the intelligence problem confronting empires, Major Kelley briefly addresses the modern critic of Bentham, Michel Foucault, "who essentially established 'Panopticism' as a byword for a whole spectrum of state surveillance and disciplinary activities." One is reminded of chilling images of the power, knowledge, and omniscience developed in George Orwell's *1984*. However, the author sharply brings readers back to the reality of our own time and problems by noting that:

> The Panopticon actually operates in reverse in the imperial context. In a system of information exchange, empires will nearly always operate at an information deficit in relation to their subjects.

This, as he notes, runs counter to the demand that the IC "know something of intelligence value about everything of interest to us, all the time."[i]

In the author's view, the substrata of the subjugated societies which he has selected for examination resemble rhizomatic biological entities. The rhizomatic model may be one artful way to describe metaphorically how societal groups merge and emerge over time, and perhaps offers a conceptual, cultural point of departure for the penetration or manipulation of a group from an Intelligence or Information Operations point of view.

In the case of the Romans, the author argues that part of the problem that permitted them to be blindsided was their world view, or perhaps better said,

---

[i] Stephen Cambone, *Statement for the Record by Dr. Stephen A. Cambone, Under Secretary of Defense for Intelligence, before the Senate Armed Services Committee Strategic Forces Subcommittee, 7 April 2004*, p. 4; at http://www.fas.org/irp/congress/2004_hr/040704cambone.pdf, accessed 31 March 2008.

lack of a view of their entire world, geographically and demographically, as we understand it, or think we do, today. How much might his approach change were he to have had access to the Emperor Trajan's memoirs from his campaigns against the Dacians? These people north of the Danube were, until incorporated into the empire by the warrior-emperor, defiantly "the other." Such a memoir certainly existed—once. The sliver of a fragment we have does read exactly like the urban-centric "itineraries" Major Kelley describes as giving sparse attention to the large population outside of urban centers.

However, the *Tabula Peutingeriana*, a medieval copy of an ancient Roman map, may take on a great deal more import with respect to the author's inferences. The map shows the entire Roman Empire save for the western-most sections (the Iberian Peninsula and most of Britain), as it is obvious that part was already lost when it was copied. It features a cartoon-like depiction not only of Roman territory, but of the broader Near East, of India as far as the Ganges, of Sri Lanka, and it even mentions China. Fully 555 cities and 3,500 other named places, many not urban sites, are depicted, and many are illustrated, all of which suggests a good deal of familiarity with non-urban places and people. Internal evidence suggests that the map is based on a fifth-century copy of a document that probably goes back to before A.D. 79, as Pompeii and Herculaneum are depicted. Educated (senatorial and equestrian) Romans were certainly urbanized, as are most Americans today if one includes the suburbs; only two percent of our population lives on the land in the classic sense. However, the author's suggestion that part of the Romans' information deficit derived from their marginalization and exclusion of the fully 90 percent or more of their population that lived on the land outside the cities and the road net of the "mapped" itineraries he discusses (think of our austere airline or train timetables), I believe to be a judgment derived from an absence of contrary evidence, which is not the same as evidence of absence.

Major Kelley does get us to think anew about the problem of dealing with "the other" in the intelligence context, and has asked some important questions about how we organize our own thought processes in tackling problem sets more generally.

Duane C. Young is a retired U.S. Army officer and an adjunct faculty member at the National Defense Intelligence College, where he has taught graduate and undergraduate courses on Strategy, Operational Warfare, and on the history and literature of the Intelligence Community. He is currently completing a PhD thesis with the Security Studies Institute, Cranfield University.

******

Major Patrick Kelley's book, Imperial Secrets, raises important questions about the form and substance of intelligence available to contemporary military and political leaders. In an age marked by the constant threat of terrorism and war, these issues emerge as compelling, not to say vital, for many. What interest does the work hold in particular for historians, especially ancient historians?

Imperial Secrets confronts a series of challenges familiar to many of those who write about the past. Sources that are never sufficiently abundant and that are, moreover, difficult to interpret, must number among these. Difficulties in interpretation arise in no small part from various reasons that are ultimately embedded in a cultural divide separating the originator of information and its ultimate consumer, as the author suggests. Perhaps most compelling are the challenges posed by the book's comparative methodology. It is clear that information available from other societies past and present is culturally constructed to the extent that meaning can alter dramatically with context, often to the mystification of the alien interpreter. This aporia is reinforced by a certain logic germane to constructionism, which in an extreme (though very common form) would deny the possibility of drawing useful comparisons between cultures.[ii] Major Kelley overcomes this difficulty by uncovering what might be described as a deep structure of Empire, whose most significant elements are located at the nexus between power and knowledge.

So his recognition, from the outset, that the United States faces "nearly unique problems in the field of intelligence" contains both a statement of the dilemma and the beginnings of a solution. The heft of this doublet lies in the quasi-oxymoronic phrase "nearly unique." We begin with an acknowledgment of the subjective, even self-referential, considerations at work in the construction of the Other, of the rhetorical, even tendentious, quality of "information," of the instability and indeterminacy of knowledge, of its "slipperiness" as it passes through various stages from initial collection to final consumption.

What emerges is a sense that if every Empire has its own problems, they share a few key elements among them. One such common feature might be labeled "information deficit disorder". Empires, we learn, typically operate at a data deficit in relation to their subjects and the outside world. In other words, they tend to "shed" information. This would be very bad news for Empire if the relationship between power and knowledge operated in the way often assumed. It is clear that management of data, meaning their validation, transmission, and elimination, when necessary, remains crucial to imperial administration. Here

---

[ii] Essential reading on social constructionism includes John R. Searle, *The Construction of Social Reality*, NY: Free Press, 1995; F. Collin, *Social Reality*, London: Routledge, 1997; Ian Hacking, *The Social Construction of What?*, Cambridge, MA: Harvard University Press, 1999.

an inverse relationship between information and knowledge is all too easily established. In this management process, marginal actors, persons whose core identity lies beyond the imperial mainstream, can play a central role, as vital data, or the understanding thereof, tend to be embedded in difference. The correlate of a deficit in information is often a deficit in understanding, but this is not inevitable. It is not simply the kind, quality, or amount of information that bodes for success or failure, but how it is cultivated and managed, handled through a technique or set of skills identified by the author as an imperial epistemology, a way of knowing.

Certainly the imperial successes (and failures) of the Romans sustain multiple and complex explanations. One can argue that the expansion of imperial rule entailed an intensive program of mapping and counting.[iii] Or that their intelligence capabilities improved over time to match an enhanced level of external threat.[iv] Or that they developed sophisticated, long-term programs that combined diplomacy with an economy of force gauged to confront diverse frontier challenges.[v] Or that their approach to such challenges was in fact much simpler, grounded in a violent competition for honor wedded to the pursuit of material self-interest, and (perhaps) informed in turn by a relative ignorance of geography.[vi] Or that stability depended on a consensus forged between the center and the periphery, with the latter often taking the initiative in soliciting and importing Roman values and, in the end, internalizing imperial ideology.[vii] Whatever view(s) one chooses to adopt, Kelley's thesis of information deficit looms large as a likely factor in Rome's eternally problematic relation to the spaces and peoples within and without its borders.

It almost seems at times that in place of a window on the frontiers looking out on the world beyond, the Romans instead installed a mirror reflecting directly back on themselves. Contemplation of the Other generated on the

---

[iii] Claude Nicolet, *Space, Geography, and Politics in the Early Roman Empire*, Ann Arbor, MI: University of Michigan Press, 1991 ([transl.] *L'inventaire du monde: Géographie et politique aux origines del'Empire Romain*, Paris: Fayard, 1988).

[iv] Norman J.E. Austin and B. Rankov, *Exploratio: Military and Political Intelligence in the Roman World from the Second Punic War to the Battle of Adrianople*, London: Routledge, 1995.

[v] Edward N. Luttwak, *The Grand Strategy of the Roman Empire*, Baltimore, MD: Johns Hopkins University Press, 1976. Luttwak's book has been subjected to searing criticism, of such a sustained and intense quality as to pay paradoxical tribute to the book's significance in setting off a long-running debate.

[vi] For different perspectives on these issues, see J.E. Lendon, *Empire of Honour: The Art of Government in the Roman World*, Oxford: Oxford University Press, 1997; Susan P. Mattern, *Rome and the Enemy: Imperial Strategy in the Principate*, Berkeley, CA: University of California Press, 1999.

[vii] Clifford Ando, *Imperial Ideology and Provincial Loyalty in the Roman Empire*, Berkeley, CA: University of California Press, 2000. It is difficult to overstate the importance of the provinces in this analysis. Emperors themselves eventually came to be made there, famously one of Tacitus' "imperial secrets": Hist. 1.4.2.

part of the Romans the image of an alternative version of Rome itself, some-times identifiable as more virtuous and/or located earlier in its development. So in the *Germania,* Tacitus is able, through relentless reference to Rome as a standard for weighing and measuring all things, to assert the Empire's supe-riority in some matters and in others to equate civilization with corruption, so that "Romanization" itself assumes a curiously double-edged quality. The author seems not so much in search of "Germany" as an ideology of Empire, complete with alternative views of Rome.[viii] The Germans were good to think with, at least about Rome.

Such "barbarians", recast in the image and likeness of Rome, made useful mouthpieces for criticism of the Empire itself. Kelley usefully locates one such example in the person of Boudica, the British queen who led a revolt against Rome in the reign of Nero. The speech invented for her by the historian Cas-sius Dio indicts the Romans for their financial and sexual exploitation of their subjects, in brief for reducing the conquered to a state of slavery.[ix] Kelley finds nothing of the "Other" in the speech itself, which retails some all-too-familiar charges against the Romans, but is able to find a view of the Other in a broader rhetorical and historical context.[x]

We cannot know for certain, but it seems very possible that Empire oper-ated as a category-killer on the level of discourse. It likely shaped in a de-finitive manner the possibilities for any serious challenge to its hegemony in ideological terms. More than this, Rome's enemies appear to have resembled Rome in terms of the techniques they adopted and the ambitions they enter-tained. The point is made by a Roman general, Petilius Cerealis, for whom Tacitus constructs a speech rebuking groups of rebellious subjects not far from the frontier with Germany.[xi] Those Germans who challenge Rome's rule allege "freedom" and other pretty slogans as pretexts, but "no one has ever conceived the desire to enslave and lord it over others without arrogating to himself that very same terminology". [xii] "Cerealis" challenges his listen-ers to distinguish between domination by the Romans, which has brought them peace and prosperity, and that of the Germans, which promises higher taxes, harsher treatment, and endless warfare. It is clear that Cerealis' critique cuts both ways, as becomes even more obvious later in the speech, when he concedes the extravagance and greed of some emperors. From this source we can perhaps derive some sense of how anti-Roman rhetoric may have mim-icked imperial claims. In the Roman conception, to be sure, the enemy offered

---

[viii] Ellen O'Gorman, "No Place Like Rome: Identity and Difference in the Germania of Tacitus." *Ramus* 22 (1993) 135-154.

[ix] Dio 62.3-5; cf. Tac. Ann. 14.35.

[x] Kelley cites Tac. Ann. 14.30 to this end.

[xi] Tac. Hist. 4.73-74.

[xii] Tac. Hist. 4.73.3.

nothing more than a warped version of their own Empire. Can we be certain that, at least in some key respects, the reality was all that different?

It seems likely that the Roman Empire, at least, shed more than just information, in the usual sense of the term. At the same time knowledge, or the appearance thereof, can work backward in an imperial setting, as we see, for example, with attempts to identify and repress the phenomenon of "Thuggee" in British India. What Tacitus and Kelley suggest, each in his own fashion, is that a certain instability of meaning carried across frontiers. Words lose their power to signify, values are overthrown, and identities undergo shifts, in the sense that it becomes difficult to locate much that is precisely and unambiguously Roman or German, on the level of ideological profession, at any rate. One advantage that the Romans appear to have possessed in this area is their practice of unrelenting self-critique, turning even the "barbarians" to good account. Perhaps here too we can identify a particular imperial way of knowing.

It would take a much longer essay to do even modest justice to the question of the relevance of Kelley's book for the interests of the ancient historian. Only one or two aspects have been touched upon here. It would be good to engage the nexus he identifies among the discourses of history, gender, and law, just to take one example. I could name further the inclination of empires to overstretch, their tendency always to be at war, and their habit of blurring the boundary between truth and fiction, as points worthy of exploration. Finally there is the disquieting argument that no meaningful distinction exists for them between domestic and foreign intelligence. These elements arguably form part of a deep structure of Empire.

It will be obvious that Major Kelley did not write this book to comfort us. No small part of the explanation for this lies in the fact that, unlike the field of Roman History, in his world, social constructions can have lethal consequences. For this reason alone, the book merits a broad readership, far beyond ancient historians and intelligence specialists. The author makes abundantly clear how good the Romans are to think with, not least about ourselves.

Thomas A.J. McGinn
American Academy in Rome/Vanderbilt University

INTRODUCTION

Jam ultima aetas Cumaei carminis venit;
Magnus ordo seclorum nascitur ab integro.

Now the last age of the Cumaean song has arrived;
A great order of ages arises anew.[1]

A serving U.S. military officer presumably has something to answer for at the very outset when writing about a topic like "Imperial Intelligence." If the issue is not one of purely academic import, and I do not believe it is, then there are obvious implications in associating the American enterprise with a highly charged term like Empire. I believe the matter is not clear-cut, and is the subject of much debate in various circles; however, what I will argue is that, regardless of how the U.S. role is characterized, it does face nearly unique problems in the field of intelligence. Nearly unique, in that these problems do not so profoundly impact traditional nation-states, but have been confronted before by historical imperial formations.

The genesis for this position lies in the immediate aftermath of September 11th, when perhaps the most urgently asked and passionately debated question was "Why do they hate us?" This seems to me the essence of the Imperial Intelligence problem. Despite its broad consideration in the media and public venues, this question does constitute an intelligence problem the answer to which requires profound insights into the hidden thoughts and desires of others and presumes a predictive as well as explanatory response. The answer, or answers, will shape the course of public policy. It is also uniquely imperial, through its implications of betrayal, outrage, and anguished incomprehension. They, presumably, have no obvious reason to hate us; and in fact, we expect a degree of gratitude and cooperation from others around the world who have been the beneficiaries of our largesse. We saved the Saudis from Saddam Hussein, the rebuttals run, we provided more foreign aid to the Egyptians than any other state, we helped the Afghans throw off the Soviet yoke. These are the kinds of questions and responses that played out in the 19th Century British press and parliament after one or another imperial subject committed some especially egregious outrage. They are not the existential questions the 20th Century Poles, for example, would have asked about Nazi Germany. As September 11 recedes, and the consequent struggle takes on a generational

---

[1] Virgil, "Eclogue IV," *The Works of P. Virgilius Maro*, trans. Levi Hart and V.R. Osborn, New York: David McKay Company, 1952, p. 17.

character, the question assumes greater urgency, as the pronoun *They* in this formulation has come to represent an ever-widening demographic.

This question, or its variants, continues to resonate as insurgencies in several theaters survive beyond their expected shelf-life. A project I was directed to undertake while serving in Afghanistan was research into "*Why Do They Fight?*" The fact that one needs to ask why local residents would fight against a foreign military power dispatched from across the globe betrays an Imperial, rather than a nation-state perspective.

Nevertheless, while these questions suggest our relation to the world has changed beyond that of a traditional nation-state—albeit a profoundly powerful one—our attempts at intelligence reform indicate our interest in answering traditional questions, just in a faster and more accurate fashion. Better interagency cooperation, sharing with partners, broader and more rapid dissemination will ultimately result in more "actionable intelligence." Not surprisingly, the catch-phrase implies a specific type of action, especially for military audiences. The concept was addressed at a forum during the 2006 Association of the United States Army annual meeting, and as a practical exercise eight individuals from the crowd were directed to locate the one insurgent in their midst. With "actionable intelligence," the problem might not have seemed so daunting, and the "insurgent" could have been killed or captured in short order. However, in our current "strategic enterprise," and given the rapidly shifting tides around names, I hesitate to commit to any single term such as Long War, Global War on Terror, Global Struggle Against Extremism, there will never be a "VE" or "VJ" day when all the insurgents and terrorists are captured and killed; the letters of capitulation signed; and the vast war-time machines of actionable intelligence dismembered, dissolved and disbanded. Success, rather, will come with an open-ended enterprise to identify ideas, values, understandings and movements that threaten an international order built around a specific set of legal principles and economic interests. It is an intelligence challenge more akin to that facing Rome in 150 CE, Istanbul in 1600 or London in 1800, than it is to that confronting Washington, DC in 1941.

Exploring history for "Lessons-Learned" which are applicable to present challenges is a well-established technique. Studies of how Napoleon, or Caesar, or Grant employed Signals intelligence, Human intelligence, Open Source intelligence, etc.—under their contemporary labels—abound. What I propose, however, is slightly more radical. I am not interested, for example, in how the British recruited informants in Waziristan per se. Rather, I am interested in the problems of *knowing* that the British faced because they were an *imperial power* in the north-west of the sub-continent: problems of language and translation, problems of framing questions in a way acceptable to consumers in London, problems of shaping an information order which would integrate antagonists into a particular legal and economic framework. Moreover, I intend to further radicalize the project by departing from the traditional "history as narrative" approach.

All narratives, including histories, are told by someone, *for* someone else, for a purpose, and not necessarily, or even frequently, is that purpose strictly to inform. There is a caveat commonly applied to intelligence report-writing which notes that a given source may have intended to "influence as well as inform." This formulation suggests there may be sources that intend purely to inform. I consider this contingency unlikely, as virtually every communication, particularly in the intelligence world, but in academic writing as well, intends to influence. Informing is more or less incidental to this purpose. Edward Said's *Orientalism*, despite decades of debate, still holds up in its critique of this operation—especially when the writers and consumers come from one context, and the object of study comes from another.[2] As an active-duty military officer in a specific context, I am as susceptible to this phenomenon as any of my Orientalist predecessors or contemporaries; but I hope to at least ameliorate the tendency through disrupting already-established narratives, many of which I frankly find appealing. That disruption will also become apparent in my writing style. This is, at least partly, by design. The absent author in official and traditional academic writing creates an illusion of objectivity in even the most partisan texts. This kind of illusion is one I wish to critique, and I will consequently avoid adopting it for my own narrative voice. These techniques collectively seek to subvert the linear approach still evident in the "actionable intelligence" discussion above—evidence of a very culture-specific attitude that demonstrates how very little U.S. security officials have adapted to the epistemological critiques which have raged in the U.S. academic community for decades.

---

2 Proceeding from the text that started it all (Edward Said, *Orientalism*, New York: Vintage, 1979), a bibliography addressing the pro-and-con jousting over "Orientalism" would probably run longer than this entire project. However, for a recent rejoinder to some of Said's more sweeping generalizations, see Robert Irwin's *For Lust of Knowing: The Orientalists and Their Enemies*, London: Allen Lane, 2006. Maya Jasanoff's review of Irwin ("Before and After Said," *London Review of Books*, 8 June 2006) provides a useful summary of the state of play in this ongoing debate.

How then to proceed? I accept as more or less true Francis Bacon's aphorism, *Ipsa Scientia Potestas Est*.[3] Knowledge is indeed power, but in a relation of mutual influence rather than direct equality. Power influences the kinds of questions asked and on what topics; it shapes the kinds of answers possible and how they are expressed. Knowledge, too, influences power; and philosophical issues about the nature of reality and understanding can shape how power is realized. Michel Foucault opens *The Order of Things* with his bemused reaction to an imaginary bestiary recounted by Borges.[4] The world's animals in Borges' work are classified as embalmed, tame, sucking pigs, frenzied, innumerable, painted with a camelhair brush, etc. in a bewildering system which reads like nonsense to the European observer, despite its presumptive rationality to the author. We are confronted, Foucault notes, with "the stark impossibility of imagining that…."[5] Foucault's book addresses the transition in European thought from a Classical to Modern mode. However, the more general challenge offered at the outset suggests there are still fruitful queries to be made regarding different and changing epistemes—the ways in which the particular menu of ideas available to knowledge producers in any given context frame and shape what can be known, what constitutes knowing, and how knowledge can be credibly expressed. This challenge remains particularly relevant for intelligence communities attempting to gain valid cross-cultural insights.

While I accept the premise of contextual framing, I wish to examine how these frames can be defined by power generally, rather than exclusively by a specific time and place—i.e. is there a distinctively "imperial" way of knowing, defined by the power relations and information requirements of the parties involved, as one world struggles with the impossibility of imagining how the other's world operates. A suggestive indication that this may be so—and which has specific intelligence relevance—comes from the British struggle against "Thuggee" in 19th Century India. British authorities of the time were confronted by a bewildering array of violence, apparently stemming from multiple, inchoate sources. In an act of sheer intellectual assertion, they identified a bloody religious cult which systematically spread terror through the

---

[3] Francis Bacon, "Of Heresies," *Meditationes Sacrae, in The Works of Francis Bacon*, Vol. 2, Boston: Houghton, Mifflin and Company, 1897, p. 179. While Bacon's aphorism is widely applied in a secular context, it was originally generated to contest "heretical" arguments regarding human free will which sought to assign a wider range to God's knowledge than to his power—a distinction Bacon denies. I find this distinction between the sacred and the divine particularly relevant to the practice of strategic intelligence in empires.

[4] Jorge Luis Borges, with Margarita Guerrero, translated by Andrew Hurley, *The Book of Imaginary Beings*, New York: Vintage, 2002.

[5] Michel Foucault, *The Order of Things: An Archaeology of the Human Sciences*, New York: Vintage, 1994, p. XV-XX.

murder of innocents. The phenomenon was highlighted in diplomatic correspondence, novels, press, "confessions" of detainees, and prompted the erection of an extraordinary legal, intelligence and police organization which defined the problem through historical studies, elaborate network analysis diagrams, and philosophical ruminations on the ideology of such movements. The modern consumer familiar with struggles to define the problem will see parallels—are *they* Al Q'aida, Al Q'aida Associated Movements, radical Islamists, Salafists, etc. *ad inifinitum*? I have personally participated in staff competitions to evolve comprehensive acronyms capturing in a single term political/religious movements/drug runners/bandits etc. Familiar too, is the kind of "intelligence" produced to explain the problem.

But if power shapes knowledge, does knowledge also shape power?

This question is not meant simply as a play on words. Rather, I wish to contest a unidirectional reading of how "knowing" works, i.e.: that an observing subject gains ever more knowledge of some given object and consequently, power over the latter accrues to the former. This presumption underlies a great deal of modern discussion regarding a national security apparatus in which intelligence aspires to be omniscient and surveillance aspires to be omnipresent.[6] The inspiring ideal, however, is far older. Writing sometime around the

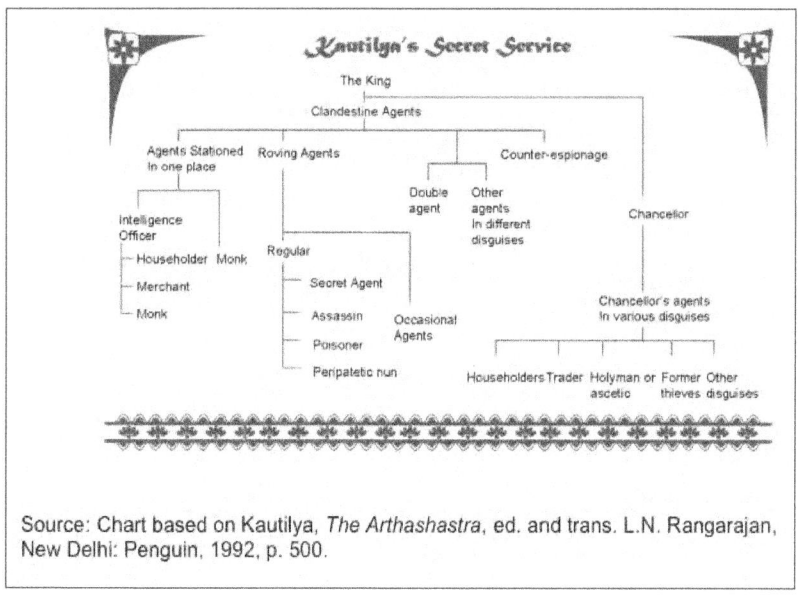

Source: Chart based on Kautilya, *The Arthashastra*, ed. and trans. L.N. Rangarajan, New Delhi: Penguin, 1992, p. 500.

---

6 Pete Hoekstra, "The Next Evolution of Geospatial Intelligence," *Military Geospatial Technology* online edition, accessed 10 Oct 2007 at http://www.military-geospatial-technology. com/article.cfm?DocID=1226.

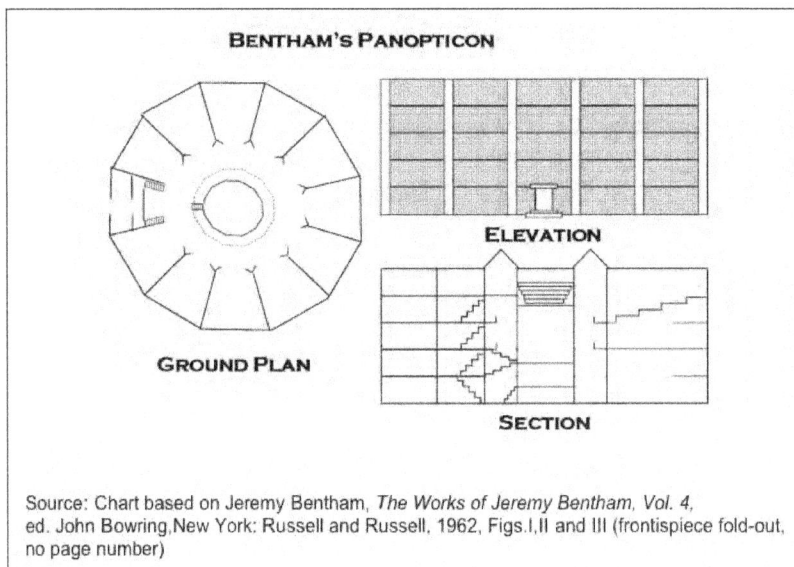

BENTHAM'S PANOPTICON

GROUND PLAN

ELEVATION

SECTION

Source: Chart based on Jeremy Bentham, *The Works of Jeremy Bentham, Vol. 4,*
ed. John Bowring,New York: Russell and Russell, 1962, Figs.I,II and III (frontispiece fold-out,
no page number)

First Century CE, the Indian strategist Kautilya argued that state power rests fundamentally upon near-omniscient state knowledge.

To this end, Kautilya proposed a near-omnipresent architecture of surveillance, observing everything from domestic court intrigue to the peccadilloes of foreign statesmen; reporting on topics from price-fixing in local markets to popular opinion regarding state policy. The cast of characters dedicated to the mission included dwarfs, hunchbacks, monks, ascetic nuns, forest dwellers, householders and tradesmen acting as agents provocateur, double agents and counter-espionage agents.[7] Less colorful, perhaps, but more widely known in the West, Jeremy Bentham articulates the same ideas in his Panopticon. Where Kautilya established a surveillance system through social networks, Bentham achieves this end architecturally.

Physically, Bentham's device is fairly simple. A series of open cells are arranged around a central observation post. From this point, an overseer enjoys unfettered visual access to all of the cells' inmates—surveillance is

---

[7] Kautilya, *The Arthashastra*, ed. and trans. L.N. Rangarajan, New Delhi: Penguin, 1992. Discussion of secret agents, surveillance and espionage occupies several chapters of the original (p. 499-540 in this translation); but the rest of the work covers nearly every conceivable aspect of statecraft in sometimes eye-watering detail. Although quotes from his masterwork adorn nearly every Indian government and military facility (the diplomatic district in New Delhi is named after him), outside the sub-continent, Kautilya is generally acknowledged only as the "Indian Machiavelli" for his *realpolitik* policy prescriptions. While true as far as it goes, this chronologically misplaced description falls short of representing the Arthashastra's scope and its potential utility as a comprehensive representation of a non-Western approach to diplomacy, intelligence and security affairs.

omnipresent—or almost. Bentham also recognized that as a practical matter—and the Panopticon was a practical proposition—no real human being could actually be looking into all of the cells, all of the time. Consequently, he conceived a Venetian blind arrangement within the central tower which concealed the observer's presence, or lack thereof, from the observed. The overseer might be watching, or he might not, but the end result would be the same—the inmates would always tend to behave as if they were being watched. The mere possibility of knowing here exerts a kind of power in shaping the behavior of the known. The relevance of these ideas to prison design is obvious, and it is in this field that Benthamite designs have been most widely applied—but the original scheme was far more ambitious. The full sub-title to the Panopticon, lengthy but instructive, reads: "the idea of a new principle of construction applicable to any sort of establishment in which persons of any description are to be kept under observation; and in particular to penitentiary houses, prisons, houses of industry, work-houses, poor-houses, lazarettos, manufactories, hospitals, mad-houses, and schools."[8] Whether one is being punished, corrected, employed, educated or cured, the panoptic vision is always present.

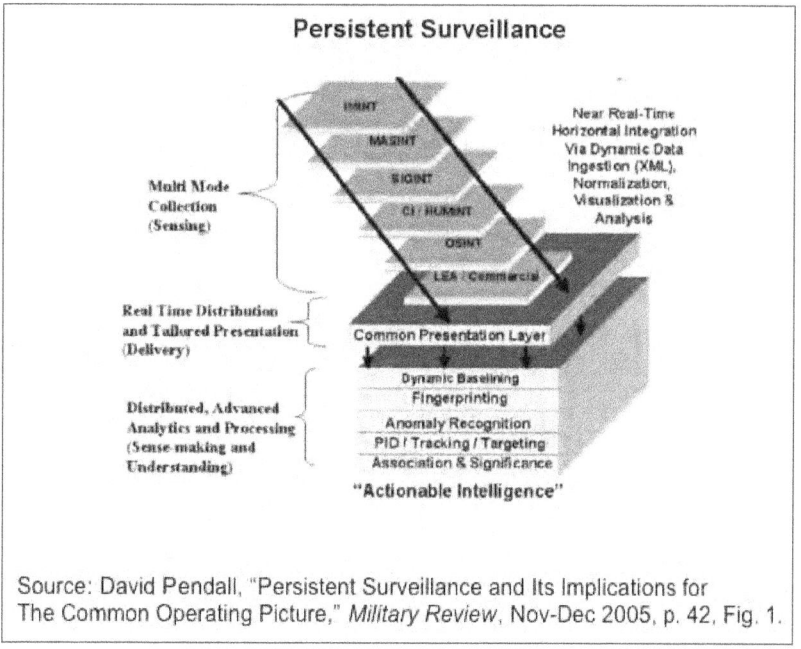

Source: David Pendall, "Persistent Surveillance and Its Implications for The Common Operating Picture," *Military Review*, Nov-Dec 2005, p. 42, Fig. 1.

---

[8] Jeremy Bentham, *Panopticon* in *The Works of Jeremy Bentham*, Vol. 4, ed. John Bowring, New York: Russell and Russell, 1962. The volume represented as the "Panopticon" was originally a collected series of letters in which Bentham ranges over a wide variety of topics associated with the management of his model institution, but the basic design from which the other concepts flow is established briefly at the outset (p. 40-45 in this edition).

The breathtaking scope of Bentham's project is relevant here on both substantive and philosophical grounds. Substantively, the broad sweep of his proposed collection targets, like those of Kautilya, mirrors the intelligence problem confronting empires—a problem extending far beyond stealing enemy secrets. Philosophically, it addresses the interaction of power and knowledge, establishing themes and tropes explicitly critiqued by later scholars like Foucault, who essentially established "Panopticism" as a byword for a whole spectrum of state surveillance and disciplinary activities.[9]

The same troika of omniscience, omnipresence and omnipotence is implicitly endorsed in modern exhortations for development of a persistent surveillance intelligence capability—or alternatively, "persistent intelligence, reconnaissance and surveillance"; "persistent stare"; and "pervasive knowledge of the enemy".[10] Etymologically all are panoptic terms, with the goal to "know something of intelligence value about everything of interest to us, all the time."[11]

Whether this ideal can be achieved has been explored extensively in the burgeoning field of post-colonial studies, with particular attention to the Indian experience. On one side of the power-knowledge equation, scholars like Bernard Cohn have argued that the way the British "knew" India materially influenced what India in fact constituted. On the other, the sub-altern studies movement (where sub-altern literally derives from "subordinate," the British Army term for a junior officer) has sought to recover alternate discourses among subject populations, opaque to their rulers.[12] In league with at least some in the

---

[9] Michel Foucault, *Discipline and Punish: The Birth of the Prison*, trans. Alan Sheridan, New York: Vintage, 1991. While the entire book is devoted to related themes, the Panopticon is specifically addressed in p. 195-228. For a more recent, contested reading of Panopticism, see *Theorizing Surveillance: The Panopticon and Beyond*, ed. David Lyon, Portland: Willan, 2006.

[10] David Pendall, "Persistent Surveillance and Its Implications for the Common Operating Picture," *Military Review*, Nov-Dec 2005, p. 41.

[11] Stephen Cambone, *Statement for the Record by Dr. Stephen A. Cambone, Under Secretary of Defense for Intelligence before the Senate Armed Services Committee Strategic Forces Subcommittee*, 7 April 2004, p. 4.

[12] While the present work is not explicitly "post-colonial" or "sub-altern," some of my arguments will apply ideas from those arenas. More fundamentally, this project has been inspired by my first encounter with these pre-fixed strains in a civilian graduate school. As an Army officer with ten years of experience writing PowerPoint bullets and one-page information papers, I literally crashed into this realm while nominally studying political-military affairs in South Asia. The emotional anxiety and hostility this encounter provoked suggested to me the potential utility in engaging genuinely alien intellectual approaches. Those with a similar background seeking a similar experience (aside from this book) might examine: Bernard Cohn's *Colonialism and Its Forms of Knowledge: the British in India*, Princeton: Princeton University, 1996; Ileana Rodriguez' edited volume, *The Latin American Subaltern Studies Reader*, Durham and London: Duke University, 2001; and the collection of essays assembled by Ranajit Guha and Gayatri Chakravarty Spivak in *Selected Subaltern Studies*, New York: Oxford University, 1988.

sub-altern school, and *contra* Foucault, I propose that the Panopticon actually operates in reverse in the imperial context. In a system of information exchange, empires will nearly always operate at an information deficit in relation to their subjects. Beyond the vaguest employment of the term, "Empire" connotes a robust imperial presence within its dominions. The overseer is there for everyone to observe—what the empire believes, does, wants, and will do is laid out in imperial media, legal codes and judicial decisions, the conduct of its agents, and the architectural and scientific "performances" of power—all in contrast to the "inscrutable oriental" who resists observation physically, linguistically, and epistemologically in his capacity rather than inability to "imagine that...."

Regardless of whether this deficit is confessed or not, it may grow as the desperate thirst for knowledge—for intelligence—rises as the empire's perceived real power flags. Empires face a distinct challenge in finding and employing intermediaries to bridge the gap—agents who can wander among the cells and report back to the tower. Almost by definition, such intermediaries are marginal to the contesting communities—whether deputed from the capital or recruited from the provinces—and must deal with shifting identities in their bodies, their minds, and their relations with others, in constant risk of losing their marginality to one side or another. T.E. Lawrence, one of the most celebrated marginals, remained intellectually an imperial agent to the core—his writings marked by the Orientalist prejudices of his day. Despite the cross-cultural sentiments publicly suggested in the well-known portraits of Lawrence in full Arab regalia, and even in his popular label as "Lawrence of Arabia," in personal correspondence the man could still express opinions of an entirely different nature:

> I'm not conscious of having done a crooked thing to anyone since I began to push the Arab Movement, though I prostituted myself in Arab Service. For an Englishman to put himself at the disposal of a red race is to sell himself to a brute, like Swift's Houyhnhnms.[13]

By way of contrast, the Ottomans performed something like the reverse of Kurtz's odyssey in Conrad's *Heart of Darkness*: "the lone white man turning his back on headquarters, on relief, on thoughts of home—perhaps; setting his face towards the depths of the wilderness, towards his empty and desolate station."[14] Recruiting among their Christian subjects to man the bureaucracy

---

13 T.E. Lawrence, letter to G.J. Kidston, 14 Nov 1919, *T.E. Lawrence: Selected Letters,* ed. Malcolm Brown, New York and London: W.W. Norton and Company, 1989, p. 170.

14 Joseph Conrad, "Heart of Darkness," *Great Short Works of Joseph Conrad,* New York: Harper and Row, 1967, p. 242.

and the janissaries, the sultans created an entire ruling class of imperial "subalterns," men eminently suitable to assess developments within the imperial dominions. By virtue of social isolation, professional advancement and education, however, this class came functionally to define what constituted Osmanli—what was *Ottoman*, defining the imperial rather than translating for it.

Finally, even where suitable intermediaries did exist, imperial policy makers faced the problems of "slippery" knowledge—data points collected, analyzed and presented in a context different from where they originally resided by virtue of imperial process. Ultimately, these data came to represent different truths for the host community and its ultimate consumers. Some of this phenomenon may be ascribed to active imperial intervention with an explicit purpose of domination (a la Cohn). Even more benign interaction, however, was likely to send imperial information collecting projects wildly awry with unintended consequences. Well-meaning British attempts to rationalize Hindu and Islamic law in India, for example, fundamentally contorted the material at hand in order to make it intelligible for officials operating from an English common-law background. Their consequent understanding misread what their subjects experienced and expected, with far-reaching ramifications for Anglo-Indian relations and the experience of religiously defined identity in South Asia.

With the basic propositions outlined above, and with respect to the central question of the nature of the intelligence of empire, this project will seek to explore two key phenomena common to the imperial collection, creation, and consumption of intelligence, or the spectrum of information an empire requires to rule and endure. The first is the interwoven relationship of power and knowledge that may be inferred from the record as preserved in texts or in other media of societal communication. The second is the marginal and shifting identity of both information and its transmitting agents as those are revealed in texts. Traced through Roman, Ottoman and British experiences, these twin phenomena will be explored cross-culturally and trans-historically to draw out the unique "Imperial" qualities common to this form of knowledge-seeking and production. Finally, I ask whether there is a distinctly imperial way of knowing.

Obviously, this is a complex proposal, and it would be easy to get lost in both the writing and the reading of it. As an expert, an old hand at getting lost—both in texts and the physical world—I want to offer a few navigational notes at the outset. As a point of basic orientation, the sites of this investigation were not chosen at random, but rather because they seem to me to resonate with one another—and with the modern world. The Roman Empire encompassed what would one day be Great Britain, and the British Empire in turn would identify itself with the Roman experience. More recently, the proliferating discourse on U.S. Empire consistently returns to these two examples despite countless others available—I haven't seen anything yet in the *Atlantic* about America as the new Qing or Quechua dynasty. Chronologically between Rome and the Raj, the Ottoman Empire also falls into the physical spaces in-between, its territory and the cultural forms it encompassed overlapping the margins of the other two, while also serving as a kind of boundary marker—a vessel into which all that was defined as "not the West" could be poured. I need not elaborate, I think, in too much detail how this prefigures the way many of the same places and forms serve a similar role for the West today.

This overlap and interconnection were viscerally evident in the course of my research for this project. My itinerary followed a conventional drift from east to west in space and from antiquity to the recent past in time. At the precise mid-point of my travels, I stepped into the Hagia Sophia in Istanbul, surrounded by the images of multiple intersecting worlds. From this ground zero, one could move forward or backward in time to follow the trajectory of political orders, up and down in space to engage with alternate spiritual visions, or laterally around its circumference to engage with the material and artistic manifestations of different worldviews. Each of these strategies would be legitimate, but a strict disciplinary allegiance to any one would do a grave disservice to the actual sensation of standing in this specific and extraordinary space—a sensation which has driven the design of this text.

Within these broad social architectures, the selection of specific time-frames to be considered were similarly subject to my own reflection. Although the precise dates are naturally open to dispute, each enjoyed a period of roughly two centuries of pre-eminence (a few outliers aside, my lines are drawn around Rome: 1-200 CE; Ottoman: 1550-1750 CE; Britain: 1730-1930 CE). During these periods each empire approached its broadest geographical extent, its members collectively recognized that they inhabited a distinctly imperial cultural space, and its elites constantly agonized over portents of its imminent demise. Once again, a quality of the times I find familiar today.

The question next arises of how to map this particular space I have in mind, a question not so much of specific places and times but of intersecting themes. The philosophical problem of mapping will return again and again in the pages that follow, but for now I will offer a more tangible illustration. My most recent posting is to Kathmandu. Despite Nepal's developing-world status, I have access to the full suite of modern amenities at my

Roman architecture, Christian iconography, and Islamic text fill the vault of the Hagia Sophia. Three different orders of power, three different ways of knowing: How does one tell the story of this space?
Source: photos by author.

home—from reliable power and hot water, to cable TV and high-speed Internet. What I do not have, however, is an address. No street, no number; you literally could not find it on a map. My home is located in representational space thus: From Dhumbari Chowk toward Bhishal Nagar, two bumps, red wall on right, left at the alley with the blue sign, second yellow house. Full stop. Even the address line on my cable bill holds nothing more specific than "Dhumbari."

This sort of relational geography can be frustrating to Westerners, and I have frequently heard expatriates complain that maps are worse than useless here—trying to show a cab driver where you want to go on your Lonely Planet street map is a sure way to get hopelessly lost. Instead, navigation works something like this: you tell the driver where you want to go, he nods in agreement, then expresses complete bewilderment once you're inside. He yells a question to a passer-by smoking on the sidewalk, drives a few blocks, slows and asks a fellow cab driver across several lanes of traffic, then eventually stops and gets out to have a conference with several people on the corner. Rinse, repeat, and ultimately you reach your destination. Geographical information is obviously available, but in a way accessible only through social networks. To those accustomed to arranging space with maps, this information resists inquiry—taken in terms of my earlier formulation, Kathmandu is then overflowing with secrets. The problem of trying to "read" a network through a map touches the very core of the problem I want to examine, and has also influenced the design of the text at hand, which at first glance may appear as bewilderingly random as the maze of Kathmandu alleys.

A book which deals principally with historical material like this one usually proceeds in a more or less standard and recognizable way. Organized along a steady, measurable forward-flowing stream of time, where one event follows another. Each point (chapter, event) derives meaning from its relationship to the points immediately before and after, as well as from its place in the overall trend line. While flipping through my daughter's choir homework, it struck me that this structure is analogous to a musical scale, with its own "themes," "resonances" and "echoes." As a way of communicating and arranging material, the scale is easy to write, easy to read and easy to perform. However, it is information-thin, and transmits little beyond the obvious in the way of meaning or affect. An alternate structure presents itself in the form of a fugue. Here, two, three or four "voices" can speak simultaneously—sometimes echoing, sometimes complementing, sometimes contesting one another. Every single note is embedded in multiple contexts. It is an information-thick architecture, which derives its meaning and affect from its simultaneity—one could play the independent voices consecutively, but then it wouldn't be a fugue. In the piece I wish to present, the three empires represent three different voices, but the issues raised by each sometimes echo, sometimes contest, and sometimes complement one another. Playing them together provides a way of enriching the meaning embedded in any given "note." It also serves as a practical experiment in escaping established information structures—maps that don't mesh with networks—a capacity I find to be a distinct genius of successful empires. The chart below gives a better picture of what I'm up to than a linear table of contents. Modeled on J.S. Bach's 2nd Fugue from the Well-Tempered Clavier (measures 7 and 8 from the end of the exposition are shown here), my three voices supplement and counter-point each other, while their tonal range is defined by common themes that also alternate.

Of course, there's also a fourth voice, which is missing from the chart, although those familiar with the milieu of modern strategic, diplomatic or operational intelligence may frequently recognize the tune.[15] Part of this

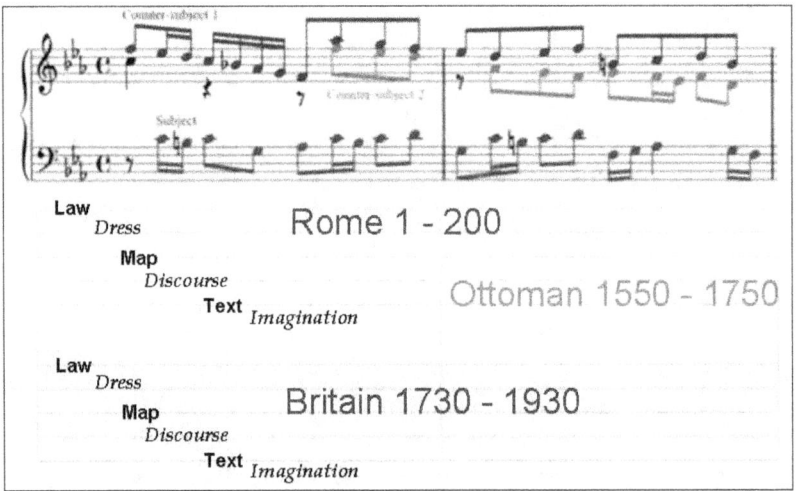

Composing History—Like the subject and counter-subject voices in a fugue, the themes raised by separate imperial experiences gain resonance and complexity when they are interspersed and played off one another. Modeled on Johann Sebastian Bach, Fugue No. 2 in C minor, BWV 847, The Well-Tempered Clavier, Book 1, Bach-Gesellschaft Ausgabe, 1866. *Source: author.*

---

15 For those who may not be familiar with the evolution of national intelligence enterprise, at least in the Western world, please see *The Intelligence Revolution: A Historical Perspective*, Proceedings of the Thirteenth Military History Symposium, U.S. Air Force Academy, Colorado Springs, CO (Washington, DC: Office of Air Force History, 1991), especially the essay by Dennis E. Showalter, "Intelligence on the Eve of Transformation: Methodology, Organization and Application," 15-37, which divides intelligence into "diplomatic" and "operational" facets. For insight into diplomatic intelligence see Adda Bozeman, *Strategic Intelligence and Statecraft: Selected Essays* (Washington, DC: Brassey's, 1992).

omission is simply a matter of capacity—every additional voice in a fugue requires exponentially greater compositional skill, and I have likely already surpassed my own with three. A second matter is that of relevance. Modern intelligence organizations and policies are always evolving, sometimes with neck-wrenching speed, and pointed comparisons made in this context would likely have outlived their shelf-life between the first drafts of this book and its printing. The opportunity to apply these ideas to ongoing problems of imperial intelligence, then, I leave mostly to others, while I will focus on those enduring topics I find to be associated with earlier empires.

An Empire of Information

It is customary at the outset of a work like this to define one's terms. What, precisely, constitutes an Empire? Is it territorial occupation or simply the hegemonic domination over the policies of subordinate states? And what about Intelligence? Is it strictly secret information (and is it secret because of its contents or due to the technique of collection)? Or is it any information that influences policy decisions? Frankly, I tend to find such exercises tedious and often irrelevant. Words are *always* polyvalent, and particularly for loaded ideas like these; they most often operate like pornography—we may not be able to define it, but we know it when we see it. In this light, it seems more appropriate to consider if "Empire" is indeed what Americans see in the mirror; is this what we imagine ourselves to be? As Arjun Appadurai would have it:

> The image, the imagined, the imaginary—these are all terms that direct us to something critical and new in global cultural processes: *the imagination as a social practice*.... [I]magination is now central to all forms of agency, is itself a social fact, and is the key component of the new global order.[16]

Languages of Empire

The jury is still out, but let's take Harvard University as a bellwether of elite imagination. On my desk, I have three recent volumes authored by Harvard professors or published by the Harvard University Press. Michael Hardt and Antonio Negri's Empire (2000), Niall Ferguson's *Colossus: the Price of America's Empire* (2004) and Charles Maier's *Among Empires* (2006). Harvard and its faculty publish a lot of books, so it's possible we're seeing merely a random efflorescence of imperial studies, but I think not. For one thing, these are not specialist academic volumes—all three were purchased at my local Border's—the little mall outlet, not the cavernous main store. For another, these are not the sort of critiques found in studies that might have been common a decade or two ago, or even in more recent vitriol like Michael Scheuer's *Imperial Hubris* (2004). Grossly simplifying, I read Hardt and Negri to say yes, America is integral to a new imperial order, though not in a traditional hierarchical sense; Ferguson sees America acting as an empire, just not a very good one, and not likely for long; and Maier hesitates to apply the label, principally because the domestic order has not yet deteriorated to the point required for

---

16 Arjun Appadurai, *Modernity at Large: Cultural Dimensions of Globalization*, Minneapolis and London: University of Minnesota, 1996, p. 31.

an explicitly imperialist polity, though he's keeping a cautious eye out.[17] No Rudyard Kipling in the bunch, but what was once a pejorative reserved for polemic from the Left has now moved clearly into polite conversation.

Regardless of the mixed conclusions here, and in many other texts, I believe the fact that the discussion is proceeding at all is instructive. The increasingly contentious struggle to work out new political science theories, or revive old ones, about how the world works echoes the strained process described by Thomas Kuhn in the natural sciences:

> Because it demands large-scale paradigm destruction and major shifts in the problems and techniques of normal science, the emergence of new theories is generally preceded by a period of pronounced professional insecurity. As one might expect, that insecurity is generated by the persistent failure of the puzzles of normal science to come out as they should. Failure of existing rules is the prelude to a search for new ones.[18]

While defining and explaining the success or failure of various U.S. overseas enterprises in the last fifty years—from Korea through Vietnam to Iraq and Afghanistan—is a problem that can, and has, filled whole libraries, I think it is probably far less controversial to claim that they have generally not "come out as they should." Imagining "Empire," rather than settling for a slightly updated version of the Westphalian order, is one approach to finding new rules. Another way to proceed, flipping this formulation back to front, is to consider how Empire imagines. How does it see the world, how does it inquire or interrogate, what does it tell? These are all questions about information, and I will suggest that one way to think about Empire is to think about it in information terms. As I protested above, I have no desire to "define" empire anew, or terrorism or intelligence or anything else, for that matter—there are already more than enough definitions, each of them at least potentially true in one regard or another. We are like the blind men in the parable, seeking to describe an elephant. It's a tree, claims one; a wall, maintains another; a snake cries a third. Focusing on the rough and folded nature of the skin, while not necessarily any more accurate than the previous perspectives, at least provides a way to address a single feature that contains and characterizes the entire beast. Information is just such a feature—in its most basic sense, it can be be seen

17 Michael Hardt and Antonio Negri, *Empire*, Cambridge and London: Harvard, 2000, p. 180-182; Niall Ferguson, *Colossus: The Price of America's Empire*, New York: Penguin, 2004, p. 286-294; Charles Maier, *Among Empires: American Ascendancy and Its Predecessors*, Cambridge and London: Harvard, 2006, p. 69-70; Michael Scheuer, *Imperial Hubris: Why the West is Losing the War on Terror*, Washington, DC: Brassey's, 2004.

18 Thomas Kuhn, *The Structure of Scientific Revolutions*, 3d ed., Chicago and London: University of Chicago, 1996, p. 67-68.

not as an abstract phenomenon, but as an expression of physical, mass-energy relations as it represents the world in which we live.[19]

One theory argues that imperial movements generally proceed along surpluses of people, of goods and of capital.[20] To this I would add information as an additional surplus, or perhaps a meta-surplus as it both drives and emanates from the others. People come along with and up against language, culture and belief. Goods and capital are inescapably tied up with ideas about exchange values, the nature of property and law. Imperial boundaries are, in general terms, liable to be less exact than those of a nation-state, but they are certainly not conterminous with the distribution of imperial people, goods and capital. Despite the shared popularity of blue-on-white pottery, the North American colonies were no more part of the Chinese empire than was the coastal region of Kerala Roman, regardless of archaeologically recovered Mediterranean coinage in that part of India. An empire's fluid boundaries may, however, generally correspond to places where imperial information about people, goods and capital predominates—where the patterning that gives meaning to physical reality follows a recognizable theme. Where was English generally understood, at least among elites? Where was Roman contract law generally

Information resists the static patterns of the state, carving its own streams along the interstices of formal and informal space—the Roman Forum in flood. *Source: photo by author.*

---

19 Paul Young, *The Nature of Information*, New York and London: Praeger, 1987, p. 73.

20 Kenneth Waltz, *Theory of International Politics*, Reading, MA: Addison-Wesley, 1979, p. 37.

recognized and enforced? Tracing the intricate patterns inscribed by information about physical people and things can provide a more accurate guide to answering questions than an abstracted map; that is, to which national state do those places in eastern Afghanistan functionally belong, where the Rupee is more widely honored than the Afghani?

Read in this way, information becomes a constitutive element of empire, rather than a subordinate component. Empire consists of a certain set of patterns that characterize the meaning and function of physical reality—Empire is information, which may almost sound like a definition, but my intent is rhetorical emphasis. Consequently, the management of information—disseminating the preferred patterns, and identifying competing patterns for elimination—becomes the core function of imperial administration. This formulation has several principal implications in my mind. The first is that availability of information of a kaleidoscopic nature has immediate and critical import for successful imperial policy; consequently, an emphasis on "secret" or explicitly security-related information, such as bomb technology or membership numbers of an armed group, is generally debilitating. Hence, my work will look at a broader spectrum of material. The second is that information circulates in a common space of exchange—a dialogue of listening to and telling stories about the world, each of which impacts the other, just as the acts of both selling and buying can alter the presumptive objective value of a given share in a stock exchange. Consequently, examining or managing only one side of the exchange in isolation—e.g. intelligence as an activity completely distinct from public diplomacy or information operations—is analogous to old Soviet-style planned economy management. By fixing ambitious output targets and devoting vast resources against them, the Soviets could achieve extraordinary results in industrial production. However, this one-sided approach ignored consumer demand feedbacks, opportunity cost comparisons, distribution constraints, etc., until ultimately much of what was produced was basically irrelevant, a wasted investment.[21] A similarly blinkered approach to the information economy is likely to produce similarly dysfunctional results.

Finally, thinking about empire—and empire as information—allows us to develop a new vocabulary, a lexical arena currently in such a state of crisis that it strikes me as one of the key features inhibiting successful innovations in policy. At the broadest level, we have nearly reached the point of exhaustion in applying prefixes to our strategic conceptions, from post-Cold War, post-modern and post-colonial to neo-conservative and neo-Marxist.

---

[21] Paul Kennedy, *The Rise and Fall of the Great Powers*, New York: Random House, 1987, p. 492-493.

Intellectually, it's as if we were talking about telephones as post-telegraphs or television as neo-radio. The analogy with technological terms becomes clearer in the context of non-English discourse. Telephones, satellites, movies, etc. have generally entered the linguistic realm in English-speaking spaces, and the English words have subsequently entered other spaces to serve as signs for previously unnamed phenomena. With my poor Hindi, I have found myself from time to time struggling with a long and particularly convoluted devnagari-script term in an Indian newspaper, only to realize in a flash of Ephesian clarity[22] that this was actually a phonetic rendering of "satellite communications technology." Sometimes the transplant proves more threatening—witness official French attempts to "purge" English terms, typically those related to technology and media, from the language. Closer to home, while stationed at Pearl Harbor, my local Honolulu public radio station had a regular feature—the "Hawaiian Word of the Day." Usually, this was something along the lines of "appreciation for a good deed," or "a hole or tear in fabric," words of long-standing application. But occasionally, there were awkward attempts at innovation to create a Hawaiian term for "carburetor" or "radio broadcast." The point is that our vocabulary for talking about—and thus thinking about—matters of strategic intelligence is limited in a similar way, with concrete consequences. For instance, the fundamental lack of a commonly accepted word for the inmates at Guantanomo Bay has ramifications for diplomacy, international law, the practical administration of justice and domestic U.S. politics. Our way of engaging these issues has "so long been associated with the interests and devices of nation-states that it is hard to conceive of a culturally rhizomatic geopolitics."[23]

Empire, however, just as the world we now live in, "seems rhizomic, even schizophrenic, calling for theories of rootlessness, alienation and psychological distance....[24] "Empires seem to combine aspects of both domestic and international politics."[25] "Empire is born and shows itself as crisis."[26] This very

22 "...the mystery made known to me by revelation..." Paul's Letter to the Ephesians, 3:3, *The Holy Bible*, New International Version, Cambridge: Cambridge Univ., 1984.

23 William Thornton, *New World Empire: Civil Islam, Terrorism and the Making of Neoglobalism*, New York and Oxford: Rowman and Littlefield, 2005, p. 38. Applying the botanical concept of rhizomes [literally, underground, horizontally spreading stems that periodically and progressively sprout roots and shoots] to politics is generally associated with Gilles Deleuze and Felix Guattari (*A Thousand Plateaus: Capitalism and Schizophrenia*, trans. Brian Massumi, Minneapolis: University of Minnesota, 1987). Over time, the idea has increasingly been associated with phenomena that seem to defy easy definition, like globalization or the Internet. I will consider how this theme might be applied to imperial information systems below in "Unity and Multiplicity".

24 Appadurai, *Modernity at Large: Cultural Dimensions of Globalization*, p. 29.

25 Michael Doyle, *Empires*, Ithaca, NY and London: Cornell University, 1986, p. 35.

26 Michael Hardt and Antonio Negri, *Empire*, p. 20.

sense of crisis and schizophrenia, both issues of the imagination, of information and how it is perceived, suggest to me something of how empires succeed—despite, rather than because of highly developed bureaucratic structures, which the polyglot nature of empire continuously subverts. All systems tend toward entropy, which is essentially a measure of lost information, when considered in its mass-energy context.[27] Creativity, however, reduces entropy by articulating new configurations that can self-organize; and creativity goes hand in hand with chaos, each engendering the other.[28] Rhizomic, hybrid, crisis-ridden information orders are prime sites for creativity, forestalling or reversing the tendency toward entropy. Chaos emerges from the contest of patterns.

Critiquing the barriers to information exchange, Gayatri Spivak observes:

> [B]orders are easily crossed from metropolitan countries, whereas attempts to enter from the so-called peripheral countries encounter bureaucratic and policed frontiers, altogether more difficult to penetrate. In spite of the fact that the effects of globalization can be felt all over the world, that there are satellite dishes in Nepalese villages, the opposite is never true.[29]

Precisely which side is the most disadvantaged by these conditions is, however, open to debate. The Nepalese villagers have daily access both to their own patterns as well as those of the metropole to a degree the Lonely Planet tourist passing through Kathmandu can only superficially approximate. The space for creativity here exists in the so-called margins, rather than the center; it is a space that empire can access through its hybrid nature, but which is denied to the hard-limits of the nation-state. Historically, empires have profited by the permeability of these borders. Describing the British experience, Thomas Metcalf notes that: "Ideas and people flowed outward from India.... Throughout the 19th Century, as the extension of empire provided security and opened trade routes.... Indian traders and businessmen followed behind the British flag."[30] In an even earlier era, "The Romans spoke Greek to the Greeks...Greek became virtually compulsory for the support of the Roman Empire."[31] Marginal identities proliferate in empires, and it is precisely among

---

27 John Archibald Wheeler, *At Home in the Universe*, Woodbury, NY: American Institute of Physics, 1994, p. 298.

28 Stephen Guastello, *Chaos, Catastrophe and Human Affairs*, Mahwak, NJ: Lawrence Erlbaum, 1995, p. 301, 320.

29 Gayatri Chakravorty Spivak, *Death of a Discipline*, New York: Columbia, 2003, p. 16.

30 Thomas Metcalf, *Ideologies of the Raj*, Cambridge: Cambridge University, 1994, p. 215.

31 Arnaldo Momigliano, *Alien Wisdom: The Limits of Hellenization*, Cambridge: Cambridge University, 1971, p. 18, 21.

marginal communities that creativity flourishes. One study of intellectual achievement in the United States concluded that 44% of the most prominent individuals measured were relative newcomers—a proportional representation seven times higher than that of families with roots stretching back to the Revolutionary era, suggesting the degree to which the interplay of different languages and cultures enhances the capacity for divergent thinking.[32] This reading of information traffic would counter Niall Ferguson's critique:

> On close inspection, America's strengths may not be those of a natural imperial hegemon. For one thing, British imperial power relied on the massive export of capital and people. But since 1972, the U.S. economy has been a net importer of capital...and it remains the favored destination of immigrants from around the world, not a producer of would-be colonial emigrants.[33]

Incoming information, embodied in physical people and things, would provide a potential source of strength for American intelligence. The complex and contested nature of those information patterns, however—the chaos that breeds creativity and reduces entropy—requires a slightly different approach to intelligence than we are accustomed to, both in the questions we pose and in the answers we expect to find in those patterns.

A Demon and a Map

"Don't give me rumors or theories, I want the facts." Certainly most intelligence analysts, and likely many of those working in similar fields, have received guidance along these lines from their bosses. Facts are something we can rely on, and presumably if we have enough of them, we may even get something like "truth." If the facts can be expressed in numbers or articulated through mathematics, so much the better. To that end, let me pose a formula: $t^1 > t$. It's short and simple, but like the better known $e=mc2$ has profound implications for the nature of the physical world. The essential idea is that if all the necessary information is known about a system at time t, the conditions prevailing at some later time t^1 can be accurately predicted. As the idea's foremost proponent, Pierre-Simon Laplace explains it:

> An intelligence that, at a given instant, could comprehend all the forces by which nature is animated and the respective situation of

---

32 Dean Simonton, *Origins of Genius: Darwinian Perspectives on Creativity*, New York: Oxford University, 1999, p. 122-124.

33 Niall Ferguson, *Empire: The Rise and Demise of the British World Order and the Lessons for Global Power*, London and New York: Basic Books, 2002, p. 368.

the beings that make it up, if moreover it were vast enough to submit these data to analysis, would encompass in the same formula the movements of the greatest bodies of the universe and those of the lightest atoms. For such an intelligence nothing would be uncertain, and the future, like the past, would be open to its eyes.[34]

By happy chance, this translation from the French original employs the term "intelligence" to denote its knowing agent, a lexical choice fitting quite neatly with another articulation which claims "intelligence [here of the political-military variety] aims at performing three principal functions: description, explanation and prediction."[35] Total Information Awareness? Laplace's Demon, as this intelligence has become more broadly known (an unintended irony, given the association I have proposed here), might have proven a suitable agent for creating the map described in a note by Borges:

In that Empire, the craft of Cartography attained such Perfection that the Map of a Single province covered the space of an entire City, and the Map of the Empire itself an entire Province. In the course of Time, these extensive maps were found somehow wanting, and so the College of Cartographers evolved a Map of the Empire that was of the same Scale as the Empire and that coincided with it point for point. Less attentive to the Study of Cartography, succeeding Generations came to judge a map of such Magnitude cumbersome, and, not without Irreverence, they abandoned it to the Rigors of sun and Rain. In the western Deserts, tattered Fragments of the Map are still to be found, Sheltering an occasional Beast or beggar; in the whole Nation, no other relic is left of the Discipline of Geography.[36]

Borges' erstwhile geographers discovered that at some point, the attempt to know with such exactitude, or to achieve real-time, all-source, persistent global coverage at a sub-national level of granularity, in a more recent formulation, becomes dysfunctional and ultimately irrelevant. The problem would not daunt Laplace's Demon or his terrestrial counterparts. Achieving such awareness might be nearly impossible for practical reasons; but given enough time, enough money, enough people, enough bandwidth and enough processing speed it could at least be approximated. The closer the Demon

---

34 Pierre-Simon Laplace, *Philosophical Essay on Probabilities*, trans. Andrew Dale, New York: Springer-Verlag, (1819) 1995, p. 2.

35 Woodrow Kuhns, "Intelligence Failure: Forecasting and the Lessons of Epistemology," *Paradoxes of Strategic Intelligence*, ed. Richard Betts and Thomas Mahnken, London and Portland: Frank Cass, 2003, p. 85.

36 Jorge Luis Borges, *A Universal History of Infamy*, Trans. Norman Thomas di Giovanni, New York: E.P. Dutton, 1972, p. 141.

comes to realizing its goals, however, the more it confronts a more fundamental challenge. "The quest for precision is not limited by its cost, but by the very nature of matter. It is not true that uncertainty (lack of control) decreases as accuracy goes up: it goes up as well," Jean-Francois Lyotard argues. He then proceeds to offer a material example of the problem:

> [M]easurement of the real density (the mass/volume quotient) of a given quantity of air contained in a sphere…varies noticeably when the volume of the sphere is reduced from 100 m^3 to 1 cm^3, although already in this range irregularly occurring variations of the order of a billionth can be observed. As the volume for the sphere decreases, the size of the variations increases; for a volume 1/10th of a cubic micron, the variations are of the order of a thousandth; and for 1/100th of a cubic micron, they are of the order of 1/5th.[37]

Feeding Laplace's Demon ultimately becomes the fatal temptation for power, a siren song that promises paradise as it lures the unsuspecting to disaster. The risk only grows greater with the seductive addition of secrecy, which masks its contents with an aura of special authority to which all information aspires. A British political letter from 19th Century Bengal captures the phenomenon:

> The Governor General observed that of late years it had been the practice to record in the Secret department generally all the correspondence with presidents of Foreign Courts and Political Agents, and all documents on subjects of a political nature, with the exception of such as related to accounts and issues of money, or such as were, strictly speaking, of a public nature, and considered Political merely because of their connection with those branches of the general administration which were cognizable in the Political Department. That by this arrangement nearly the whole of the Political proceedings of Government had been recorded in the Secret Department, which had occasioned the necessity of addressing our several letters on almost all political subjects to the Secret Committee, although many of these subjects were not strictly of a secret nature.[38]

---

37 Jean-Francois Lyotard, *The Postmodern Condition: A Report on Knowledge*, trans. Geoff Bennington and Brian Massumi, Minneapolis: University of Minnesota, (1979) 1993, p. 56.

38 L/P&S/6/17, Political Letters from Bengal, Vol. 2, p. 64-66, Cited in Martin Ian Moir, *A Study of the History and Organization of the Political and Secret Department of the East India Company, the Board of Control and the India Office 1784-1919 with a Summary List of Records*, thesis in support of University of London Diploma in Archive Administration, August, 1996, p. 81.

The language may be a bit tortured and the specific administrative units dated, but the general theme undoubtedly recognized by anyone familiar with the alphabet of acronyms and color-coded badges that has steadily seeped out to deform even apparently irrelevant spaces of social information like YouTube. Once secrecy sets in, it is a weed profoundly difficult to uproot.

So, no definitions, and a fair amount of abstraction here at the start; but before we ascend too far into the ethereal, I want to turn to a viscerally physical incarnation of these issues. This concrete rooting is, I believe, vital when discussing a phenomenon as intangible as information. The idea of patterns suggests something incorporeal and free-floating, but ultimately these patterns only adopt meaning when manifested in arrangements of "mass-energy relations." Gayotri Spivak captures this in her assessment of a sometime pseudonym for empire:

> Globalization is the imposition of the same system of exchange everywhere. In the gridwork of electronic capital, we achieve that abstract ball covered in latitudes and longitudes, cut by virtual lines, once the equator and the tropics and so on, now drawn by the requirements of Geographical Information Systems…The globe is on our computers. No one lives there. It allows us to think we can aim to control it. The planet is in the species of alterity, belonging to another system; and yet we inhabit it, on loan.[39]

Spivak's distinction between the globe and the planet captures a key conundrum of knowledge, and intelligence, production. The risk of drawing virtual lines and imposing order on the grand confusion of reality is not simply that our lines may be imperfect, our approximation inexact. Rather, these virtual creations can become so comfortable and accessible that we come to inhabit them as real, producing "knowledge" about things and places that don't actually exist. Reality as such then enters into the "species of alterity"; it literally becomes something foreign and other—opaque, if not irrelevant, to our attempts to understand it. I now want to look at a particularly striking example of such reality construction in British India. Given these prefatory notes about globalization, the discussion begins appropriately with the fictional harbinger of the phenomenon: *Around the World in 80 days.*

---

[39] Gayatri Chakravorty Spivak, Death of a Discipline, New York: Columbia, 2003, p. 72.

Thuggee: Making the Invisible Visible

It was thereabouts that Feringhea, the Thuggee chief, king of the stranglers, held his sway. These ruffians, united by a secret bond, strangled victims of every age in honour of the goddess Death, without ever shedding blood; there was a period when this part of the country could scarcely be travelled over without corpses being found in every direction. The English Government has succeeded in greatly diminishing these murders, though the Thuggees still exist, and pursue the exercise of their horrible rites.[40]

Jules Verne only noted the phenomenon of Thuggee in passing, and we never learn in *Around the World in 80 Days* how the phlegmatic Phileas Fogg, embodiment of empire, might have dealt with them. Presumably he didn't have the time. But this brief sketch outlines the key points of the problem—secrecy, conspiracy, religious fanaticism, the wholesale slaughter of innocents, and a capacity for eluding legitimate government. The threat embodied by Thuggee has remained a resonant one over a century after Verne's novel, confronted later by popular heroes from Cary Grant and Douglas Fairbanks, Jr. (*Gunga Din*, 1939) to Harrison Ford (*Indiana Jones and the Temple of Doom*, 1984). More to the point, it does not require a vast imagination to see how those definitive qualities might be applied to other real-world phenomena in modern times. Take, for example, comments in the April 2006 U.S. National Intelligence Assessment regarding terrorism (unclassified extract):

> Although we cannot measure the extent of the spread with precision, a large body of all-source reporting indicates that activists identifying themselves as jihadists, although a small percentage of Muslims, are increasing in both number and geographic dispersion. If this trend continues, threats to US interests at home and abroad will become more diverse, leading to increasing attacks worldwide….We assess that the global jihadist movement is decentralized, lacks a coherent global strategy, and is becoming more diffuse. New jihadist networks and cells, with anti-U.S. agendas, are increasingly likely to emerge. The confluence of shared

---

[40] Jules Verne, *Around the World in 80 Days*, trans. Michael Glencross, London: Penguin, 2004, p. 61.

purpose and dispersed actors will make it harder to find and undermine jihadist groups.[41]

Not only are the groups described here secret, religiously inspired and implacably hostile, but they are spreading. Although employing slightly more hyperbolic rhetoric, the fictional Thug captive in the bestselling 1839 novel *Confessions of a Thug* expresses similar sentiments in this foreboding assessment:

> Yet Thuggee, capable of exciting the mind so strongly, will not, cannot be annihilated! Look at the hundreds, I may say thousands, who have suffered for its profession; does the number of your prisoners decrease? No, on the contrary they increase; and from every Thug who accepts the alternative of perpetual imprisonment to dying on a gallows, you learn of others whom even I knew not of, and of Thuggee being carried on in parts of the country where it is least suspected, and has never been discovered till lately.[42]

Let the reader then compare the American government response to modern perils with this note from G. W. Swinton, Chief Secretary to Government, Fort William, 4th August 1830:

> With regard to these organized Bands of inhuman wretches whose profession and livelihood is cold blooded murder, the Governor General in Council deems it of the greatest importance to endeavor to break up if possible, the whole system by the apprehension of the principal leaders who must be well known…. By the secret employment, under due precautions of some of the witnesses and approvers stimulated by the promise of a liberal reward on the conviction of the Leaders in question, such a knowledge might be acquired of their plans for their next annual excursion as might greatly facilitate their apprehensions by the British Authorities, if timely apprized of the probable scene of their operations.[43]

Beyond this emotive concurrence between past and present, what strikes me as intriguing and enduringly relevant about the issue is the way in which the imperial situation shaped the government's attempt to understand this problem, and the way authorities constructed and marshaled "knowledge" to defeat the perceived threat.

---

41 *Declassified Key Judgments of the National Intelligence Estimate "Trends in Global Terrorism: Implications for the United States,"* dated April 2006, accessed 7 Feb 2007 at *http://www.dni.gov/press_releases/Declassified_NIE_Key_Judgments.pdf.*

42 Meadows Taylor, *Confessions of a Thug,* New Delhi and Madras: Asian Educational Services, 1988 (First printed 1839), p. 1.

43 *Oriental and India Office Collections,* Mss. Eur., D1188, p.5.

Despite its many fictional embellishments, the phenomenon broadly described by the term "Thuggee" does in fact denote historically recorded violence, with European accounts of Indian robbers who principally employed deception and strangulation dating back to the late 17th Century.[44] Mughal rulers in the same period were equally aware of the problem, illustrated by emperor Aurungzeb's 1672 *firman* [royal mandate or decree], describing appropriate punishments for stranglers who were particularly "habitual" and "notorious" for their practices.[45] More broadly, by the early 19th Century India was wracked by a rise in banditry brought on by economic and political dislocation.[46] Basic components of the story were thus well established by the time the 3 October 1830 edition of Calcutta's *Journal of Belles Letters, Science and the Arts* printed an anonymous letter, shocking its readers with a host of revelations about the heretofore invisible menace in their midst (the original runs to near 6,000 words):

> Kali's temple at Bindachul, a few miles west of Mirzapor on the Ganges, is constantly filled with murderers from every quarter of India between the rivers Narbada, Ganges and Indus, who go there to offer up in person a share of the booty they have acquired from the victims strangled in their annual excursions.... If they die by the sword in the execution of these murderous duties by her assigned or sanctioned, she promises them paradise in its most exquisite delights.... It is an organized system of religious and civil polity prepared to receive converts from all religions and sects and to urge them to the murder of their fellow creatures under the assurance of high rewards in this world and the next.[47]

Within fairly short order, the author of the letter was revealed to be a relatively obscure captain serving as a district officer, who became ultimately Major General Sir William Sleeman. A special task force was set up to combat the problem, led by Sleeman and operating outside the authority of the civil administration. By 1836, a Thuggee Act was established which allowed: prosecution with retroactive effect, for Thug association inside or outside British administered territory; with no customary regard for local Indian legal pre-

---

44 Jean de Thevenot, *The travels of Monsieur de Thevenot into the Levant*, London: Printed by H. Clark, for H. Faithorne, J. Adamson, C. Skegnes, and T. Newborough, 1687, p. 369-70.

45 Cited in Kim Wagner, "The Deconstructed Stranglers: A Reassessment of Thuggee," *Modern Asian Studies*, Vol. 38, No. 4 (October 2004), p. 942-943.

46 Sandria Freitag, "Crime in the Social Order of Colonial North India," *Modern Asian Studies*, Vol. 25, No. 2 (May, 1991), p. 233.

47 *Calcutta Literary Gazette, Journal of Belles letters, Sciences and the Arts*, in George Bruce, *The Stranglers: The Cult of Thuggee and Its Overthrow in British India*, New York: Harcourt Brace, 1968, p. 82-83.

rogative, and on evidence largely provided by the testimony of apprehend-
ed Thugs; all without ever defining precisely what constituted the crime of
"Thuggee."[48]

All this extraordinary legal innovation took place at the precise moment
official policy sought to legitimize British paramountcy through establishing
the "rule of law," and despite widespread and vocal protests of many British officers who noted quite clearly how radically despotic this activity really was.[49]
Moreover, outside the claims of Sleeman, his newly empowered associates,
and the less-than-disinterested testimony of his informants ("Approvers'),
there is little independent evidence, contemporary or modern, to suggest any
particular organization, conspiracy or specific religious theme to the violence
afflicting the early 19th Century Indian countryside.[50]

This apparent disconnect between the genuine security threat (clearly,
"something" was happening on the roads), the available evidence, and avowed
British legal principles is symptomatic of the problems confronting imperial
intelligence. As the British empire in India expanded, it encompassed an increasing expanse of human and physical terrain which it did not fundamentally understand, prompting the series of "information panics" which characterized the British experience in the sub-continent.[51] The entire discourse of
Thuggee captures this anxiety, and is "troped by figures of darkness, mystery,
inscrutability, unpredictability, and unexpected menace."[52] Even when captured, tried and convicted, the Thuggee managed to escape the moral and
corporeal censure of the state, laughing on the way to the gibbet in a way that
both fascinated and horrified British witnesses: each individual placed the
rope around his own neck, and "as soon as he had adjusted the noose, jumped
off the beam and launched himself into eternity."[53]

The real issue, in this reading, is not so much the actual crime or its ultimate
punishment; but rather the "not knowing" which threatens a more total loss
of control. The challenge of Thuggee then was principally about information,
rather than the information's practical employment, and it is this formulation

---

[48] Radhika Singha, "'Providential' Circumstances: The Thuggee Campaign of the 1830s
and Legal Innovation," *Modern Asian Studies*, Vol. 27, No. 1 (February 1993), p. 83-84.

[49] Upamanyo Pablo Mukherjee, *Crime and Empire: The Colony in Nineteenth-Century Fictions of Crime*, Oxford: Oxford University, 2003, p. 99.

[50] Stewart Gordon, *Marathas, Marauders, and State Formation*, Delhi: Oxford University,
1994, p. 9.

[51] C.A. Bayly, *Empire and Information: Intelligence Gathering and Social Communication
in India, 1780-1870*, Cambridge and New York: Cambridge University, 1996, p. 143, 149,
171-3, 316.

[52] Parama Roy, *Indian Traffic*, Berkeley: University of California, 1998, p. 54.

[53] Fanny Parks, *Begums, Thugs and White Mughals*, London: Sickle Moon, 2002 (originally
published as *Wanderings of a Pilgrim in Search of the Picturesque*, 1850), p. 89, 120-121.

Tangled jungles and rocky thickets were the presumed haunts of the thugs, in the unmapped spaces which physically resist imperial vision.
Source: photo by author.

of the problem which explains William Sleeman's remarkable success—not because he was able to "exterminate" Thuggee, which still lurked about for Jules Verne's characters decades later, but because he was able to explain it.

> As the sole authority on Thuggee, Sleeman constructed a religion and a thug language based on a few informers and subsequently made sweeping assertions where single statements became dogma and thugee took on the appearance of a religious cult.[54]

In short, Sleeman made the inchoate world of Indian violence "knowable." Better still, he constructed this knowledge in a way that looked and felt scientific, with the form providing as much comfort as the content. Beyond the depositions and confessions used in criminal trials, Sleeman and other anti-Thuggee officers conducted long interviews with captured Thugs in a sort of early anthropological field project, publishing their findings for a wider British commercial audience.[55] From these conversations, Sleeman built up

---

54 Wagner, "Deconstructed Strangler," p. 947.

55 Martine van Woerkens, *The Strangled Traveler: Colonial Imaginings and the Thugs of India*, trans. Catherine Tihanyi, Chicago: University of Chicago, 1995, p. 114.

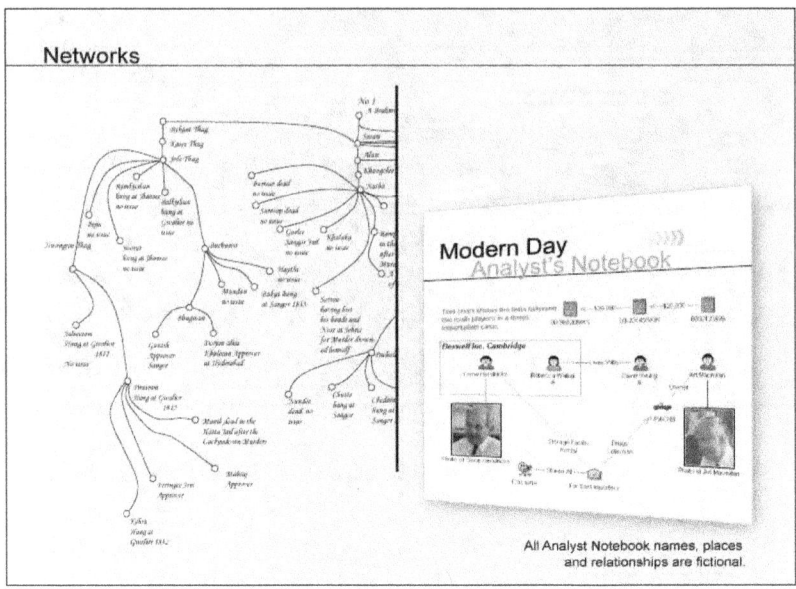

Networks drawn by Sleeman (from his Ramaseeana, 1836; modified from original) and by desktop link analysis (notional).

a vocabulary of the Thugs' "secret language," rendering them thereby culturally legible.[56] Additionally, he built up family trees, operational diagrams and charts—the architecture of social science—to make the invisible, visible.

The modern effort to delineate, classify, and assign structure to movements which are "decentralized" and "diffuse" but share "anti-American agendas" suggests a similar sense of anxiety and response. In form, if not precise substance, it is illuminating to compare a sample link analysis screen—from a popular information management tool within the U.S. intelligence community—with another "link diagram" prepared more than a century ago with similar aims in mind. While Sleeman draws only longitudinal connections, which the modern analogue supplements with latitudinal links for a more sophisticated grid, the operation is fundamentally the same. By physically and visually drawing a line between two points, a new mote of information is created, literally out of thin air. When I first encountered Sleeman's drawings as a graduate student, I was captivated by this image of a cephalopodic network of sinister conspiracy. It was only later, after learning how these apparent connections were generated, that the tenuousness of the entire enterprise became clear. Later, in my early postings on intelligence

---

56 James Hutton, *Thugs and Dacoits of India*, Delhi: Gian, 1981 (First published 1857), p. 41-47.

assignments, I experienced the same sense of fascination and disenchantment with more recent varieties of the same technique. The "aha" moment for me in seeing these two charts came not because they were technically identical—the cross-connections of Analyst Notebook and the like are distinctly different—but rather because the representative effect is the same. The image of connection, the portrayal of a system, has an impact all its own, ordering the way we see relationships in much the same way that latitude and longitude lines materially influence the way we imagine space.

These charts are not simply images or containers for information, but are also explicit performances. The drawing of lines represents a literal "striation" of "smooth" space, which otherwise threatened to overwhelm imperial administration with its "nomadic" resistance to British categories of understanding.[57] Once harnessed by this network grid, the blank spaces could then be filled up with careful, sometimes touching, annotation: e.g. "Pucholee adopted Rambutkho Jemadar, for whose apprehension 500 Rupees reward was offered, supposed to be in the service of Gruikwhan at Baroda," or "Bodhooa shot himself for love."

In articulating a spatial operation here, I think it worth noting the physical space in which Sleeman's campaign took root. First encountering the Thugs in his own area of administration, a sort of gray area at the cusp of British expansion,[58] Sleeman noted in the Calcutta Gazette letter cited above that: "In the territories of the native chiefs…a Thug feels just as independent and free as an Englishman in his tavern," while at the same time "so may these men be found often most securely established in the very seats of our principal judicial establishments." In other words, they defy domestic/foreign distinctions and physically embody the problems of marginal identity and space inherent to the imperial situation.

Despite this critique, as a purely practical affair I must confess a degree of sympathy with Sleeman and his project. My professional identity as a U.S. Army Foreign Area Officer—specifically trained in foreign culture and language to perform duties which span the diplomatic/military divide (and a South Asia specialist, to boot)—is not terribly different from that of the military officers on deputation to the Political Department in the Raj. I, too, have sat confronting a

---

57 Derived from the works of Gilles Deleuze and Felix Guattari, *A Thousand Plateaus: Capitalism and Schizophrenia*, Minneapolis: University of Minnesota press, 1987, my use of "nomadic" throughout this text refers to people and concepts that defy fixed categorization in time, place or description. Best exemplified by Bedouin tribes, First Peoples and Pirates, Nomads in this sense are counter-poised to the rigid social categories embodied by the State, the Caste, the census, etc.

58 Singha, "'Providential' Circumstances," p. 89.

blank sheet of paper, or a computer screen, and an apparently random mass of places, names and violent incidents demanding to be analyzed and ordered. Like Sleeman, I have "constructed" grids for containing information. I even came up with an acronym that went into common usage—perhaps the high point of a mid-grade officer's career. Nevertheless, all that familiarity simply adds to my concern in considering his body of work, and what this phenomenon represents. For if the construction of Thuggee and all its associated texts represents an operation of power on knowledge, that knowledge also worked back on the power which constituted it.

Once Thuggee had been established as a distinct category, it could be articulated in fiction as well as official discourse, until the Queen of England became an avid and breathless consumer of the story.[59] The appeal of this narrative as explanation, obviously established well "outside," made alternative, "inside" explanations more difficult to recognize. In particular, enamored as they were with this scintillating cult, the British were unable to detect the way their own operations in India had created major disruptions in the market for military labor—the surplus of which was ultimately responsible for much of the violence labeled as Thugee.[60] This "knowledge" consequently created a sort of feedback loop, inhibiting other kinds of knowledge and potentially more effective applications of power. Similarly, once the form of Thuggee had been established, the kinds of questions applied to suspects took on a ritual quality, and not surprisingly the kinds of answers driven by this process took on an almost identical aspect in thousands of cases.[61] Again, knowledge worked backward—constraining what might otherwise have been learned—to shape the activities and exercise of power. More broadly, the seduction of Thuggee as an information container gradually expanded to encompass almost any variety of misconduct from routine banditry to kidnapping and poisoning, ensuring it could never genuinely be defeated, and ultimately shaping the way the imperial power would engage with its subjects in years to come, sometimes with disastrous results.[62]

From this perspective, the 1830s campaign is not—as the hagiographers would have it—"the ghoulish and sinister story of the secret Thug societies of India and how 150 years ago William Sleeman, a young Bengal Army officer

---

[59] Meadows Taylor, *The Story of My Life*, New Delhi: Asian Educational Service, 1986 (First published 1882), p. 117, 120.

[60] Gordon, *Marathas*, p. 21-22.

[61] Van Woerken, *Strangled Traveler*, p. 60.

[62] Roy, *Indian Traffic*, p. 54-55.

[63] Bruce, *Stranglers*, Preface.

led the twelve-year campaign that broke them up and suppressed them."[63] Rather, it is a cautionary tale about the seductions and ramifications associated with knowledge production. The urge to fill up the blank spaces on the page, with press reports, official documents, scientific studies, or fiction, can conceal as much as it reveals, calling to mind the original Sanskrit root, sthag: "to cover, recover, to hide, to veil, to make invisible, to disappear."[64] Consequently, circumspection is most merited precisely when knowledge seems most certain, particularly when claims like Sleeman's own are made.

> I have, I believe, entered in this vocabulary everything to which Thugs in any part of India have thought it necessary to assign a peculiar term; and every term peculiar to their associations with which I have yet to become acquainted. I am satisfied there is no term, no rite, no ceremony, no opinion, no omen or usage that they have intentionally concealed from me; and if any have been accidentally omitted after the numerous narratives that I have had to record, and cases to investigate, they can be but comparatively few and unimportant.[65]

Lack of such circumspection has consequences beyond simply failing to properly address the problem at hand. The drive to create information, to feed the insatiable appetite of Laplace's Demon, can undermine the fundamental architecture that supports the construction of knowledge. Let us take, for example, an internal dispute over the guilt of a specific individual accused of Thuggee. Despite the abundant and creative production of knowledge surrounding the broader discourse, here at the sharp end of the law, guilt or innocence usually came down to the testimony of a few individuals, themselves generally already convicted and then turning "state's witness" to testify against former partners in crime. The individual here in question, one Abji, had been detained by the Thagi and Dacoity[66] Department based on the testimony of three such witnesses, or Approvers in the parlance of the time. When later judicial review called this evidence into question, the Department protested that the three Approvers had been confined separately, and had given independent testimony as to the accused Thug's identity. In support of this argument, a chart was provided setting out this testimony in which each of the Approvers describes the suspect's particulars.

---

64 Van Woerkens, *Strangled Traveler*, p. 116.

65 W.H. Sleeman, *Ramaseeana* (1836) cited in Roy, *Indian Traffic*, p. 57.

66 Dacoity = armed robbery.

Approver	Parentage	Caste	Age	Residence	Height	Color	Body
Bhopru	unknown	Rajpot	30	Serolia	short	dark	medium
Dewa	unknown	Rajpot	35	Seolia	short	dark	thin
Unkar	Gopal	Rajpot	22	Seolia	short	dark	thin

Clearly, there was a short Rajput with dark hair living in Serolia, though beyond that the issue becomes a bit hazy. The Thagi and Dacoity official helpfully notes that natives were "notoriously unreliable" when it comes to assigning age—here more than a decade's difference.[67] The British were well aware how dubious the whole affair was always in danger of becoming, as the controversy around this particular case indicates. The record preserves a series of documents racing up and down the administrative hierarchy, capturing some of the passionate and visceral nature of this debate over knowledge, hand-written notes with barely concealed personal animosities giving way to typed memoranda thick with the discourse of bureaucratic department rivalry. One particular letter from the judicial department captures the problem, noting how presumptively objective fact-finding can become when conflated with prosecutorial intent. In any era of extraordinary renditions and special military tribunals, the text is an evocative, cautionary note on the reliability of information under-girding those projects:

> The Prosecution in these cases very naturally assumes a man accused by the approvers, to be guilty, and bends all the circumstances to that conclusion, but let it be assumed that the man is innocent and let the case be regarded under this aspect. A resident in a village in the Bellary districts of the Madras Presidency, an ignorant and indigent man, is suddenly arrested, and taken off some two hundred miles into another Presidency, and charged before a special court with the commission of Dacoitee about (12) twelve years before the date of his arrest. Against the man thus removed far from his own friends, and acquaintances, appears a Prosecutor, the experienced head of a formidable Department, and witnesses, who have themselves committed various Dacoities, against whom convictions have been recorded, and who have been pardoned on the condition of bearing evidence against their accomplices. Can it be said that the accused has that reasonable opportunity afforded to him of proving his innocence which justice demands, and that the scales are held equally between the Government and the Prisoner at the bar.[68]

---

67 *National Archives of India*, Home, Thagi and Dacaity, B 1. No. 16, 1890.

68 *National Archives of India*, Home, Thagi and Dacaity, B. 1, No. 8, 1868 [1858], p. 5-6.

As I argued earlier, information traffic has a two-way function, and the very act of collection—what questions are asked, and how, as well as what constitutes valid knowledge—is also an act of transmission. The reliance on Approvers told a story about the British to an Indian audience with unsavory implications, as noted by the Mysore Commissioner's Office:

> As this is the second occasion on which the Panchayets [village councils], who have sat on the Thug Trials, have recorded their opinion of the false and contradictory evidence of some of the approvers, the Commissioner apprehends that such repeated instances of falsehood will not only tend to shake the confidence of the Panchayets in the veracity of the approvers, but also to render these individuals less scrupulous in their observance of truth if a deviation from it is permitted to pass with impunity.[69]

Despite these protests and controversies, the perceived threat of Thuggee continued to empower the Department established to combat it through extraordinary measures of knowledge production. Far from being esoteric matters of technique and administration, these ultimately had consequences for imperial political legitimacy, the very nature of knowledge and the British sense of their own identity. Modern counterparts might note the anguish expressed by Bhurtpoore's Political Agent in 1832:

> The object of my dispatches was to point out the objectionable method (as it appeared to me) pursued by this party of Thug Hunters in apprehending persons upon mere hearsay evidence without receiving the defence of the parties apprehending and without asking or obtaining the sanction of the Local authorities. I now learn, I must confess, with no little astonishment that however "extraordinary" the measures adopted may have been, still they were both just and necessary because Thuggee cannot otherwise be checked. In other words that the end sanctifies the means, a doctrine which I had erroneously supposed to have been long since exploded, alike from morals as politics.[70]

Extraordinary as the problem of Thuggee may have seemed to British administrators, however, the issue would have been familiar to earlier imperial agents in both the Ottoman and Roman empires. A century earlier and hundreds of miles to the west of Bhurtpoore, Ottoman jurists were applying their own special terminology to those malefactors who resolutely refused to fit into the architecture of imperial legal space.

---

69 *National Archives of India*, Home, Thagi and Dacaity, B.1, No. 4, 1838, p. 6-7.

70 *Oriental and India Office Collections*, Eur. Mss. D1188, p. 165.

Sai bil' fesad: Fomenting Evil in the World

Mulla Nasrudin and his wife came home one day to find the house
burgled. Everything portable had been taken away.
'It is all your fault,' said his wife, 'for you should have made sure the house
was locked before we left.'
    The neighbors took up the chant:
    'You did not lock the windows,' said one.
    'Why did you not expect this?' said another.
    'The locks were faulty and you did not replace them,' said a third.
    'Just a moment,' said Nasrudin, '- surely I am not the only one to
blame?'
        'And who should we blame?' they shouted.
        'What about the thieves?' said the Mulla.[71]

The hapless Mulla Nasrudin's misadventure hints at a number of "secrets"—vital pieces of information not immediately susceptible to direct observation—which nevertheless are key to understanding what is happening in his world. Beyond the most obvious (Who were the thieves?), there are questions of intent (Did Nasrudin consciously neglect his duties or simply forget?), responsibility (Who really enjoys "agency" in this world?), and expectation (What does reasonable analysis suggest the future holds?). Presuming Nasrudin escapes his wife's wrath—a constant threat in his picaresque life—these various kinds of concealed knowledge will ultimately be matters for the courts—matters of law.

As Foucault would have it, and I am inclined to believe him in this regard, "the exercise of power is always formulated in terms of law."[72] But it is more than that, and by providing a mechanism for encoding basic cultural assumptions, the law also constitutes a form of "local knowledge."[73] Suspecting, as I have from the outset, that an "imperial way of knowing" involves a distinct interplay of knowledge and power, the law then appears to me as a particularly fascinating site of such interplay. I have already suggested how this phenomenon might have manifested itself in the British context, but with

---

[71] Idries Shah, *The Pleasantries of the Incredible Mulla Nasrudin*, New York: E.P. Dutton, 1971, p. 50.

[72] Michel Foucault, *The History of Sexuality*, Volume I, trans. Robert Hurley, New York: Pantheon, 1978, p. 87.

[73] Clifford Geertz, "Local Knowledge: Fact and Law in Comparative Perspective," *Local Knowledge*, New York: Basic Books, 1983, p. 167-234.

the multiplication of legal identities and legal spaces in the Ottoman realm, the issue becomes more pronounced. This is a problem applicable as well to the Roman world.

Like Roman law, the Ottoman system involved constructing the identity of individuals in order to locate them within a specific legal space. Beyond the Latin bi-polar categories of "Roman citizens" (*ius civile*) and "everyone else" (*ius gentium*)—a simple line—the geometry of Ottoman legal space involved a network of intersecting and overlapping bifurcations: free/slave, male/female, Muslim/non-Muslim, and taxpayer (*reaya*)/elite (askeri). As Leslie Peirce puts it:

> It was not an ideal of the premodern Ottoman legal system that its justice be blind. Not until the mid-nineteenth century was the idea entertained that the law should encounter the individual as a notional entity rather than as a particular combination of social and civil attributes to be scrutinized and entered into the calculus of judgment[: hence] the labels employed by scribes to identify all litigants who were not freeborn Muslim men—namely, Christians and Jews, freedmen, slaves, minors and females.[74]

Amplifying the complexity, any combination of the above might be enmeshed in "law" emanating from the *sharia* and its textual attendants, the Sultan's decrees (*kanun*) and customary law established among the various guilds. Cleary, such a kaleidoscope does not lend itself to neat interior/exterior identifications; however, it does suggest how information critical to imperial rule might flow throughout the system.

Key to this perspective is an understanding of law which is "not separate from culture but is an integral part of culture. Likewise, it does not stand aloof from the consciousness of members of the culture but is partly constitutive of it."[75] Such an understanding is perhaps not terribly controversial regarding law generally, but it takes on a confrontational air when counterposed to a commonly articulated vision of law within an Islamic context, where:

> …in theory at least, it is not society and its needs which make the law, but the law which shapes society and to which men's needs

---

[74] Leslie Peirce, *Morality Tales: Law and Gender in the Ottoman Court of Aintab*, Berkeley, Los Angeles and London: University of California Press, 2003, p. 143.

[75] David Delaney, "Making Nature/Marking Humans: Law as a Site of (Cultural) Production," *Annals of the Association of American Geographers*, Vol. 91, No. 3 (September 2001), p. 489.

must perforce be conformed. Over the whole world of Islam, with its heterogeneous races and cultures, the Shari'a stands supreme, exacting one standard, prescribing unified norms, and exercising—in theory—an exclusive authority over every aspect of human life.[76]

Divergence between these two perspectives, as actually realized in practice, is the subject of a vast body of literature, perhaps ultimately no more amenable to resolution than differences held in the social sciences between the roles of discourse and ideology. However, like the latter distinction, both interpretations of law refer to a consciousness that "is borne through language and other systems of signs, it is transmitted between people and institutions and, perhaps most of all, *it makes a difference.*"[77] The manifestation of that common consciousness—the law—is a kind of knowledge product, circulating between the rulers and the ruled.

From the nominal centers of power, the provision of law is most obviously a message about sovereignty, albeit of a very specific and imperial type. At one level, as the inscription over Suleyman the Magnificent's mosque portal formulates it, the Sultan is "Promulgator of Sultanic Qanuns;" but more broadly, he is also the one who "makes manifest the Exalted Word of God."[78] In other words, not only is the Sultan's administration competent to issue specific technical orders and decrees to its subjects necessary for the day-to-day conduct of governance (the business of a state), but it also enjoys a special relationship to universal laws applicable to all mankind (the business of empire). One may agree or disagree on the specifics, but it is quite clear which variety of law the U.S. Secretary of State had in mind when addressing the American Bar Association:

> The advance of freedom and the success of democracy and the flourishing of human potential all depend on governments that honor and enforce the rule of law. Today, America's belief in the universal nature of human liberty, a belief we expressed in our Declaration and enshrined in our Constitution, now leads us into a world to help others win their freedom and secure it in law.[79]

---

[76] J.N.D. Anderson, "Law as a Social Force in Islamic Culture and History," *Bulletin of the School of Oriental and African Studies, University of London*, Vol. 20, No. 1/3, Studies in Honour of Sir Ralph Turner, Director of the School of Oriental and African Studies, 1937-57 (1957), p. 17.

[77] Trevor Purvis and Alan Hunt, "Discourse, Ideology, Discourse, Ideology, Discourse, Ideology..." The *British Journal of Sociology*, Vol. 44, No.3 (September 1993), p. 474.

[78] Colin Imber, *Ebu's-su'ud: The Islamic Legal Tradition*, Stanford: Stanford University, 1997, p. 75-76.

[79] States News Service, "Rule of Law is Key to Advancing Democracy, Rice Says," Washington, DC, 9 November 2005.

Law and text, space and power—the inscribed gateway to Suleyman's Mosque.
Source: photo by author.

By its arrogation of universal value, imperial law transmits information beyond that overtly expressed in texts, and in its normalizing linguistic maneuvers, both then and now, defines legal identity in ways which privilege certain positions.[80] Ottoman practice, in particular, as it wrestled to reconcile the dictates of shari'a and day-to-day exigency, highlights this crucial aspect of privileging certain perspectives—emphasizing adherence to normalized values over actual conduct. A legal opinion authored by Suleyman's chief legal advisor illustrates the problem:

> Zeyd is a wine-drinker. While he is drinking wine, he—we take refuge in God—curses, using the f. word, and says: 'Wine's a brilliant thing. I'll so-and-so anybody's wife who doesn't drink it!' 'Amr applauds Zeyd, saying: 'You're right!' What should happen? Answer: They are both infidels. It is permissible to kill them.[81]

At issue here is the statement of support for illicit action (an offense against the community) rather than the actual illicit act itself (a matter between the subject and God). Yet despite these mechanisms for relating the state's priorities and concerns, the law also served as a vehicle for transmitting information back up the system—revealing issues within the body politic perhaps not visible through other means.

One such mechanism is in the practice of customary law. The Ottoman guild system, as mentioned earlier, permeated society, and by creating a body of regulations to govern their internal conduct, the guilds established an equally sprawling and penetrating body of supplementary law which, not surprisingly, typically related to commercial affairs. What is striking about this phenomenon is that despite its relatively autonomous development, this "law" was nevertheless adjudicated through government courts. Once a case was brought before a judge, the state's representative would inquire as to the customary practice in the matter, and then apply that practice as a binding rule. In this arrangement, information about values, relations, financial practices and moral norms grew up from the body politic, was circulated though the legitimizing organs of the state and returned as inviolate as the imposed laws of the Sultan or the *shari'a*.[82]

---

[80] David Armstrong, "Law, Justice and the Idea of a World Society," *International Affairs (Royal Institute of International Affairs, 1944-)*, Vol. 75, No. 3 (July 1999), p. 558.

[81] Cited in Imber, *Ebu's-su'ud*, p. 92.

[82] Haim Gerber, *State, Society and Law in Islam: Ottoman Law in Comparative Perspective*, Albany, NY: State University of New York, 1994, p.113-114.

While the guild issue may represent a comparatively innocuous encounter between the law of the state (or of the divine) and that of custom, specific social practice and tradition could also directly contradict the universal. In this case it was not "the law which shapes society and to which men's needs must perforce be conformed," but rather quite the reverse. A striking case is that of usury, a practice clearly prohibited by the Koran.[83] Despite this overt prohibition, the practice was managed in a roundabout way throughout the Ottoman area of influence through the institution of *waqf*, or the charitable endowment. These were originally envisioned in Islamic law as the dedication in perpetuity of specified real, durable properties toward some public benefit—the proceeds of which could be enjoyed tax-free by the endowing agent and his designees—or hers, as women were well represented in the practice. An Ottoman innovation was to apply the *waqf* conditions to purely cash endowments, in direct contravention of established shari'a construction. Interest-bearing loans were the chief means of deriving income from the dedicated "property."[84] When interested religious scholars took umbrage at the almost explosive growth of the practice, the empire's chief legal/religious officer made the following ruling:

> It is recognized absolutely that throughout the lands of the provinces of Rum [that area of Anatolia conquered from the Byzantines and hence "old" Rum (i.e. Rome)] cash waqf is popular and generally practiced, that most of the awaqf of mosques and welfare establishments are based on cash, that judges past and present relying on the aforementioned citations have ruled in favor of its permissibility, that up till now military judges and provincial governors have been ruling in favor of its validity and irrevocability, and no one has spoken out against this. The practice is perfectly sound and irrevocable.[85]

I find the *waqf* question interesting not only because it contests the too-facile argument that the *shari'a* is static and universal, but principally because it suggests something about the function of law in successful empires. While republics, whether ancient or modern, may structure laws reflecting popular sentiment—or at least that of enfranchised elites—via the electoral process and legislation, the heterogeneous political structure of empires renders such an option problematic. The universal pretensions of imperial law only exacerbate

---

83 Tahir Mahmood, "Interaction of Islam and Public Law in Independent India," *Perspectives on Islamic Law, Justice, and Society*, ed. R.S. Khare, Lanham, MD: Rowman and Littlefield, 1999, p. 117.

84 Gerber, p. 101-102.

85 Cited in Jon Mandaville, "Usurious Piety: The Cash Waqf Controversy in the Ottoman Empire," *International Journal of Middle East Studies*, Vol. 10, No. 3 (August 1979), p. 297.

the problem. The capacity of imperial administrators, however, to detect and legally articulate common practice among imperial subjects—to incorporate the production of particular knowledge into the universal—suggests a particular strength within the transactions of imperial information.

The success or failure of such an enterprise can be detected in a community's legal participation, which—beyond its immediate value as a kind of referendum on imperial legitimacy—provides a variety of additional information sources. We may ask: Who uses the courts? In the Ottoman context, the answer to this legal question makes publicly real a whole segment of society otherwise almost entirely and privately invisible—i.e. women. Women, at least among the upper classes, are almost entirely physically concealed, a quality matched by their statistical absence from the fiscal records of the tax census, which count only individual men and male heads of households. In the courts, however, women come into their own, visibly enmeshed in a host of family, property and criminal affairs. They play an active role in over a quarter of the cases brought to the Galata court in 1789.[86] An equally striking appearance is made by non-Muslims, who frequently appear in the empire's shari'a-oriented courts for matters both personal and commercial, despite the availability of autonomous legal bodies for adjudicating issues within their communities.[87] This cast of characters brings before the courts—and into the view of the state—a wide spectrum of complaints, which, collected into various registers and compendia, provide great depth and range of insight into imperial conditions ranging from petty domestic disputes to the ill-defined, but apparently frequently reported sai bil' fesad—"fomenting evil in the world"—a category outside the matrix of routine criminal law, occupying the same "no man's land" of legal space where we find the Thugs.[88]

The relevance of the issue today appears in various contested political spaces. In Afghanistan, imperial power transmits information about its priorities, values and expectations through its construction of law, both in the broad universal terms indicated above, and in practical specifics by decisions such as that to build a Judicial Reform Act primarily around counter-narcotics concerns.[89] Conversely, Afghans communicate both their assessments of

---

86 Fatma Muge Gocek and Marc David Baer, "Social Boundaries of Ottoman Women's Experiences," *Women in the Ottoman Empire: Middle Eastern Women in the early Modern Era,* ed. Madeline Zilfi, Leiden, New York, Koln: Brill, 1997, p. 51.

87 Najwa Al-Qattan, "Dhimmis in the Muslim Court: Legal Autonomy and Religious Discrimination," *International Journal of Middle East Studies,* Vol. 31, No. 3 (August 1999), p. 430.

88 Gerber, 73.

89 Nancy Powell, testimony before the House International Relations Committee, "Policy in Afghanistan," *Congressional Quarterly,* 22 September 2005.

government and the priority of their concerns when they turn to Taliban courts to resolve their disputes, which chiefly revolve around land ownership.[90] A similar body of information was communicated by rural Nepalis turning to Maoist courts in order to resolve land disputes prior to the government-insurgent rapprochement.[91]

These recent examples, alongside the construction and practice of Ottoman law, highlight a recurrent theme of imperial intelligence. Namely, the strategic information most fundamental to a successful imperial order—information about beliefs, identity, authority and allegiance—does not appear as some "golden nugget" at the end of an operational or tactical tasking order. Rather, it circulates along networks of exchange, akin to an economy in which information serves as currency. Careful management of the messages transmitted and of the infrastructure enhances the potential of successful reception along the same networks. This was a challenge confronted by Roman administrators, as well as their Ottoman and British intellectual descendents. Leaping backward now a millennium and one half, we return to the same theme, now initially played in a key perhaps familiar to many readers, albeit in a very different context.

90 Paul Watson, "Democracy in the Balance," *Los Angeles Times*, 18 December 2006; and Pajhwak Afghan News, "Afghanis turn to 'Taliban Courts' to solve legal disputes," *Asia Pulse*, 7 June 2006.

91 Kantipur, "Nepal Maoists close down 'People's Court' in Kathmandu,' *BBC Monitoring*, 8 July 2006.

Rome: Concealing and Revealing

Just as he was speaking, Judas, one of the Twelve, appeared. With him was a crowd armed with swords and clubs, sent from the chief priests, the teachers of the law, and the elders.

Now the betrayer had arranged a signal with them: "The one I kiss is the man; arrest him and lead him away under guard." Going at once to Jesus, Judas said, "Rabbi!" and kissed him. The men seized Jesus and arrested him.[92]

Responding to this piece of "actionable intelligence," Roman authorities and their proxies successfully identified, located, seized and subsequently executed the leader of a sect which appeared to threaten the imperial order, most likely around 29 CE.[93] Nevertheless, the supreme leader of this same imperial order would confess the divinity of the victim some three centuries later, with Constantine's at least nominal conversion to Christianity—suggesting that despite this tactical success, the Romans in some fundamental way failed to perceive the nature of the threat. The obstacles to perception, both structural and self-imposed, highlight many of the "intelligence" challenges confronting any imperial power.

Overlaid and freighted with theological and contested readings though they are, the penultimate chapters of the three synoptic Gospels nevertheless narratively portray issues raised earlier regarding the interplay of knowledge and power—expressed through the construction of legal space. Understanding how this space is experienced by both rulers and ruled is a fundamental problem of imperial knowledge about the world. As Thomas McGinn has it: "To put the matter in a more general way, law qualifies as a constitutive rhetoric; in the sense that it constitutes reality. This reality is a 'culture of argument, perpetually remade by its participants.'"[94]

While two millennia of scholarship and debate have opened up the events surrounding the crucifixion to broad investigation, the imperial agent at the point of contact is working at a marked information deficit. What Pontius Pilate says and does, and the punishment he imposes, are by design highly visible and rendered in words and images widely heard and seen. Jesus, in contrast,

---

92 Mark 14: 43-46, *The Holy Bible*, NIV.

93 Leo Depuydt, "The Date of Death of Jesus of Nazareth," *Journal of the American Oriental Society*, Vol. 122, No. 3. (July-September 2002), p. 478.

94 Thomas McGinn, *Prostitution, Sexuality and the Law in Ancient Rome*, New York and Oxford: Oxford University, 1998, p. 348.

is almost entirely silent, and Pilate is forced to resort to local intermediaries—mediators in language, power and culture—in order to understand the problem with which he is faced. Expressing a variety of local agendas and internal contests that are equally resistant to imperial understanding, these intermediaries levy a variety of charges from blasphemy to treason against the emperor.

Confronted by both silence and cacophony, Pilate imposes punishment without ever clearly rendering a verdict on the supposed crime, an omission likely native to the texts for their own internal reasons; but the context of the proceedings suggests how he views the issue. Barabbas, the man sent free in lieu of Jesus, has been convicted of murder in the course of insurrection; while Jesus is ultimately crucified in company of less clear affiliation—the other two crosses on Golgotha occupied by thieves, robbers, rebels or revolutionaries, depending on the translation.[95] Jesus of Nazareth, like so many other problems which defy imperial understanding, is tossed into the legal netherworld broadly occupied by "bandits."

Eric Hobsbawm begins his study of the bandit issue by noting that:

> For the law, anyone belonging to a group of men who attack and rob with violence is a bandit, from those who snatch payrolls at an urban street corner to organized insurgents or guerrillas who happen not to be officially recognized as such. Historians and sociologists cannot use so crude a definition.[96]

He then proceeds to articulate and explore a more limited category of "social banditry" in a process of scoping and definition followed by other scholars pursuing related topics. Hobsbawm and others provide useful insights into their specific categories of study; but at the outset it is specifically the "crude definition" above which interests me, for it is not simply the anonymous "law" which sees things in this all-encompassing way, but historical imperial powers. The British in India tried to capture a wide variety of ill-defined violence under the rubric of "*thuggee* and *dacoity*," following the Roman practice of applying the label *latrones* (and derivatives thereof) to: "bands of robbers living in the countryside…pretenders to the throne…individuals, as opposed to groups, who broke into buildings and stole…and to barbarian raiders across the Rhine and Danube."[97] As the list of offenses here

---

95 Mark 15: 7, 27—"robbers" in the NIV, "thieves" in the King James Version, "revolutionaries" in the New American Version and "rebels" in *The Complete Gospels*, ed. Robert Miller, San Francisco: HarperCollins, 1994.

96 E.J. Hobsbawm, *Bandits*, New York: Delacorte Press, 1969, p.13.

97 Ramsay MacMullen, *Enemies of the Roman Order: Treason, Unrest and Alienation in the Empire*, Cambridge: Harvard University Press, 1966, p. 255.

The Panopticon in reverse. The imperial palaces on the Palatine Hill were visible to all, while the real life of Rome ran along a mythical subterranean network, accessible only through the mouth of the Umbilicus Urbis at city center.

Source: photos by author.

suggests, the phenomenon represented by *latronicium*, generally translated as "banditry," was a vague and all-encompassing one. This was distinct, I feel, from the more explicit challenge posed by later movements like the bagaudae, a term which generally describes peasant insurrections in 3rd Century CE Gaul involving large-scale violence, attacks on towns, etc. This may represent the real difficulty of defining a kaleidoscopic issue, as I think it was in part for the British, but the catch-all category also has utility for the expansion of state power, and it was applied regularly during the Roman conquest of Europe.[99]

Suggesting that the problem of nomenclature for such disparate threats retains its relevancy, a modern survey of academics asked to define "terrorism" produced 109 different responses.[100] Such broad definitions may have tactical utility—one can crucify a murderer, a thief and a prophet without too much legal wrangling—but they cripple as well as enable. How does one identify and understand such disparate phenomena, how does one declare war on "banditry?" One way, at least, is through a campaign of discourse which shapes what happens in the physical battle.[101]

By deliberately accepting the cruder definition of the law—the variety which has been applied in practice, rather than scholarship—I propose that banditry, and its like terms, constitutes a particularly imperial problem of knowing: how to gain insight into spaces, languages, cultures and minds that resist interrogation by the imperial power. Hobsbawm's definition notes that banditry flourishes where a "central or state apparatus is absent or ineffective," and assesses that banditry consequently declines with the onset of modernization and strong states.[102] The very conditions of empire, however—ancient or modern—involve significant gaps in state effectiveness in various regions over time, particularly as empire disrupts and reorganizes power and the legitimacy of violence within the spaces under its influence. I noted earlier how many of the problems associated with Thuggee may be seen as unintended consequences of British success and a subsequent condition of surplus in the military labor market—a connection between labor, social change and irruptions of illegitimate violence noted by Roman observers.[103] The modern problem of rising "terrorism" in the wake of Afghan Demobilization, Disarmament and

---

99 Michael Bhatia, "Fighting Words: Naming Terrorists, Bandits, Rebels and Other Violent Actors," *Third World Quarterly*, Vol. 26, No. 1 (2005), p. 14

100 Alex Schmidt and Albert Jongman et al., *Political Terrorism*, Amsterdam: Transaction Books, 1988, p. 5.

101 Michael Bhatia, "Fighting Words," p. 7.

102 Hobsbawm, p. 82, 15.

103 Cassius Dio, *Roman History: The Reign of Augustus*, trans. Ian Scott-Kilvert, London: Penguin, 1987, 52.27; 55.34.

Reintegration (the last part being the real trick) and the disbanding of the Iraqi Army, suggests the issue may not be a mere historical artifact.

One function of the bandit category is to conceal the gaps in imperial control. Cassius Dio noted the satisfaction Octavian took in directing that the doors to the temple of Janus be closed in 29 BCE, a symbolic gesture representing the return of peace to the empire. Almost as an aside, he added a brief note admitting:

> It is true that the Treveri, who had called in the Germans to help them, were still under arms, as also were the Cantabri, the Vaccaei and the Astures....and there were many other disorders taking place in various regions. But since no consequences of importance resulted from them, the Romans did not consider that they were at war at that period, and for my part I have nothing of note to record about them.[104]

The prevalence of non-state violence throughout the Roman Empire is directly attested by a wide variety of imperial documents—with guidance to various officials to root out bandits, requests for assistance against bandits, guidance for the legal processing of bandits, etc.—and in multiple funerary epigraphs noting the cause of death as *interfectus a latronibus* ("killed by bandits").[105] Indirectly, the issue arises as a legal caveat, articulated as a qualifier to various contracts (on par with natural disasters or acts of God) and as legitimating the formation of local para-military units.[106] Similarly, casual references to pirates are replete in classical sources, suggesting they were a common feature of Mediterranean life; although they reside in the same legal space as bandits.[107] Cicero notes that one is free to break oaths with or deceive pirates with moral impunity, as their status lies outside the legal sphere.[108]

But if such violence is so widespread just outside the city walls, just what kind of sovereignty does the empire enjoy? The contest with *latrones* provides just enough urgency to enjoin various extraordinary legal measures without implying a genuine threat to the regime from a *bellum iustum*, in the sense of "genuine" rather than literally "just" war.[109] This style of defining constitutes

---

104 Cassius Dio, *Augustus*, 51.20.

105 MacMullen, p. 257-259.

106 Brent Shaw, "Bandits in the Roman Empire," *Past and Present*, No. 105 (November 1984), p. 8-9, 18.

107 Philip de Souza, *Piracy in the Graeco-Roman World*, Cambridge: Cambridge University, 1999, p. 150.

108 Cicero, *De Officiis*, trans. Walter Miller, Loeb Classical Library, Cambridge: Harvard, 1913, III:29.

109 Ibid, p. 6.

a "protective fiction," a fantasy "where statehood takes hold and binds its subjects, and then, unequal to its own injunctions, lets slip just a little."[110] While the passage below addresses banditry, much of its assessment could be more broadly associated with Thuggee, *sai bil' fesad* and the like.[111]

> For the people of the Empire, the bandit was not so much a physical threat as a psychological one, a symptom of anxiety. People lived in open or hidden fear of the bandit. According to Velleius Paterculus...thanks to the *Pax Augusta* every inhabitant of the Roman Empire, even those in the most distant regions, needed no longer fear attack by bandits (*metus Latrocinium*). This was propaganda. It was part of the standard repertoire of the propaganda of the Roman ruler, and the more it emphasized *pax, securitas* and other endlessly lauded blessings of human existence, the more it suggested how bad these really were.[112]

Such rhetorical moves mask complex and little understood threats to imperial power; with a single pejorative term, legions of opposition become functionally invisible. Moreover, the terms help to conceal the role imperial and state power may have initially shared in creating these phenomena, just as 17th and 18th Century legitimate privateers were lexically converted into 19th Century illegitimate pirates.[113] My concern, here at least, is not so much with the principle of propaganda; but rather, that such language choices take on a life of their own and can constrain the agents of empire just as surely as empower them. Once these essentializing masks are applied, it becomes increasingly difficult to see the more complex reality behind them, for analysts and administrators as well as for the general public.

This textual imagining is replicated visually in Roman articulations of space. For the most part, bandits in their various guises operate in rural spaces, those the empire does not fully or often even tentatively control—a cartographic no-man's land, a blank space which echoes the bandit's negative legal space. This location has its modern corollary in our own negative vocabulary: our enemies are principally defined as being *il*-legal combatants, who fight *ir*-regular and

---

110 Jacqueline Rose, *States of Fantasy*, New York: Oxford University Press, 1996, p. 14.

111 Sai bil' fesad refers to an Ottoman legal category encapsulating generic "fomenters of evil." While the parallel between Thuggee, *latronicium*, and *sai bil fesad* is inexact, all three suggest the struggle faced by imperial powers trying to construct an identifiable legal space around those who are more than mere domestic criminals but less than conventional foreign enemies.

112 Thomas Grunewald, *Bandits in the Roman Empire: Myth and Reality*, trans. John Drinkwater, London and New York: Routledge, 1999, p.32.

113 Janice Thomson, *Mercenaries, Pirates, and Sovereigns*, Princeton: Princeton University, 1994, p. 107-108.

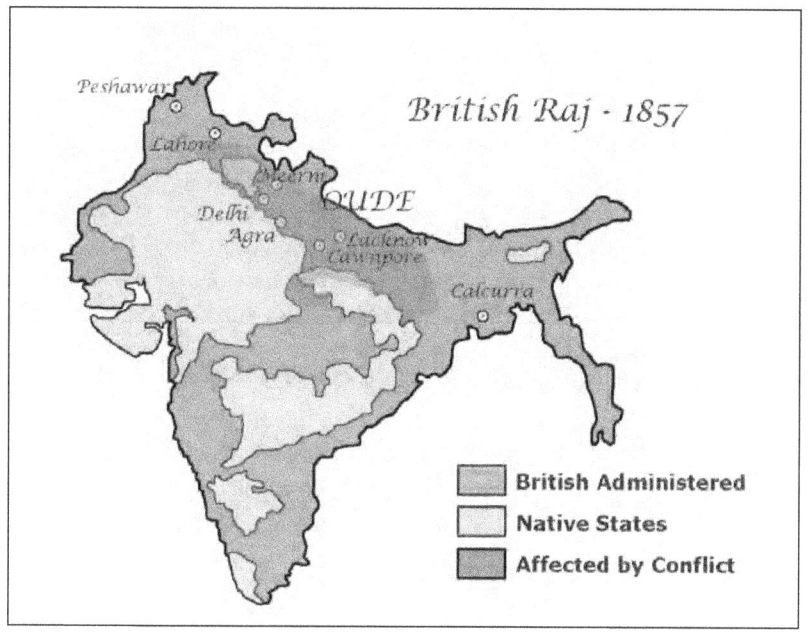

A Map of Empire. *Source: Author's modification and distillation of various British maps.*

a-symmetric campaigns; their terrestrial orientation being *under*-ground or in the ubiquitous "caves" of the Afghan border regions. Just as *latrones* as a concept simplifies and reduces the image of contestants to power, simplifying and reducing the expression of contested spaces can anticipate rather than reflect reality.[114] The British practiced a form of cartographic manipulation, perhaps familiar to the modern observer, by simply painting over these spaces in charts constructed at the height of Imperial power around the turn of the last century. Although partly a question of scale, a world map portrays the entire Indian subcontinent as a British Possession, while more detailed consideration reveals less than half this landmass is genuinely (legally) British administered. An actual laydown of British forces and local presence would prove even more limited, but to the imperial eye in London these spaces are comfortably "Pink."

The Romans achieved essentially the same end by more radical means, simply eliminating the contested spaces altogether. Although detailed charts exist for developed urban areas and a few examples of recognizably topographical maps have survived or been described in texts, for the most part

114 Thongchai Winichakul, *Siam Mapped: a History of the Geo-Body of a Nation*, Honolulu: University of Hawaii Press, 1994, p. 130.

Romans depicted their domains in the form of itineraries listing the major towns, travel distances/times, and any major features which might impact movement.[115]

Rome in this depiction is an urban capital, its empire composed of subordinate urban centers. The spaces in between—the spaces of the *latrones*—simply don't exist. As comforting as such a "protective fiction" might be, however, such places manifestly *did* exist, along with all the myriad contestants to power within them. These hybrid places and their occupants—not truly Roman, but not quite the enemy either—constituted a distinct space, and consequently demanded distinctly imperial ways of knowing about them. One can still sense this framework by beginning at the remains of the Forum's Golden Milestone, physically representing the center of the empire, and proceeding along the old Roman road out to the first of innumerable milestones that choreograph imperial space. The Ottomans repeated this centering and Greenwich echoes on it a global scale. The Roman example below gives the flavor of these one-dimensional "maps":

> From the shrine of Zeus Urios to the River Rheba are 90 stades. From the Rheba to the Black Point it is 150 stades. From Black Point to the river and the village of artane it is 150 stades. Artane also has a little harbour for small boats and nearby lies a small island that shelters the harbour.[116]

The foreignness of this articulation for a modern reader stems from the absence of cardinal directions and unfamiliar metrics, but the basic principles of cartography, as we would think of it, were not unknown in the ancient world and large-scale graphic representations of the earth's surface were produced as early as the 5th Century BCE.[117] More important, however, may be the *meanings* of space as articulated through different representations. Not far from the forum, one of Augustus' principal post-mortem requests was the posting of the *Res Gestae*, a text unique in antiquity.[118] Along with

---

[115] N.J.E. Austin and N.B. Rankov, *Exploratio: Military and Political Intelligence in the Roman World from the Second Punic War to the Battle of Adrianople*, New York: Routledge, 1995, p. 115.

[116] Cited in Benet Salway, "Sea and River Travel in Roman Itinerary Literature," *Space in the Roman World: Its Perception and Presentation*, eds. Richard Talbert and Kai Brodersen, Munster: Lit Verlag, 2004, p. 55.

[117] Claude Nicolet, *Space, Geography, and Politics in the Early Roman Empire*, Ann Arbor: University of Michigan, 1991, p. 70-71.

[118] *Res gestae*—literally "things done"—is generally applied as a legal term describing statements of unusual spontaneity and credibility. In this case, it describes the list of "things done" during Octavian's career—a text far more calculated than spontaneous, and obviously designed as much to influence as to inform.

All roads may lead to Rome, but first they lead from Rome. People, power and information progress outward—Mile One on the *Via Antiqua. Source: photo by author.*

lists of Octavian's principal achievements, the inscription includes a list of the territories annexed or subjected under his rule—a sort of textual atlas of the empire.[119] This act of inscribing—of writing rather than drawing or otherwise depicting—constitutes for the Romans, as for the Ottomans and

119 Ibid., p. 19-21.

those industrious inscribers, the agents of the Raj, an act of possession: "Inscription archived, and thus immobilized, the subject population."[120] The ordering of space in this context is less about correspondence to geo-physical reality, than about correspondence to a world of honor—equally real if less tangible.[121] Reading space in this way provides an alternate, far more rhizomic and schizophrenic way of imagining Roman strategy, in contrast to the kinds of conventional understandings which presume a coordinated military and political network of roads and fortifications, expressed in spatial depictions which the Roman generals and administrators, as far as the record reveals, never employed.[122]

I want to emphasize here this different imagining of space for two fundamental reasons of modern relevance. The first is that our current cartographic vision of the world is not "natural." It is not a given, and it is clearly possible, and perhaps necessary, to imagine the world with a different set of benchmarks. The planet, unlike the globe in Spivak's formulation, is not striated with latitudes and longitudes. Despite its artificiality, the geo-political map of states remains our primary frame for viewing space:

> Despite its increasingly active competitors for identity and affiliation, it continues to dominate the determination of how things are valued, actions are interpreted, and persons are assigned identities. Representing the structure of approved sovereignties, it is the primary force determining recognized political subjectivity.[123]

Michael Shapiro's assessment has a specific social-justice intent, but even a far more cynical perspective could read dysfunction in adherence to increasingly antiquated geographic frames. The U.S. military, intelligence agencies and State Department all provide handbooks, write assessments, write campaign plans and assign funding for the war in Afghanistan; a war which, absent continued adherence to a 19th Century artifact of cartography, would

---

120 Peirce, *Morality Tales*, p. 279-280.

121 Susan Mattern, *Rome and the Enemy: Imperial Strategy in the Principate*, Berkeley: University of California, 1999, p. 171-172.

122 Edward Luttwak, *The Grand Strategy of the Roman Empire: From the First Century A.D. to the Third*, Baltimore and London: Johns Hopkins, 1976, p. 4, 138. While Luttwak would likely not have used the term, "schizophrenic" here applies in two regards. First, what to our eyes is the self-evidently spatial nature of the physical world is re-imagined in terms of text and honor, largely disassociated from that spatial physicality—a form of un- or alternate reality, i.e. schizophrenic. Additionally, I consider the Roman case to be a particularly vivid example of a problem facing all cartography, and imperial cartography in particular, which is reconciling—or failing to reconcile—distinctly different, and frequently antagonistic aspects of the world the discipline seeks to represent.

123 Michael Shapiro, *Violent Cartographies: Mapping Cultures of War*, Minneapolis and London: University of Minnesota Press, 1997, p. 16.

Striking in its bare simplicity, the Peace Altar of Augustus achieves its effect by what it leaves out—mirroring the *Pax Romana*, achieved principally through ignoring the sustained violence which characterized it.
Source: photo by author.

be far more accurately described—and fought—as the war in Pashtunistan. Absent similar constraints on imagination, it would likely not have required four years of inconclusive violence in Iraq to re-center the primacy of other constructions of space and power, both sub and supra-national.

A second issue is the dialogic nature of space in the Roman understanding. The categorization of space in terms of honor mimics a similar construction in law, with which it is intimately related.[124] I earlier noted how the law creates reality through discourse and argument, which presupposes at least more than one party. The same can be said of honor generally—no action, for the Romans at least, was intrinsically honorable or dishonorable, but was made so through the perception of *others*.[125] The meaning of space thus, and similarly, becomes the subject of negotiation, rather than of imposition.

To understand and administer these negotiated spaces, the Romans required a similarly hybrid class of agents. Institutionally, a distinctly imperial

---

124 McGinn, *Prostitution, Sexuality and the Law*, p. 342.

125 J.E. Lendon, *Empire of Honor: The Art of Government in the Roman World*, Oxford: Clarendon, 1997, p. 37.

intelligence *apparat* grew along with the formation of the empire itself. Classical texts of the Republican era refer to various intelligence-related organizations like the *exploratores* and *speculatores*—generally military detachments—conducting reconnaissance in advance of legionary operations against one or another of Rome's enemies.[126] However, with the transition to the Principate, the latter began to take on duties inside the established sphere of Roman influence, indicating to some scholars that:

> There seems to have been a difficulty in maintaining a clear division between external intelligence and internal subversion. The danger was always present that a ruler would use the speculatores for a political purpose.[127]

Concurrently, military officials formerly associated with acquisition of grain for the legions, the *frumentarii*, began to perform duties associated with information collection and transmission—giving rise to their description in academic literature as the early incarnation of Rome's domestic Secret Service.[128] I contend, however, that both the latter appellation and the implied external/internal confusion represent anachronisms reflecting epistemes grounded in a formal nation-state with its more or less clear foreign and domestic distinctions. The unique intelligence problem of empire, in contrast, is precisely that such distinctions do not exist—or rather that they exist in over-abundance, with inside/outside fractures splintering and overlapping ad infinitum within and between spaces, communities and individuals under the imperial umbrella.

The frumentarii themselves embodied such dichotomies. Selected from the serving legions, they remained attached to their administrative parent units and answered to their respective governors, while simultaneously constituting

---

126 Both *exploratores* and *speculatores* were involved in information gathering and their roles evolved over time; but generally *exploratores* acted more as traditional military reconnaissance, and *speculatores* took on an increasing domestic role, including service as imperial bodyguards and executioners.

127 Rose Mary Sheldon, *Intelligence Activities in Ancient Rome: Trust in the Gods, but Verify*, New York: Frank Cass, 2005, p. 166.

128 William G. Sinnigen, "Two Branches of the Late Roman Secret Service," *The American Journal of Philology*, Vol. 80, No. 3 (1959), p. 238-239. While the *exploratores* and *speculatores* were designed more or less explicitly as intelligence organizations, the *frumentarii* represent a more organic development. The title originally applied to officers assigned to managing corn acquisition in the provinces—the military contracting officers of their day—who consequently developed extensive information networks both within their own community and inside the host society. These networks ultimately proved a ready-made resource for turning to intelligence collection and distribution purposes.

a separate corps serving the emperor.[129] When in Rome, they were housed in the *Castra Peregrinorum*—the "Camp of the Foreigners"—although epigraphic evidence describes them as *milites*, and thus Roman citizens.[130] Moreover, although in accordance with growing legionary practice they were largely recruited locally in the provinces and frontier zones, prevailing custom was to deploy them to regions where such local expertise—and potentially compromised loyalties—could not come into play, thus compounding multiple layers of "foreignness."[131]

All three voices have now played their initial notes—Roman, Ottoman and British; and now we can develop their respective themes along multiple axes. Establishing Egypt, a province of the Roman Empire, as a geographic pole, we can slide forward in time to its Ottoman administration—specifically to consider a corresponding transformation in the meaning and social occupation of space.

---

[129] Austin, 136.

[130] P.K. Baillie Reynolds, "The Troops Quartered in the Castra Peregrinorum," *The Journal of Roman Studies*, Vol. 13 (1923), p. 168-169. *Milites* represent members of the formal Roman Army, consisting of legal citizens, as opposed to those foreigners enrolled in allied and supporting formations.

[131] Sheldon, 255.

Barzakh: The Intermediate World

The office of the Zabit has been mentioned. He is now the chief of police. His officers, who have no distinguishing mark to render them known as such, are interspersed through the metropolis; they often visit the coffee-shops and observe the conduct, and listen to the conversation, of the citizens. Many of them are pardoned thieves. [132]

This vignette of surveillance operations, described by an Englishman visiting Egypt in the mid-1800s, forms a sort of *mis en abyme*, a scene-within-a-scene which portrays multiple issues of Ottoman imperial intelligence captured in miniature. Through this portal, we can begin to trace the "rhizomic" information spaces of the Ottoman Empire.

Lane's account took place in a specific place, a site embedded multiple times over in the geography of power. At the broadest level, the setting was a province of an empire which, echoing Rome, had established at least a nominal *Pax Ottomanica* around the southern and eastern Mediterranean littoral. This particular province enjoyed special status, as Ottoman Egypt, again echoing Latin precursors, played a key role as imperial granary, as well as guarding the *hajj* routes. Nevertheless, highlighting the tenuous nature of imperial identity, from its conquest by Selim I in 1517 until the arrival of Napoleon in 1798, the province was wracked by at least eight major incidents which threatened imperial control. [133] Depending on its status at any particular time, then, this particular place could be inside the empire, outside, or in some transitory stage—rendering problematic the nature of intelligence about events there. Regardless of its shifting secular status, however, as a Muslim polity Egypt remained within the *dar ul-Islam*, as did many other societies which the Ottomans conquered, and in which rebellion was repeatedly suppressed. [134] The imperial necessity for practices more appropriate to the *dar ul-harb* in this context cast issues of identity even further in doubt, undermining the Qu'ran's thematic logocentrism between male/female, free/slave, and Muslim/non-

---

[132] Edward William Lane, *The Modern Egyptians*, New York: E.P. Dutton, 1936.

[133] Caroline Finkel, *Osman's Dream: the Story of the Ottoman Empire 1300-1923*, New York: Basic Books, 2005, p. 120, 180, 359.

[134] Based on the religious affiliation of a community's governing political arrangements, Islamic legal tradition maintains a distinction between the *dar ul-Islam*, the Abode of Peace, and the *dar ul-harb*, the Abode of War. An Islamic polity faces distinctly different obligations and permissions in its choices regarding policy, diplomacy and warfare depending on which abode another community resides in.

Its interior beauty illuminated only by external light, the Pantheon is neither entirely inside, nor quite outside—it is an architectural realization of imperial space *par excellence*. *Source: photo by author.*

Muslim in ways that would ripple across the imperial administrative apparatus and influence both the substance and form of its information architecture.[135]

This distinction between the "Abode" of peace and the "Abode" of war highlights another geographic theme—the domesticity of power. The "household" of the Sultan in Istanbul served as the locus of imperial power through the multitude of administrators and soldiers who were technically personal slaves of the Sultan;[136] and this domestic constellation was emulated by elites within the provinces.[137] These contested series of nested "residences" emphasize a fundamental issue unique to imperial intelligence that I have outlined previously—specifically, the uncertain distinction between foreign and domestic. As an illustrative aside, it is perhaps worth noting here that the English word "foreign" entered the language in the 13th Century to describe a chamber within the home, and for the next four hundred years was gradually applied to those things perceived as alien and other, yet within the purview of the domestic state.[138]

Returning to Lane's Cairo, despite these domestic macro frames, at the micro level surveillance did not take place at the site of a proper home, but rather at a place somewhere in between the public and private. Coffeehouses—like bath houses and other marginal spaces—were singled out for special attention by those seeking information.[139] These "meeting places of the people, and of mutinous soldiers" provided a convenient site where various strata of society could mingle and pass information, enjoying an escape from the enclosures of the home without the constraints of the formally public.[140] It is the imagined nature of this space that ruptures boundaries between public and private, rather than its physical situation, which allows for the exchange of otherwise concealed information. Though the silent figures bent over their MacBooks in the neighborhood Starbucks—or the Kathmandu equivalent—may not be

---

[135] Colin Imber, *The Ottoman Empire, 1300-1650: the Structure of Power*, New York: Palgrave Macmillan, 2002, p. 244-245.

[136] Suraiya Faroqhi, "Civilian Society and Political Power in the Ottoman Empire: A Report on Research in Collective Biography (1480-1830), *International Journal of Middle East Studies* Vol. 17, No. 1 (February 1995), p. 111-112.

[137] Jane Hathaway, "The Military Household in Ottoman Egypt," *International Journal of Middle East Studies*, Vol. 27, No. 1 (February 1995), p. 40-41.

[138] David Campbell, *Writing Security: United States Foreign Policy and the Politics of Identity*, Minneapolis: University of Minnesota, 1992, p. 43.

[139] Cemal Kafadar, "Self and Others: The Diary of a Dervish in Seventeenth Century Istanbul and First Person Narratives in Ottoman Literature," *Studia Islamica*, LXIX, 1969, p.144-145.

[140] Ralph S. Hattox, *Coffee and Coffeehouses: the Origins of a Social Beverage in the Medieval Near East*, Seattle: University of Washington, 1985, p. 89, 102.

physically sited in such a rupture, the blogosphere populated by their rapid-fire typing suggests that the attraction of such spaces persists. This is the same imagined space manifested in the bazaars of British India:

> The duality of this space is inescapable. It harbors qualities that threaten one's well being (strangers embody these qualities). Yet it provides a venue for linkages across communities (linkages with strangers).... Politically, the bazaar was seen as a den of lies and rumors...the place where conspiracies and rebellions were plotted and carried out.[141]

It is there, between the known and unknown, that we find what the Sufi mystic Ibn 'Arabi (d. 1240 CE) called *barzakh*—"the intermediate world."[142]

> Intelligence is the shadow of objective Truth.
> How can the shadow vie with sunshine?
>
> Jalaludin Rumi (d. 1273 CE)[143]

Sufi observations on knowledge and intelligence enter the narrative here, where Lane's *mis en abyme* winds down to its most dense concentration, at the inky bottom of a coffee cup, before expanding outward again into a new and wider scene. Coffee drinking was introduced to the Arab world by Yemeni Sufis in the fourteenth century, who likely adopted the beverage as a surrogate for wine, which weighed heavily in Sufi symbolism.[144] Like the secular counterparts they would inspire, the Sufi practices included social gatherings which drew in people from across the social spectrum. Recording the important aspects of his life, a Sufi diarist of the mid-17th Century thought it particularly relevant to note both the refreshments on offer at such affairs and the range of attendees, from artisans to members of the imperial administrative elite.[145]

Like the coffeehouses, these Sufi associations (*tarikkats*) provided a kind of social "intertext."[146] Muslim by confession, their tendencies toward religious

---

141 Dipesh Chakrabarty, *Habitations of Modernity: Essays in the Wake of Subaltern Studies*, Chicago and London: University of Chicago, 2002, p. 74, 76.

142 Adonis, *Sufism and Surrealism*, trans. Judith Cumberbatch, London: Saqi, 2005, p. 61.

143 Idries Shah, *The Way of the Sufi*, New York: E.P. Dutton, 1970, p.105.

144 Alan S. Kaye, "The Etymology of 'Coffee': The Dark Brew," *Journal of the American Oriental Society*, Vol. 106, No. 3 (July-September 1996), p. 557.

145 Kafadar, ibid., p. 142.

146 A *tarrikat* encompasses a group of Sufi practitioners affiliated with a specific individual teacher or a more extensive tradition associated with a specific chain of transmission among successive teachers. Tekkes serve as places of meeting, study and devotion for these groups—identified more by these functions than by architectural design, which ranges from adapted private homes to purpose-built lodges.

Imperial sunset. Dominating the Istanbul skyline, the Blue Mosque is an information broadcast device, telling a story about who rules and what they value.
Source: photo by author.

heterodoxy and synthesis generated chronic tension between the Sufi orders and the more orthodox, who questioned in which "Abode" the Sufi genuinely resided—occasionally leading to violence.[147] This was not merely a problem

147 Madeline C. Zilfi, "The Kadizadelis: Discordant Revivalism in Seventeenth Century Istanbul," *Journal of Near Eastern Studies*, Vol. 45, No. 4 (October 1986), p. 251-252. Sufism appears within both Shia and Sunni communities, and its more esoteric aspects echo mystical elements within Christianity, Buddhism and Gnosticism more faithfully than any of these traditions mesh with their more formal respective variants.

of the pulpit, but a contest over who can access the divine, who can speak the truth, who can participate in society's discourse—a contest over information which shaped the infrastructure of empire. The growth of Sufi facilities spurred an equal or greater burst of orthodox madrassas and mosques, built across from or above Sufi institutions throughout Anatolia.[148] In the imperial capital, the presence of Islam was architecturally scripted in two dominating themes: the huge, visible skyline of mosques and madrassas representing the righteousness of Islam and of the Sultan; with a contrasting theme of Sufi *tekkes*, modest and non-descript, built with the funds of ordinary individuals, shifting almost imperceptibly from place to place and from one *tarikkat* to another.[149]

This architectural point and counterpoint mirrors that of imperial Rome. In both the capital and the provinces, the architecture of impersonal state power was meant to be seen, elevated and designed to visually bind the empire together.[150] By way of contrast, informal Roman associative cults (where social classes could also mix) like that of Mithras were designed to be pursued in iconic caves, distant from the shrines, seats and alters of the Olympian gods.[151]

Sufism further echoed Mithraism in its appeal to the military, and the elite Janissary corps had a longstanding relationship with the dervish orders, particularly the Bektashi.[152] In sixteenth-century Egypt, the relationship grew so close that emirs and viziers would go into the hills to consult with a retired Army officer turned mystic, while another Sufi was considered such a popular distraction among Turkish soldiers and officials that he was forced into complete seclusion to avoid exile.[153] Beyond affiliation with agents of government, the Sufi were also associated with broader social functions the government deliberately abjured.

> By Ottoman theory, the sole attribute of rule was the right to possess all sources of wealth together with the authority to exploit those sources. So all wealth in the empire lay in the ultimate possession of the Sovereign, the Sultan. The obligations and powers of the Ottoman ruling class therefore were limited only to those

---

[148] Godfrey Goodwin, "The Dervish Architecture of Anatolia," *The Dervish Lodge: Architecture, Art and Sufism in Ottoman Turkey*, ed. Raymond Lifchez, Berkeley and Los Angeles: University of California, 1992, p. 62.

[149] Raymond Lifchez, "The Lodges of Istanbul," and Klaus Krieser, "Dervish Living," in *The Dervish Lodge*, p. 50, 74.

[150] Henri Stierlin, *The Roman Empire*, Köln and New York: Taschen, 1996, p. 132-135.

[151] Leroy Campbell, *Mithraic Iconography and Ideology*, Leiden: Brill, 1968.

[152] Franklin, 9.

[153] Michael Winter, *Society and Religion in Early Modern Egypt: studies in the writing of 'Abd al-Wahhab al-Sha'rani*, New Brunswick and London: Transaction Books, 1982, p. 105

matters directly connected with the tasks of enlarging, protecting and exploiting that wealth for the benefit of the Sultan.[154]

Anachronisms regarding the proper functions of government aside, consider the description of the Ottoman administration above with that of Sufi functions below.

> By the sixteenth century Sufism was established as a fundamental element of Ottoman Islamic society. Sufi brotherhoods were important in the organization of Muslim town and rural life where they provided a focus for devotional, charitable and educational activities.[155]

From the standpoint of information collection, understanding and transmission, these contrasting functions suggest a deficit on the part of the formal government in relation to entities more intimately bound up with the practicalities of daily life. Dervishes—Sufi devotees—who "guarded passes and caravan routes, introduced new crops and propagated more specialized agriculture"[156] were liable to enjoy insights akin to those available to modern Non-Governmental Organizations (NGOs), in contrast to conventional military forces.

By virtue of the fluid social interactions inherent in the *tarrikats*, the Ottoman elite were likely able to exploit at least some of this information access. Members of a lodge in remote areas of the empire could at the very least pass on grievances regarding failures of the local administration to their brothers in Istanbul, and those contacts in the capital could use local associations or personal access to the Sultan's household to press complaints with more urgency than formal processes.[157] These same networks would have been suited for passing a wide variety of information to the court. Despite such utility, the ambiguous, social-border-crossing nature of Sufi identity also suited them for literal border-crossing and affiliation with enemies of the regime, such as the Safavids, the 16th-18th Century Persian Shia dynasty which alternated with European regimes as the Ottomans' chief antagonist. Consequently, imperial policy frequently vacillated between supporting Sufi orders and ruthlessly

---

154 Stanford J. Shaw, "The Dynamics of Traditional Ottoman Society and Administration," *Ottoman Bureaucracy: Two Papers*, Bloomington, IN: Comparative Administrative Group, American Society for Public Administration, 1967, p. 2.

155 Ira M. Lapidus, "Sufism and Ottoman Islamic Society," in *The Dervish Lodge*, p. 28.

156 Omar Lufti Barkan, cited in Suraiya Faroqhi, "The Tekki of Haci Bektas: Social Position and Economic Activities," *International Journal of Middle East Studies*, Vol. 7, No. 2 (April 1976), p. 183.

157 Suraiya Faroqhi, *Subjects of the Sultan: Culture and Everyday Life in the Ottoman Empire*, London and New York: I.B. Tauris, 2000, p. 68.

suppressing them.[158] This apparatus of observation likely exacerbated the imbalance of trade in the imperial information economy. An associate of the French ambassador to the Sublime Porte in the mid-1500s claimed:

> ...after council meetings the Grand Vizier would go to report to the Sultan all the truth: what had been discussed and matters of importance. At this time, lying is mortal, because often the Sultan is listening at a window overlooking the said chamber without being seen or noticed. And even if he were never there, one always thinks that he is.[159]

Despite the Panopticon-style assertions of the Sultan's omniscience, the Sufi networks suggest how many more eyes may have been watching the doings of the court "without being seen or noticed."

Finally, from the perspective of the imperial information consumer, while the Sufi may have participated in an alternative information order, they were also involved with the organs of the state, functioning in fact, if not through law, as part of the governing apparatus—again, much like modern mainstream NGOs which have achieved consultative status with formal government bodies.[160] As one critic puts it:

> Alternative development collectives, national-local health care, ecology and literacy collectives have been in place for a long time, and play a critical role at the grassroots level. Why are they seldom heard? These oppositional structures are indigenous NGOs.... The NGOs that surface at the "NGO Forums" of the UN conferences have been so thoroughly vetted by the donor countries, and the content of their presentations so organized by categories furnished by the UN, that neither subject nor object bears much resemblance to the "real thing," if you will pardon the expression.[161]

Truly alternative information networks—the places where surprises come from—may circulate among these "oppositional structures" and associations of more genuinely state-separated "civil society" like modern incarnations in the liberation theology movements of Latin America or the exploding Christian

---

158 John Robert Barnes, "The Dervish Orders in the Ottoman Empire," in *The Dervish Lodge*, p. 35-37.

159 Imber, p. 157.

160 Scott Turner, "Global Civil Society, Anarchy and Governance: Assessing an Emerging Paradigm," *Journal of Peace Research*, Vol. 35, No. 1 (January 1998), p. 31.

161 Gayatri Chakravorty Spivak, *A Critique of Postcolonial Reason: Toward a Vanishing History of the Present*, Cambridge: Harvard, 1999, p. 371.

The lodges of the Sufi orders, like this one tucked away in the lanes of Galata, represent information alternatives to empire. Small, dispersed, omnipresent, this architecture can listen as well as speak. *Source: photo by author.*

Pentecostal churches of sub-Saharan Africa in the 1980s.[162] The challenge of both accessing and understanding these alternative networks remains an enduring one, highlighted by the assessment below of U.S. intelligence shortfalls more than three full years after the beginning of the Iraq war:

> We rely too much on others to bring information to us, and too often don't understand what is reported back because we do not understand the context of what we are told.[163]

The issue of context is not without its complications, from the broadest level of imperial understanding down to the most discrete individual interactions. Unless we are vainly seeking to feed Laplace's Demon with all the conceivable conditions relevant to a system's operation, there will always be some selection of which context, precisely, actually matters. More often than not, the context considered vital to a Bangladeshi women's relief organization in Khowst is unlikely to be the same context considered vital to a U.S. soldier in the same place and time. Alternative context, however, is much of what such

---

162 Paul Gifford, "Some Recent Developments in African Christianity," *African Affairs*, Vol. 93, No. 373 (October 1994), p. 531-532.

163 James A. Baker, III and Lee Hamilton, Co-Chairs, *The Iraq Study Group Report*, New York: Vintage Books, 2006, p. 94.

interactions can provide—an alternate frame of reference, sometimes more valuable than whatever apparently substantive information is being framed. Frustrated by the ornate and flowery Persian of their Indian informants, British officials preferred a blunt and forthright style—antecedents of our Keep It Simple Stupid and Bottom Line Up Front professional writing guides. Consequently, they routinely deleted "irrelevant" poetic references from their translations—"But the 'verses' they pointedly left out may well have conveyed much more than the guarded and complex prose around them."[164]

Consider this "intelligence report" received by agents of the Northwest Province of British India during the revolt of 1857, and imagine seeking to separate the wheat from the chaff. I can recognize quite quickly in a single reading what I would delete before forwarding to my superiors, as certainly as can my readers. But perhaps the next time one of these arrives in an imperial office, we should consider at least one more time what really matters:

KHUREETA, OR OFFICIAL LETTER FROM THE RANA OF DHOLPORE TO THE LT. GOVERNOR AT AGRA, DATED 3D SEPTEMBER 1857.

[The original is on native paper, sprinkled all over with gold leaf, and with gilt floral border and heading. It is written in the best style of Persian calligraphy.]

NAWAB SAHIB [proper style of address for Lt. Gov], of high dignity, appreciator of merit, affectionate and kind to me, your humble servant, may your dignity increase!

After paying such respects as a suppliant should offer, and expressing my desire for the honour of serving you (your service having the virtue of changing the base into the noble, which is the dearest wish of my heart), I beg to submit to your exalted mind of sunlight splendour the following information. To-day, the 3rd September 1857, news arrived, conveyed verbally by a trustworthy person, that yesterday, Wednesday the 2nd inst., the infantry of Indore with the troops of the Nawab of Bhopal, having marched from Morar, have encamped at the resident's house in Lashkar, Gwalior: and to-day, Thursday, they would halt there. The rumour is that on Friday they are marching in this direction. The troops of Morar and Indore are united in purpose, "You go one stage ahead, and we will follow stage by stage." It is necessary that you should be informed of this, so I now send you this letter. Whatever you wish I am ready to do. I am but an old dependent and sincere well-wisher of the Government of

164 C.A. Bayly, *Empire and Information: Intelligence Gathering and Social Communication in India, 1780-1870*, Cambridge: Cambridge University, 1996, p. 78.

the East India Company. Night and day do I cherish the desire that it may prosper, and be victorious. I trust that you will kindly continue to favor me by sending me letters with tidings of your health.

May the star of your dignity and glory shine brightly![165]

The troops of Indore, Morar and the Nawab of Bhopal are currently in Lashkar and will presently move by stages toward Dholpore. Full stop. The rest is largely window-dressing, of more interest to the protocol officer than the intelligence section. But the language of protocol is full of import regarding power and allegiance, where how something is said is frequently more important than what is said, requiring a different facility for translation. I encountered this issue as a student with the Indian military in Tamil Nadu, struggling to master the bureaucratese peculiar to every hierarchical organization. I think I ultimately managed the various paragraph formulations, indentations, numbering conventions, etc. required in an official letter—but I ran up hard against a wall when I attempted the signature block. As a U.S. Army officer, I am quite happy to sign off to superiors with a "Very Respectfully," and would never dream of dropping the "Very." The Indian Army version, however, required a few additional modifiers—along the lines of Most Humbly and Sincerely Respectfully. I simply couldn't do it, as those extra adverbs felt like crossing the line from respect to obsequiousness. It was a small and silly thing, utterly beside the point of the letter's substance; but the struggle over those five or six words essentially captures my entire year-long engagement with my Indian counterparts, far more so than any operations order, tactical appreciation or academic thesis I produced during that period. The implied issues of power and subordination inspired such emotional attachment that it ultimately became a disciplinary issue. After being called on the commandant's carpet, I felt honor had been satisfied by my "resistance" and ultimately relented. The point is that frequently sound analysis isn't about paring away the extraneous to reveal the "bottom line" or to identify the "center of gravity." Rather, more fruitful results may often open up from exploring marginal aspects of context, picking a single stray thread and pulling until the fabric unravels, or tugging at a single weed until an entire underground network of roots emerges from the earth.

---

[165] William Coldstream, ed., *Records of the Intelligence Department of the Northwest Provinces of India During the Mutiny of 1857. Vol. I*, Edinburgh: T & T Clark, 1902, p. 397.

Rhizomes: Unity and Multiplicity

He saw that a moon arose from the holy man's breast and came to sink in his own breast. A tree then sprouted from his navel and its shade compassed the world. Beneath this shade there were mountains, and streams flowed from the foot of each mountain. Some people drank from these running waters, others watered gardens, while yet others caused fountains to flow. When Osman awoke he told the story to the holy man, who said "Osman, my son, congratulations, for God has given the imperial office to you and your descendants and my daughter Malhun shall be your wife."[166]

or

Life has always seemed to me like a plant that lives on its rhizome. Its true life is invisible, hidden in the rhizome. The part that appears above the ground lasts only a single summer. Then it withers away—an ephemeral apparition. When we think of the unending growth and decay of life and civilizations, we cannot escape the impression of

Plant with rhizomatic root compared to isolated tree image. *Source: created by author.*

---

166 Rudi Lindner, *Nomads and Ottomans in Medieval Anatolia*, Bloomington, IN: Indiana University, 1983, p. 37.

absolute nullity. Yet I have never lost the sense of something that lives and endures beneath the eternal flux. What we see is blossom, which passes. The rhizome remains.[167]

Two dreams of empire are on display here: two images of how they grow, draw sustenance from their environment, and spread their influence through the world around them. But which does the Ottoman Empire—or any empire for that matter—more closely resemble, the rhizome or the tree?

The question is not merely a figurative one, because it impacts both the information experiences of imperial powers in situ and the expectations of outsiders attempting to study those experiences. Living as I do in a modern nation-state, and a servant of the state's most structured hierarchy to boot, it is perhaps less than surprising that I am inclined toward the arboreal approach—embodied in the terms of reference for the project at hand. Consideration of the Roman, Ottoman and British "Empires" presupposes that the term represents a discrete and limitable entity. This supposition is vulnerable to any number of attacks on the grounds of time, space and social affiliation; but something identifiable remains, at least in the self-perception of imperial elites. Clearly, participants have believed that they belong to a particular social order that was identifiable and distinctly imperial—illustrated above in the purported dream of the Ottomans' eponymous imperial founder, which played a key role in the self-imagining of empire.[168]

In a more material sense, this formation calls to mind adolescent memories of sweaty and back-breaking summer jobs with a landscaping company. The new owner, say, of a carefully constructed suburban lot in West Bloomfield, Michigan, would decide that the dwarf Japanese Maple (*Acer palmatum*) planted by his predecessor would look better in the northeast—rather than northwest—corner of his yard. I would carefully spade into the surrounding earth (perhaps eighteen inches out and twenty-four down), wrap the root ball in burlap, gasp and groan as I dragged this awkward mass across the lawn, and plop it down into a new excavation. With a little water and luck, the tree (self contained and physically circumscribable) would bloom in its new location, all evidence of the former location quickly vanishing beneath some shovelsful of topsoil and some grass seed. On less happy days, however, a lot would need to be cleared of some weed or tangle like that of the Canada thistle (*Circium arvense*). A single spade stroke could once again destroy a standing plant, but the same shovel would turn up a root network leading to yet another and another, *ad infinitum* until a whole day passed, spent with my playing a

---

167 Carl Jung, *Memories, Dreams, Reflections*, New York: Vintage Books, 1965, p. 4.
168 Finkel, 2.

scratched and dirty Theseus winding up a ball of roots with no way out of the Minotaur's maze, and inevitably the same lot would need to be cleared of the same weed come next summer. The difference lay in Jung's *rhizomes*, although articulated rather more elegantly in his imagination than in mine. This sub-surface root network of connections, which defies equally observation and eradication is "reducible neither to the One nor the multiple...it is comprised not of units but of dimensions, or rather directions in motion."[169]

Gilles Deleuze and Felix Guattari, the writers most widely associated with applying the concept of the rhizome in political theory—in opposition to the tree—have done so explicitly as a matter of Marxist critique. The common sub-title of their key works, *A Thousand Plateaus: Capitalism and Schizophrenia and Anti-Oedipus: Capitalism and Schizophrenia* gently hints at their position. But this tool of specific critique might also prove useful for more general analysis, as suggested by Jung's original formulation of growth, decay and resilience. These qualities are especially pertinent in the imperial context, where the associations of empire historically appear and reappear, sprouting perennially in the same fields from some subterranean root despite visible cycles of rise and fall. The Roman Empire is a case in point. Reaching backward from the formal rule of the Latin city-state over the Mediterranean rim, this polity incorporated so many principles of governance, architecture, art and literature from its predecessors that the phrase Graeco-Roman is frequently required to speak meaningfully of this cultural complex. Leaning forward, in its seminal articulation, Rome "fell" for almost twelve hundred years, with Gibbon's opus ending only in 1453 CE after the conquest of Constantinople by the Ottomans, encompassing what other authors consider an almost entirely independent Byzantine imperial manifestation. So too for the Ottomans, in an imperial construct which incorporated both the territories and cultural forms of earlier regional empires from the Abbasids to the Seljuks and Mamluks. Despite its apparent decline in the early twentieth century, the rhizome of that imperial space persists.[170] In the current "long war" there is more than coincidentally familiar association among the key players. Perhaps descriptions of the United States as a "new" empire, whether in critique or applause, are just slightly misplaced—with Washington actually playing Constantinople to London's Rome. We ask, Who devotes the highest percentage of forces? To the hardest fights? Which language is spoken in coalition headquarters? Who

---

169 Gilles Deleuze and Felix Guattari, *A Thousand Plateaus: Capitalism and Schizophrenia*, Minneapolis: University of Minnesota press, 1987, p. 21.

170 Efraim Karsh, *Islamic Imperialism: A History*, New Haven and London: Yale, 2006, p. 232.

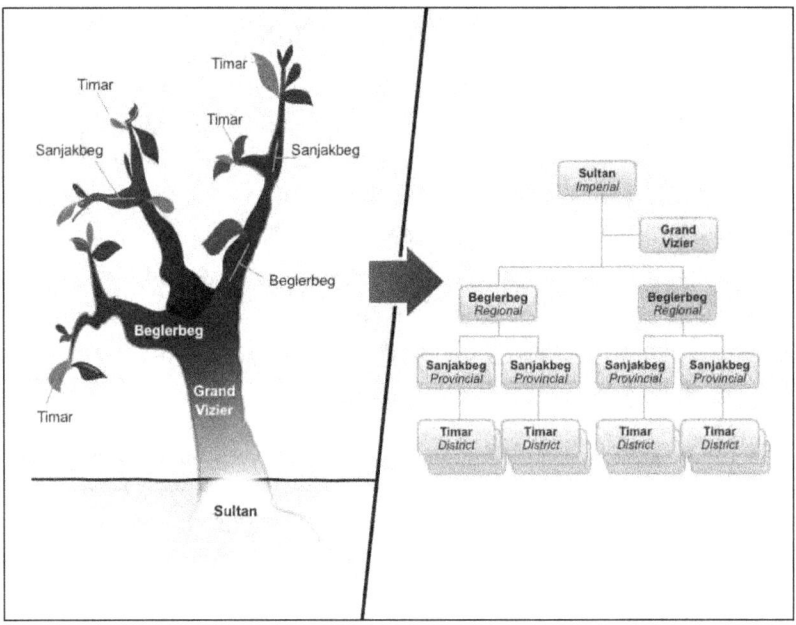

An Arboreal arrangement, whether in the natural world or a powerpoint chart, channels the flow of vitality, information and power in ways that progressively restrict multiple connections and vectors of escape or growth.
Source: created by author.

shares the most sensitive intelligence with whom?[171] The issue of intelligence sharing, while tactically specific in its connotations above, speaks to the potential rhizomatic qualities of imperial information in its subterranean and concealed transversality. This aspect of information provides an alternative model for considering how intelligence flows and works, and delineates a way to escape the persistent imperial topologies in a fashion beyond the well-worn models of hub-and-spoke.[172]

Taking Osman at his word, what might the Ottoman Empire look like in arboreal form? While the dramatically simplified trace above neglects much of the regional variation and layers of bureaucracy, it essentially captures the nature of authority in the imperial state, which springs from the navel of the Sultan. Power and guidance flow outward from the roots of sovereignty in the palace, via the administrative functioning of the Grand Vizier, along the limbs of regional *beglerbeglik*, to the branches of provincial *sanjakbegs*, ultimately

171 Greg Sheridan, "A friendship to offer lasting dividends," Sunday Telegraph (Australia), 30 July 2006; "U.S., Britain in Intelligence, Defence Deal," Indo-Asian News Service, 27 May 2006.

172 Alexander J. Motyl, "Why Empires Reemerge: Imperial Collapse and Imperial Revival in Comparative Perspective," *Comparative Politics*, Vol. 31, No. 2 (January 1999), p. 128.

terminating in the proliferation of district and village *timariots*.[173] Mimicking photosynthesis, the system also provides feedback as the *timars* collect wealth and information from the environment around them and pass it back down to nourish the roots. Such information is itself frequently about wealth and its protection or exploitation. The addition of judicial and administrative functions to what is essentially a military model would lend greater verisimilitude, but the trunk and branch aspect would remain the same—recognizably familiar to a modern organizational chart, which basically articulates the same vertical theme in reverse.

Attractive and convivial to Ottoman mythology as the chart may be, however, it misrepresents the flows of both power and information. While in theory the Sultan stood at the apex (or the root) with absolute authority, in practice "The nature of the Ottoman system in fact left the sultan with very limited power."[174] This is not to say that information did not reach the Sultan, or his immediate underlings; and in fact the central bureaucracy generated enormous paperwork.[175] Rather, it is the utility and relevance of this information to imperial functioning which is open to question. First, because as Baudrillard has observed, "the profusion of information corresponds to a tendency of the rate of knowledge to fall."[176] Second, because the nature of the Ottoman state privileged a certain world view and prioritized a certain *kind* of knowledge.

The Ottoman conception of rule and the role of government revolved around wealth and its extraction, a preoccupation reflected in the imperial archives. The bulk of these documents, *defters* comprising provincial surveys of population and revenue from the fifteenth century onward, more or less follow a predictable pattern.[177] After a preamble outlining the fiscal rules and usage of the province (usually carried over from a previous regime, whether Ottoman or not), the chief towns, districts and villages are broken down first

---

[173] Specified members of the provincial cavalry were authorized to derive an income—called a timar— from agricultural taxes raised in their assigned villages, hence this dual military-administrative role was known as a *timariot*. Several of these villages together constituted a *sanjak*, the basic Ottoman territorial administrative unit, managed by a *sanjakbeg*. Similarly, a collection of *sanjaks* was coordinated by a *beglerbeglik*. Norman Itzkowitz, *Ottoman Empire and Islamic Tradition*, Chicago and London: University of Chicago, 1972, p. 40-42.

[174] Stanford Shaw, *History of the Ottoman Empire and Modern Turkey, Volume I: Empire of the Gazis: the Rise and Decline of the Ottoman Empire, 1280-1808*, Cambridge, London and New York: Cambridge, 1976, p. 165.

[175] Norman Itzkowitz, *Ottoman Empire*, p. 55.

[176] Jean Baudrillard, *The Intelligence of Evil or the Lucidity Pact*, trans. Chris Turner, Oxford and New York: Berg, 2005, p. 128.

[177] *Defter* was the technical title for the cadastral tax surveys.

by the list of male inhabitants, followed by an accounting of the geographical unit's revenue by type of production and value.[178] Classification of individuals takes place along two axes: 1) Taxable status (taxable households, taxable bachelors and tax exempt), and 2) religion (Christian and Jew separated out for additional tax identification, with non-taxable Muslims lumped together regardless of affiliation).[179] Notable in these categories is the residual quality of religious faith, a factotum incidental to the more crucial issue of financial status. In the world of official Ottoman information, man is primarily "*homo fiscalus*," despite the emphasis, both in Ottoman self-mythologizing and later Western historiography, on the empire as the manifestation of a ghazi[180] ethos "blazing forth the way of Islam from the East to the West."[181] In this matrix, the key criterion of knowledge lies in wealth, rather than faith.

Administering an empire, however, naturally requires a variety of information types. A gap between what imperial powers *want* to know—determining what kinds of questions they routinely ask—and what they *need* to know creates a tension in intelligence requirements and production, leading to innovative narratives.[182] One such product is the *Nizamname-i Misir*, an assessment of conditions in Egypt preparatory to proposed military operations. The text is initially interesting simply in its context. The author was likely an old "Egypt hand" at the imperial court, writing between 1758 and 1775.[183] More than two centuries after the initial "conquest" of Egypt, the dating of such a project

---

[178] Bernard Lewis, "Registers on Iran and Adharbayan in the Ottoman Defter-I Khaqani," in *Studies in Classical Islam* (7th-16th Centuries), London: Varorum Reprints, 1976, XIX, p. 3-4.

[179] Lewis, "Studies in the Ottoman Archives—I," *Studies in Classical Islam*, XVI, p. 474-476.

[180] The term ghazi and its lexical associates has had different meanings in different contexts, but here generally captures the nomadic bands which prefigured the conquest and establishment of the Ottoman state. Although in practice they were frequently little more than mercenaries or bandits living off plunder, they were imagined as holy warriors waging war on the infidels—a sort of Anatolian *mujahideen*. For the Ottomans, this image of both rough martial freedom and piety in action was an important self-referent in a society increasingly less characterized by either.

[181] Karsh, 88.

[182] John Bodnar makes a case for the distinction between intelligence *wants* and *needs* in a modern systems-theory context. Current intelligence and tactical warning in this formulation are essentially feedback inputs to some particular course of action already selected by a senior decision-maker; intelligence collection then principally responds to the specific requirements of that decision maker (what he wants). Strategic warning, by way of contrast, is analyst driven as it attempts to reach beyond multiple decision making cycles into the future, where specific intelligence requirements may be unforeseen or dramatically different than those anticipated (consequently it seeks to anticipate what a decision maker will ultimately need). See Bodnar's *Warning Analysis for the Information Age: Rethinking the Intelligence Process*, Washington, D.C.: Joint Military Intelligence College, 2003, p. 69-71.

[183] Uriel Heyd, review of Stanford Shaw, *Ottoman Egypt in the Eighteenth Century*, *Bulletin of the School of Oriental and African Studies*, Vol. 26, No. 1 (1963), p. 188.

highlights the shifting status of the province noted earlier. Moreover, as genre it represents a departure from the *defter* type of information described above, as well as from the corpus of reference material available to the court in the form of *inca* (examples of correspondence); "mirrors for princes" (in the vein of Machiavelli or Kautilya); and collections of anecdotes and literary excerpts, the *adab*.[184] It represents a requirement for alternatives, and a forum for teasing out new differences. Although the work is framed by military action, the actual differences constructed in the text are only peripherally military in nature. Basic topography and military dispositions are noted, but the bulk of the material focuses on other kinds of questions. Who are the key religious and popular leaders? What are their connections to one another and to the civil authorities? What are the psychological predispositions and susceptibilities of the population?[185] Issues associated with other types of documents merit consideration of their own in delimiting the information environment, but I raise this one here—as a relatively obvious kind of imperial intelligence product—for what it says about the multiple information spaces operating in the empire and what structures had access to them. Although the *Nizamname* shows an official at a time of crisis attempting to synthesize various strains of knowledge in a kind of "extra-canonical" format, intelligence regarding these themes—from the military and political to the religious and social—would already have been extant, but spreading and flowering through arrangements outside the "imperial tree."

A rhizomatic approach suggests how these arrangements might be portrayed, by marginalizing the position of the sultan, and focusing on the subterranean associations which connect the visible efflorescence of formal institutions, as represented here.

A key rhizome function was performed by one of the distinct practices of the Ottoman Empire: the *devshirme*. This "collection" was conducted periodically by Janissary officers at the Sultan's direction to replenish the manpower of the formal imperial state. Rural Christian households, principally in the Balkans, would be identified and enumerated for contributions to this levy and would be compelled to provide a set number of young men for imperial service. After being physically and mentally evaluated, the subjects of this process would be circumcised, converted to Islam and enrolled in a series of academies established in Istanbul specifically for training this corps—a process known as the *ghulam* system. Depending on their performance and

---

184 Joel Shinder, "Early Ottoman Administration in the Wilderness: Some Limits on Comparison," *International Journal of Middle East Studies*, Vol. 9, No. 4 (November 1978), p. 506.

185 Percy Kemp, "An Eighteenth-Century Turkish Intelligence Report," *International Journal of Middle East Studies*, Vol. 16, No. 4 (November 1984), p. 500-501.

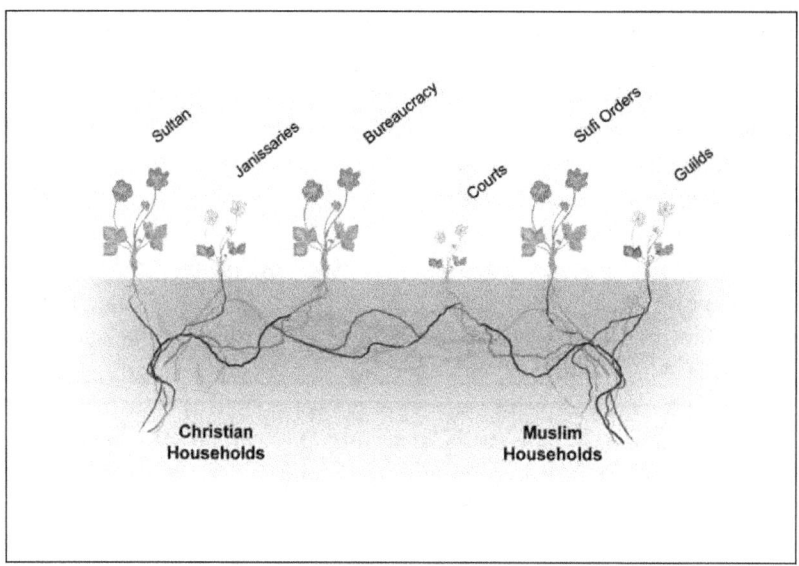

A Rhizomatic arrangement is chiefly characterized by its practically limitless possibilities for variety and connection—a design uniquely suited for resilience and expansion. *Source: created by author.*

fortunes, they would eventually pass out of the system at one of several sequential gates for service in the Janissaries, the administrative bureaus or the Sultan's personal household staff—a position from which they could rise to the highest offices in the empire.[186]

Legally, despite their exalted functional rank, the men taken in by the *devshirme* were slaves of the Sultan (and in a practical sense, his right of life-and-death over them was routinely exercised), but the mutable description of this status in the Ottoman context—blurring the distinction between servant and slave—suggests something unique.[187] Moreover, the practice among some urban Christians and Muslims of bribing officials or sending their children out to the countryside in order to allow them to be drawn up in the collection indicates how desirable this type of slavery could be.[188] Ideally, this process would create and replenish a body of the state cut-off from any other base of power or social connection—the administrative violence of the levy having ruptured ties of kin, language and faith. Officially, it did so, and the language, dress, faith and customs of the court became more important signals of "Ottoman" identity than national origin: "Turk" even being a common

---

[186] Itzkowitz, 49-54.

[187] V.L. Menage, "Some Notes on the 'Devshirme,'" *Bulletin of the Journal of Oriental and African Studies,* Vol. 29, No. 1 (1966), p. 66.

[188] Shaw, *History of the Ottoman Empire,* 114.

epithet for the uncouth. At the same time, however, this "machine" drew into the innermost workings of the empire knowledge of other worlds and other ways of knowing, among men who developed enduring relationships among themselves, even as they maintained connections to the people and places (and faiths) of their origins.[189] I noted earlier the polyvalent functions of the Sufi orders and their intersection with the Janissaries, marking yet another "subterranean" association; and the imperial practice of frequently rotating the assignment of regional officers—while intended to reduce the potential for the growth of autonomous power bases—would have provided another serial process of geographically dispersed connection-building.[190]

In their administrative functions, the more-or-less practically minded products of the *devshirme* would have interacted with another rhizomatic strain, the *ulema*—a social class educated in Muslim jurisprudence, not occupants of formal legal positions. As an alternative mode of advancement for the children of Muslim families ineligible or too scrupulous for the levy, religious training provided a route through a series of positions at various madrassas and as judges throughout the imperial space, including the possibility of passing over into more traditionally administrative roles.[191] Islamic judges could bridge the dichotomies between *shari'a* (law based on the text of the Quran and traditions of the early Islamic community), and *kanun* (law based on the prerogative of the Sultan for setting out rules governing the conduct of his subjects). Within their own community, the *ulema* could functionally move back and forth between traditions, with Ottoman Hanafi judges ready to pass jurisdiction over certain cases to their Shafi'i or Maliki counterparts as circumstances required.

Finally, even those not drawn into the networks of official and semi-official association above would have been enmeshed in a near-ubiquitous grid of professional guilds which included virtually every actor in society. Overlapping the connections already noted, these alignments also bridged spaces and functions of government, faith, and profession.[192] The point of tracing all these lines is not to argue the arboreal nature of sultanic authority,

---

189 Metin Ibrahim Kunt, "Ethnic-Regional (Cins) Solidarity in the Seventeenth Century Ottoman Establishment," *International Journal of Middle East Studies*, Vol. 5, No. 3 (1974), p. 238-239.

190 Karen Barkey, "In Different Times: Scheduling and Social Control in the Ottoman Empire, 1550 to 1650," *Comparative Studies in Society and History*, Vol. 38, No. 3 (July 1996), p. 460.

191 Suraiya Faroqhi, "Social Mobility Among the Ottoman 'Ulema in the Late Sixteenth Century," *International Journal of Middle East Studies*, Vol. 4, No. 2 (April 1973), p. 216.

192 Gabriel Baer, "The Administrative, Economic and Social Functions of Turkish Guilds," *International Journal of Middle East Studies*, Vol. 1, No. 1 (January 1970), p. 29, 33.

capturing every member of society in a tangle of interlocking limbs, but rather to highlight the sense that "any social subject is essentially decentered, that his/her identity is nothing but the unstable articulation of constantly changing positionalities."[193] This imperial identity, transiting and intersecting multiple points of association, is not merely an artifact of history, but prefigures the "thought experiment" generated by a study group chartered by the U.S. National Reconnaissance Office (NRO) to interpret alternative, future worlds. To explain the "underlying movement of people and ideas" they found associated with the evolution toward future worlds, three participants in the experiment observe:

> That the sheer number of identities and loyalties an individual possessed increased, with a concurrent tendency toward confliction. Schizophrenia of a sort set in for many…for some, the reaction to complexity was not schizophrenia but entrenchment. For these people, continuity dictated extremely narrow and rigid loyalties that shifted only under extreme pressure.[194]

For me, the rhizome seems an appropriate model for articulating this fluid social position (both then and now), which opens possible lines of exploration for following the flow of information even as it threatens the possibility of schizophrenia.

Finally, a number of additional qualities suggest themselves from the imperial image above. The first is that the sultan—or any institution—could be cut down without fundamentally damaging the rhizome. Not a reassuring prospect for the sultan, perhaps, but a guarantor of imperial formations, which can sprout again in the same soil come another season. The second is that one can enter the construct at virtually any point without resort to hierarchy or primacy. On a visit, I consciously followed this process by entering this thematic space from an Egyptian coffee house rather than the Topkapi Palace. "All roads may lead to Rome" eventually, but they stop at many other places as well. A third aspect is the relative independence of the individual plants–connected, but not nested—which I think is distinctly imperial. This is not a case of immature administrative coordination, just as grapes are not simply immature bottles of wine—they are something different. As polities develop more homogenous and consolidated networks, as they progressively come to resemble "states" in the modern sense, they lose access to the more heterogeneous information resources demanded of heterodox imperial space.

---

[193] Ernesto Laclau, "The Impossibility of Society," *Canadian Journal of Political and Social Theory*, Vol. 7, p. 22.

[194] Michael Loescher, Chris Schroeder, Charles Thomas, *Proteus: Insights from 2020*, Washington, D.C.: 2000, p. 52.

A key function of the rhizome in this sense is to serve as an avenue of translation—not so much of language or even culture, necessarily, as of meaning. Whether in the case of classical historiography or Ottoman tax administration, the idea of what constitutes knowledge changes depending on the contexts of both consumers and producers—eliminating these differences in some form of epistemological Esperanto may produce consensus and clarity, but it also sheds the information embedded in those differences.

Consequently, translating within the different extrusions of a single rhizome can and perhaps should be as difficult as translating from one distinct entity to the next.

The struggles inherent in this study suggest something of these translation challenges. Crude stereotypes aside, the U.S. security establishment has its intellectual side—in addition to Thucydides, the Army Chief of Staff reading list recommends books both of and on history, as well as historiography and social issues. These interests drive a significant body of professional publications, just as they do among academics, but the two intellectual "sprouts" often seem to emerge in entirely different atmospheres. While academic fashion may be only slightly less volatile than the textile variety, the fact that an online search for "Foucault" (December 2006) showed exactly two items (both dismissive footnotes) among war college publications might strike those familiar with academic writing in the humanities as slightly dissonant. In a more emotive example, the authors of the NRO study cited above recount that a senior former intelligence officer simply walked out of a workshop which questioned the issue of the world's fundamental intelligibility—a central preoccupation within many of the humanities. This officer dismissed concerns regarding the potential for unforeseen and turbulent future developments by observing, "We would know it."[195]

These kinds of easy dismissals are likely to become less and less acceptable as U.S. intelligence tackles some of the more "imperial" issues I outline here. From a substantive perspective, cultural intelligence is gaining increasing prominence as a suitable topic of investigation, and the United States Marine Corps is developing a concerted institutional approach to the issue. So far, however, this is largely a case of devoting established analytical procedures to a new problem set, establishing checklists, defining categories and so forth.[196]

---

[195] Ibid, 43. The fact that the Proteus project now operates under co-sponsorship of the U.S. Army War College and the Office of the Director of National Intelligence is of interest. See http://www.carlisle.army.mil/proteus/index.cfm.

[196] Troy Thomas, *Beneath the Surface: Intelligence Preparation of the Battlespace for Counterterrorism*, Washington, DC: Joint Military Intelligence College, 2004, p. 57-58.

A shorthand example of the issue can be found in the military acronym employed to guide mission analysis. When I began military training as a Reserve Officer Training Corps cadet, the acronym was METT (Mission, Enemy, Terrain and weather, Troops available). In short order, this was amended to become METT-T (METT plus Time available). More recently, the term has been expanded once again to METT-TC (METT-T plus Civilian considerations). A whole new realm of knowledge has been included with this additional "C," but framed in a way consistent with more traditional frames of military knowledge. It is precisely this framing, however, which presents such a significant challenge—one which will ultimately have to be confronted by the U.S. security establishment. The language and themes employed in this work are, by design, not those normally found in official U.S. defense and intelligence discourse; but they do not arise solely from some intellectual ghetto of French philosophy or avant garde sociology. Efforts to create and successfully employ organizations like Human Terrain Teams, incorporating academic personnel with backgrounds in history, anthropology and linguistics, will require engaging genuinely alternative approaches to knowledge production. I have a friend on one such team who produced a far more expert version of my own amateurish *Why They Fight*, but I have trouble imagining how this superior text would have fit into a military briefing context. Similarly, during my research for this project, multiple discussions indicated an academic unease with how military and intelligence organizations approach cultural knowledge methodologically—an unease even more pronounced than concerns regarding the perception of complicity with politically volatile policy goals.[197]

Traversing along our own rhizomes then, translating these connections, may prove equally as daunting as attempting to understand those of our "enemies." At least in the attempt, one might take solace from the comments of the French philosopher Gilles Deleuze:

> How else can one write but of those things which one doesn't know, or knows badly? It is precisely there that we imagine having something to say. We write only at the frontiers of our knowledge, at the border which separates our knowledge from our ignorance and transforms the one into the other. Only in this manner are we resolved to write. To satisfy ignorance is to put off writing until tomorrow—or rather, to make it impossible.[198]

---

[197] The question of academic support to intelligence projects has generated a heated debate, most notably between anthropologists David Price and Felix Moos, many installments of which are widely available on the Internet. For an introduction to the discussion, see David Price, "America the Ambivalent; Quietly Selling Anthropology to the CIA," *Anthropology Today*, Vol. 21, No. 5 (December 2005), p. 1-2.

[198] Gilles Deleuze, *Repetition and Difference*, trans. Paul Patton, New York: Columbia, 1994, xxi.

The conundrum Deleuze raises strikes me as that confronted by any large organization which attempts to institutionalize creativity or promote innovative thinking. Such pursuits are always sketchy, hazardous, and prone to failure. Rhizomatic thinking is particularly vulnerable, equally likely to result in navel gazing, wild goose chases, and extraordinary new insights. The risk of the first two, however, is the price of the third. Failure to pay it will ultimately foster a transition from the dynamic and expansive to the static and claustrophobic—an intellectual analogue to the architectural transition between the tent and the house.

Nomads and States: Tent of Osman/House of Osman

The *Seraglio*, wherein the *Grand Seignor* resideth with his Court, is wonderfully well situated, being directly in that place where *Byzantium* stood; upon a point of the Continent, which looketh toward the mouth of the *Black-Sea*, and is in form triangular, two sides whereof are compassed with the *Thracian Bosphorus*, and the third joineth to the rest of the city of *Constantinople*. It is enclosed with a very high and strong wall, upon which there are diverse watch towers, and is, by computation, about three *Italian* miles in compass.[199]

Any discussion of Ottoman information networks, whether they begin in a Cairene coffeehouse or wander in purposefully aimless fashion with Evliya Celebi,[200] must ultimately come to Istanbul and the *sanctum sanctorum*—the

Physically circumscribed from view—a rare tile of blue sky shows only the Sultan's perch—the harem stood at the center of alternative information networks.
Source: photo by author.

---

[199] Ottavio Bon, *The Sultan's Seraglio: An Intimate Portrait of Life at the Ottoman Court* [from the *Seventeenth Century Edition of John Withers*], London: Saqi Books, 1996

[200] Evliya Celebi, Seyahatname (Book of Travels), published in Arabic 1896-1928. Also see Robert Dankoff, *An Ottoman Mentality*: The World of Evliya Celebi, Leiden and Boston: Brill, 2004.

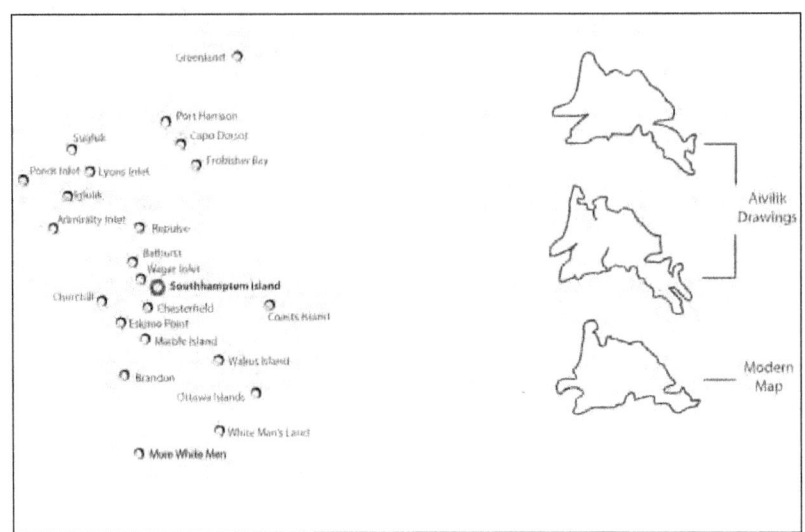

Aivilik Maps—Are you hungry or are you lonely? Depending on whether you view the world around you chiefly as a space filled with resources or with social communities, your map of that space may be dramatically different.
Source: Modified from Edmund Carpenter, Frederick Varley, Robert Flaherty, Eskimo, Toronto, University of Toronto, 1959, p. 3-4.

harem within Topkapi Palace. Mirroring my roundabout narrative approach, the physical roads leading into and through the capital would have been a haphazard affair in the imperial period, narrow, dusty and labyrinthine in their apparently random layout.[201] Along the way, an observer would have passed through the network of mosque/madrassas and Sufi *tekkes*. In addition to the messages embodied in the position and distribution of those establishments, their respective architectural forms provide an early indicator of how the physical construction of space directly shapes and more generally represents the flow of social information. While larger than the dervish lodges, the façades of the madrassas were far less revealing of what went on inside them, with shuttered windows and closed doors meeting the gaze of society at large—representing and physically acting out the separation of governing elites and the diverse governed. The *tekkes*, in contrast, were pierced with doors and large windows deliberately oriented to the main thoroughfares, drawing in observation, interest and participation form all and sundry. [202] The

---

[201] Cem Behar, *A Neighborhood in Ottoman Istanbul: Fruit Vendors and Civil Servants* in the Kasap Ilyas Mahalle, Albany: State University of new York, 2003, p. 46.

[202] Ethel Sara Wolper, *Cities and Saints: Sufism and the Transformation of Urban Space in Medieval* Anatolia, University Park, PA: Pennsylvania State University, 2003, p. 66-69.

Sufis, despite their reputation for mysticism, principally viewed the "secret" as a problem of insight rather than concealment.[203]

In consequence of this contrast, the capital can be viewed as a sort of tic-tac-toe grid, punctuated alternatively by devices—structures—which through their organization of space and architectural form either absorb and disseminate information, or deny and enclose information. While the relation between issues of practical engineering and the esoterica of information may seem a tenuous one, it continues to physically resonate, with 2006 marked by a flurry of literally tearing down walls between intelligence departments at both the Central Intelligence Agency and the Joint Chiefs of Staff. At a broader level:

> Space is crucial in thinking about culture and ideology because it is where ideology and culture take on physical existence and representations. These material forms embody, reinforce, and order universes of power and belief. People learn them, absorb them as part of the "as it is," everyday nature of things. Definitions of those universes may also be imposed and maintained by certain groups over others, and these groups will therefore have quite different experiences and apprehensions of space.[204]

The profound interplay between social roles, how space is conceived of, and what kinds of information are encoded in those conceptions are vividly illustrated by a set of maps collected in the early twentieth century among Aivilik Eskimos living on Southampton Island at the entrance to Hudson Bay. When asked to sketch out their environment, two male hunters provided outlines of the island which proved remarkably similar in their topographical coastline detail to a modern depiction assembled from aerial photographs, the chief discrepancy being an enlargement of the southeast peninsula, reflecting its importance as their chief hunting ground. By way of contrast, women responding to roughly the same task provided a radically different image—essentially a scattering of dots representing all the settlements known to them through either experience or hearsay. This map too was accurate after a fashion, the directions and relative distances being generally correct, but this is clearly a different kind of space with very different kinds of priorities.[205]

203 Michael Gilsenan, *Recognizing Islam: Religion and Society in the Modern Middle East*, London and New York: I.B. Tauris, 2000, p. 116-117.

204 Ibid., p. 187.

205 Edmund Carpenter, Frederick Varley, Robert Flaherty, *Eskimo*, Toronto, University of Toronto, 1959, p. 3-4.

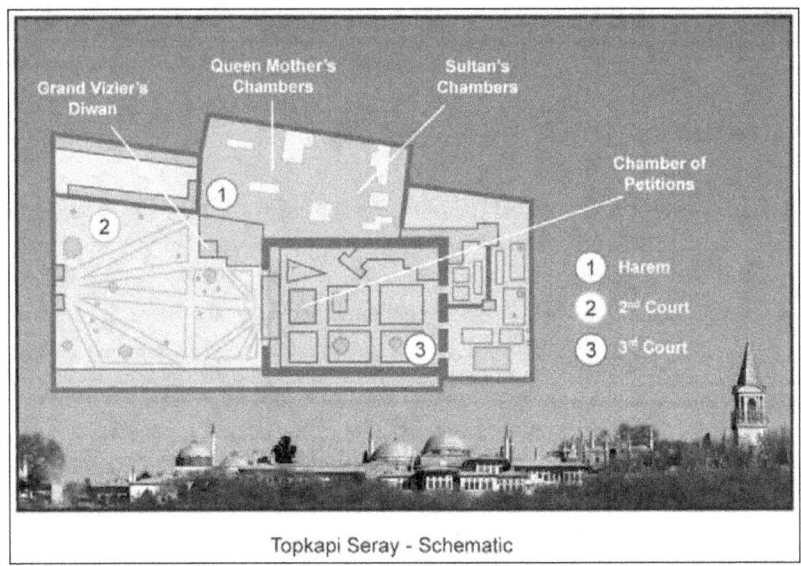

The spaces of Topkapi Palace. *Source: modified from tourist brochure.*

Returning from the Artic to the Mediterranean, the approach to Topkapi is a prolonged one, as the palace is deliberately set at some remove from the core of the city, reflecting an intentional position manifesting Ottoman political ideas within the broader context of Islamic governance generally—a context marked over preceding centuries by a sustained pattern of increasing architectural isolation.[206] Having come this far, military officers, judges, administrative officials and petitioners from across the empire—the physical transmitters of information—would emerge onto the broad, public open spaces of the palace's First Court. At the far end of this area, scattered with a few buildings and flanked by extensive gardens, selected visitors would pass through the Middle Gate into the Second Court, leaving behind the architectural, visual and aural cacophony of the city (a riot of signs) for the well-ordered realms of the administrative elite. Our visitor (representing a bundle of information in human form) would then transit this expanse of lawn to approach the Grand Vizier's Diwan chamber, where petitions and reports would be heard and deliberations taken among the most senior imperial officers.

---

[206] Jere L. Bacharach, "Administrative Complexes, Palaces and Citadels: Changes in the Loci of Medieval Muslim Rule," in *The Ottoman City and Its Parts: Urban Structure and Social Order*, eds. Irene Bierman, Rifa'at Abou-El-Haj, and Donald Preziosi, New Rochelle, NY: Aristide D. Caratzas, 1991, p. 11-112.

In practical contrast to the omniscience claimed by the Tower of Justice, information was progressively screened by the structures of empire, literally reduced to whispers and silent hand gestures once it passed the Gate of Felicity. *Source: photo by author.*

At this point, the Sultan might conceivably be party to the affair, listening unobserved from a hidden chamber through a screen with access into the Grand Vizier's chamber. Otherwise, once the routine council session concluded (four times a week), the chief officers in attendance might each in turn carry their issues to the Sultan (twice a week) within the Third Court's Chamber of Petitions. Here they would enter a realm marked by "the very silence of death itself."[207] Throughout this space of uttermost interiority, pages, attendants, ministers and even the members of the royal family would communicate largely through a system of nods and signs, bringing the contrast with the outside world to a point of nearly unbearable contrast.[208] Having consumed whatever parcels of information might pass through such an extraordinary sieve, the Sultan could then mount the Tower of Justice to enjoy the practically infinite view stretching out across his dominions.

I have sketched out this rather tedious bureaucratic sequence because I believe it tells a number of stories about the interaction of space, information

---

[207] Cited in Barnette Miller, *Beyond the Sublime Porte*, New Haven: Yale, 1931, p. 158.
[208] Bon, *Sultan's Seraglio*, p. 79-80.

and power. The first is the most obvious—that for which these places and processes were scripted. In the scripted version, this formation sends a clear message to the imperial audience that the Sultan enjoys the supreme prerogative of power—i.e. seclusion. While the harem has variously been imagined in the West as a site of sexual license, Oriental luxury, and the confinement and oppression of women, it was intended to represent a principle which cascaded down the Ottoman social hierarchy and across genders, whereby the "degree of seclusion from the common gaze served as an index of the status of the man as well as the woman of means."[209] Seclusion without parallel suggests an equally unique and exalted status. The palace's siting, the series of gates and courts, the army of intermediaries are all ways of telling this story—they write a plot through ritualized space. As Bernard Tschumi would have it:

> The use of a plot may suggest the sense of an ending, an end to the overall organization. It superimposes a conclusion to the open-endedness of the transformational (or methodological) sequence. Whenever a program or "plot" (the single family house, or "Cinderella") is well known (as are most architectural programs), only the "retelling" counts: the "telling" has been done enough.[210]

The "plot" of Topkapi Palace responds to both of Tschumi's points. There is indeed an ending, where absolute power and absolute silence meet in a profound fashion. Moreover, there is a sub-plot regarding intelligence, which concludes here in conjunction with the main theme of power. Namely, not only do these structures represent the Sultan's omnipotence, but also his omniscience. Himself concealed, the Sultan sees through the offices of his agents throughout the empire, through the latticed window above the Grand Vizier, and from his perch atop the tower of justice: "What is each window, but an eye opening to the whole world, to watch ceremonies and spectacles/What is each tower, but from head to foot a tongue to praise and eulogize the just shah?"[211] But it is precisely at this point that we reach Tschumi's second argument. The "telling" has been done enough.

What of the retelling? At the outset, it is worth noting that the Sultan may pretend (and believe) that he knows all; but while he may see a great deal, sequestered among his mutes and signing, nodding functionaries, he doesn't "hear" much at all—a systematic privileging of perception fraught with import.

209 Leslie Pierce, "Beyond Harem Walls," *Gendered Domains: Rethinking Public and Private in Women's History*, eds. Dorothy Helly and Susan Reverby, Ithaca and London: Cornell, 1992, p. 45.

210 Bernard Tschumi, *Architecture and Disjunction*, Cambridge: MIT, 1996, p. 164.

211 Cited in Gulru Necipoglu, *Architecture, Ceremonial, and Power: The Topkapi Palce in the Fifteenth and Sixteenth Centuries*, Cambridge: MIT, 1991, p. 85.

From the Tower of Justice, the Sultan could look out over two continents, seeing and knowing his empire without obstruction in the timeless dream of "persistent surveillance." *Source: photo by author.*

Responding to the world through sight differs from responding to it through the other senses in several important respects. For instance, seeing is "objective;" seeing—as the expression goes—is believing, but we tend to distrust information obtained through the ears; it is "hearsay" or "rumor." Seeing does not involve our emotions deeply…. The world perceived through the eyes is more abstract than that known to us through the other senses. The eyes explore the visual field and abstract from it certain objects, points of focus, perspectives.[212]

Compound this restriction in sense perception with the structural winnowing of imperial architecture both material and political, and the amount of information arriving at the policy-making end rapidly approaches nil. Whether driven by considerations of status or force protection, the blinding and deafening effects of isolation are the same—a consideration with contemporary relevance when one contemplates the series of barrier upon barrier, guard and gate that wall off U.S. outposts in precisely those places where information about the surrounding environment is most dear, from military headquarters in Kabul to the U.S. Embassy in Islamabad, or even more benign environments like New Delhi. Certain kinds of information about what the United States represents and intends are passed by such structures—although not necessarily those that policy-makers might desire—even while they restrict the kinds of information that might pass inside the structures, which potentially policy-makers might desire most.[213] My most recent posting provides a perfect example, as we moved operations to a new embassy complex shortly after my arrival. This facility—based on a standard model common to all new embassy construction worldwide—is modern, sanitary, safe from bombs and earthquakes, and plausibly attractive, depending on one's aesthetic; all attributes we would presumably like associated with America. As a practical matter, however, its prominent fortress-like appearance at the top of the hill has inspired local rumors regarding the 800 Marines secretly sequestered inside and the CIA rendition facility in the basement, and prompted my driver and cook to ask "Why does America want to take over Nepal?" As a local editorial puts it:

> From an architect's perspective—full points to the US embassy. It has achieved what most architects can only aspire for—that the building's physical form and lack of harmony with the site embodies and reflects the culture and ethos of its inhabitants.[214]

The recently published U.S. Army Field Manual 3-24 offers a zen-style koan in its "Paradoxes of Counterinsurgency:" *Sometimes, the more you protect your*

---

212 Yi-Fu Tuan, *Topophilia: A Study of Environmental Perceptions, Attitudes and Values*, Englewood Cliffs, NJ: Prentice-Hall, 1974, p. 10.

213 Richard Feinberg, "Get Out of Our Garrisons: Fortress Embassies Damage Diplomacy," *Washington Post*, 24 May 2007, p. 31.

214 "Arrested in Kathmandu: Does the New US Embassy Need a Hijab?" *Nepali Times*, #368 (28 Sep 07 – 4 Oct 07); accessed 11 Oct 07, online at: *http://www.nepalitimes.com/issue/368/NepaliPan/14007.*

A triangle or three cut-out circles? *Source: created by author.*

force, the less secure you may be.[215] While specifically cited in the context of infantry patrols, the same principle of risk-and-reward applies to traffic in information. Moreover, the "counterinsurgency" aspect indirectly suggests the imperial condition. As I have noted briefly in both the Roman and Ottoman periods—despite official rhetoric of the time, and backward-looking studies which tend to reify constantly mutating entities—empires are almost always being challenged from within, and counterinsurgency as a theme is almost inextricable from the consistent practice of imperial governance; that is, "Long Wars" never really end.

So this is one retelling of the Topkapi plot—strictly speaking a simply negative one—in which what appears to be near-omniscience is in fact near-

---

215 U.S. Army Field Manual 3-24, *Counterinsurgency*, Washington, DC: Headquarters, Department of the Army, 15 December 2006, p. 1-27.

ignorance, by way of bureaucratic sclerosis. But are there other possibilities? Despite this structural self-strangulation, the Ottoman Empire was among history's longer-lived. If we choose to assume intelligence is not simply irrelevant in the long run, perhaps there are alternative ways to read the Topkapi story in a "positive" light, though "positive" as a category becomes a bit problematic. Does this image portray a triangle or three cut-out circles? The optical confusion here is an old trick familiar in art, but the relationship between foreground and background, where two streams of information trace each other out, appears in systems as diverse as number theory and baroque fugues.[216]

The same theme applies to information flows within the Ottoman administration, both as narrated in the text and illustrated in the Topkapi schematic above. Nowhere in my text do women appear, and their residence in the harem is distinctly and intentionally marginal to the linear flow of both power and information along the axis running from the outer world, through the series of gates, and ending in the Chamber of Petitions. They are literally beside the point, mere background to the foreground of imperial theater.

I noted earlier one aspect of this double-image in discussing the role of the devshirme levies. These young men were brought into the palace as slaves, and the most select were trained for positions as pages within the Third Court, from which fortune and competence might lead them to high administrative office—a sort of progressive slippage from background to foreground. While the women of the harem did not have the same opportunity to transgress these frames, despite their relative physical confinement (their inability to see as well as be seen) they were able to establish broad networks of communication and influence outside the formal articulation of power. At the peak of this structure stood the queen mother, the woman who played a critical role in the training of the future sultan as well as key ally in the inevitable struggle for succession. Once her son was ensconced more or less firmly on the throne, she would frequently enjoy the consequent pre-eminence for years. It is worth noting the close proximity of the queen mother's chambers to the Sultan's within the harem—the two shared a bath, and she resided between the Sultan and the quarters of his concubines and other family members. In addition to her own connections, the queen mother from this site would be able to influence the multiple networks established by other women in the harem. Princesses of the royal family would eventually be married off, sometimes in serial fashion to five or six husbands in succession, while concubines who did not bear the sultan's sons would frequently be married to high-ranking officers across the

---

216 Douglas Hofstadter, *Gödel, Escher, Bach: An Eternal Golden Braid*, New York: Basic Books, 1999, p. 71-73.

empire, and female slaves of the more pedestrian variety would periodically be manumitted as an act of piety, leaving the harem to marry men of various vocations.[217] Personally connected via a rhizomatic arrangement of marriage and patronage, these women then enjoyed access to information in abundance. The consequent influence of the harem's residents rose to the point where it ultimately earned the sobriquet, the "Sultanate of the Women."

So, while the official organization of power and information, articulated in a rigid construction of imperial space, grew ever more restricted, unofficial networks among the marginals of the palace—women and *devshirme* levies, not to mention the legions of eunuchs and other functionaries—proliferated. Although this weed-like profusion of connections was a cause for great alarm among contemporary political commentators outside the administration (no less reluctant then than now to offer frequent criticism),[218] it suggests to me a characteristic of the successful imperial order.

If absolute power corrupts absolutely, it also tends to isolate completely—twin tendencies any executive authority risks as it ascends to the heights of imperial power. Bureaucracies rise in tandem with that isolation, providing the intellectual equivalent of walls and gates; but subverting that intellectual structure by act of will can prove nearly as impossible as escaping from the physical walls for reasons of either status or security. As Max Weber has it, "When those subject to bureaucratic control seek to escape the influence of the existing bureaucratic apparatus, this is normally possible only by creating an organization of their own which is equally subject to the process of bureaucratization,"[219] a dismal prescription for those hoping to avoid the deafening silence of the Third Court. Competing here are two different kinds of space, both material and mental, the *striated* and the *smooth*. Official imperial information—the *deftdars* and intelligence reports, the court decisions and petitions—moves through a striated space, measured and marked out as deliberately as palatial geometry. The information of the harem moves through a smooth space of marriage and whisper and rumor—as shifting and resistant to boundaries as the sea or the desert. A facility for combining these two kinds of space is rare, and one to which only the more successful empires may be predisposed.

---

217 Leslie Pierce, *The Imperial Harem: Women and Sovereignty in the Ottoman Empire*, New York and Oxford: Oxford University, 1993, p. 143-149.

218 Virgina Aksan, "Ottoman Political Writing, 1768-1808," *International Journal of Middle East Studies*, Vol. 25, No. 1 (February 1993), p. 54.

219 Max Weber, *From Max Weber: Essays in Sociology*, eds. and trans. H.H. Gerth and C. Wright Mills, New York: Oxford University, 1946, p. 338.

Windowless, narrow and cramped—here at the core of the harem, female knowledge networks connect with the male spaces of power along the private corridor linking the Queen Mother's chambers to those of the Sultan.
Source: photo by author.

In employing the *smooth/striated* model, I am following in part the formulation of Deleuze and Guattari, who integrate this idea with a dialectic between social assemblages described respectively as the *nomad* and the *State*:

The variability, the polyvocality of directions is an essential feature of smooth spaces of the rhizome type, and it alters their
cartography. The nomad, nomad space is localized and not de-
limited. What is both limited and limiting is striated space [the
space of the State], the *relative global*; it is limited in its parts,
which are assigned constant directions, are oriented in relation
to one another, divisible by boundaries, and can interlink; what
is limiting (*limes* or wall, no longer boundary) is this aggregate
in relation to the smooth spaces it "contains," whose growth it
slows or prevents, and which it restricts or places outside.[220]

The authors are curiously determined to avoid conceding a scheme of historical development between the two, positing each in a kind of temporal
suspended animation. Nevertheless, these articulations might well describe
the start and end points of various hybrid historical entities. One begins as
a fleet of more-or-less official pirates sailing around the globe, and ends as
"Cool Britannia." One begins as a tribe of *ghazis* galloping along the steppes,
and ends as Turkey. One begins as a band of cowboys riding across the Great
Plains and ends as...well, we'll see, I suppose.

In any event, the interesting part of this arc is in the middle, where smooth
nomadic spaces overlap with statist striated ones—empire, in a word. The
foreground/background reading of both space and information inside the
Topkapi Palace suggests just such an overlap, as does the concept of counterinsurgency as a condition of imperial governance. *A Thousand Plateaus*
argues that the nomad assemblage resembles a "war machine," a smooth
principle distinct from the striated nature of the state's "military institution."
But empires, so long as they remain empires, constitute a hybrid—they make
manifest Foucault's proposed reversal of Clausewitz, in which the politics of
peace are simply war carried out by other means.[221] That formulation provides a frame establishing context for another observation, relevant to both
the Ottoman and modern contexts:

The universalism of Islam, in its all-embracing creed, is imposed
on the believers as a continuous process of warfare, psychological
and political, if not strictly military.... The Jihad, accordingly, may

---

220 Gilles Deleuze and Felix Guattari, *A Thousand Plateaus: Capitalism and Schizophrenia*,
trans. Brian Massumi, Minneapolis: University of Minnesota, 1987, p. 382. Literally "path,"
limes refers to the system of fortifications built up along Roman military roads, such as
Hadrian's Wall in Great Britain. Easily identifiable as a visible symbol of "hard" borders, they
functioned both as a military obstacle and as a site of cultural interchange, suggesting the
permeable and fluid nature of the concept.

221 Michel Foucault, *Power/Knowledge: Selected Interviews and Other Writings, 1972-1977*,
ed. Colin Gordon, trans. Colin Gordon, Leo Marshall, John Mepham and Kate Soper, New
York: Pantheon, 1980, p. 90.

be stated as a doctrine of a permanent state of war, not continuous fighting.[222]

And what of the modern world, what can we draw from the Ottoman example? Walls, and guards and gates we have in abundance. With bureaucracy, too, we are blessed by an embarrassment of riches. I myself have even resorted to a bit of sign language on occasion when lurking in the outer vestibule of a three-star general's office. Concubinage and palace slavery are thankfully out of vogue, but these precise institutions are, perhaps ironically, once again beside the point for my purposes. They remain instructive because they demonstrate ways in which smooth space can escape the striated. I have discussed earlier the value of heterogeneous sources and voices outside the established architecture of power. The harem institutions, however, represent voices at the literal heart of the state, operating in nomadic ways across statist *limes*.

The most obvious counterpart to these systems is the almost paradigmatically rhizomatic Internet. For intelligence producers at almost every level, the Web availability of information can frequently seem an almost insuperable headache. Rare indeed must be the analyst or briefer, from the deployed brigade tactical operations center to those addressing congressional committees, who has not been caught out by open-source press reporting—some "scoop," whether valid or not, racing from smooth space like a nomadic raid into the plodding timescale of striated space. Within institutions, and a more precise analogue to the harem networks—e-mail—plays a similar dangerously uncontrolled function. U.S. Army units in Iraq have created local Web-based information-sharing arrangements not entirely in accord with top-down direction, increasing their battlefield efficiency despite the discord and confusion such ad hoc arrangements can breed.[223] During a variety of crises in the Pacific Theater, from the 2004-2005 tsunami disaster to the downfall of Nepal's King Gyanendra, I have seen extraordinary networks of information request, retrieval, communication and dissemination erupt literally overnight between attaches, military commands, civilian agencies and foreign governments. None have borne even the slightest resemblance to any formal intelligence-cycle model or knowledge management plan—they are smooth, nomadic, and incredibly fast. They are also disorganized, piecemeal and often infuriatingly frustrating, particularly when your boss is on a particular e-mail distribution list and you are not. Inevitably, as the crisis

---

[222] Majid Khadduri, *War and Peace in the Law of Islam*, Baltimore: John Hopkins, 1955, p. 64.

[223] Thomas McNaugher, "The Real Meaning of Military Transformation: Rethinking the Revolution," *Foreign Affairs*, Vol. 86, No. 1 (January-February 2007), p. 143.

subsides, striated space reasserts itself. In the after-action reviews, consistent themes are criticism for failure to comply with established protocols or well-meaning attempts at restructuring those protocols to resemble what actually took place. Some elements of the Army have moved to describing the process as discovering "lessons observed" rather than "lessons learned".

With the Ottoman context in mind, the point for me in this discussion is not that these incidents represent failure, but rather strength. Bounding information and structuring its flows represents an inevitable and largely salutary function of government institutions. Just as necessary, however, is maintaining the capacity for "sailing" across the smooth space of information—a capacity calling for strategy rather than institutionalization. In this struggle to contain and manage information, I submit another counterinsurgency koan: *sometimes doing nothing is the best reaction.*[224] Difficult as that admonition may be to practice, it becomes even more complicated in dealing with issues of time—a temporal "space" subjected to contesting "smooth" and "striated" tensions which can have profound effects. To broach this topic, appropriately enough, we sail forward into another imperial era.

---

[224] FM 3-24, 1-27.

Chrono-Politics: The Accelerating Archive

In the entrance-hall stood the larger figures of the Greco-Buddhist sculptures done, savants know how long since, by forgotten workmen whose hands were feeling, and not unskillfully, for the mysteriously transmitted Grecian touch. There were hundreds of pieces, fragments of statues and slabs crowded with figures that had encrusted the brick walls of the Buddhist stupas and viharas of the North Country and now, dug up and labeled, made the pride of the Museum.[225]

In the Archives of our Time, knowing is never neutral. Old and new, the British Museum represents knowledge as power, its façade a complement to images of political and military might. *Source: photos by author.*

---

[225] Rudyard Kipling, *Kim*, London: Macmillan, 1944, p. 8.

Thus Kim's peripatetic companion, the Tibetan lama, is introduced to the "Wonder House" (the Lahore Museum—still there and very much as Kipling described it). Among the grey schist and stucco sculpture depicting the life of Buddha, the lama would find that "'Tis all here. A treasure locked'.... For the first time he heard of the labours of European scholars, who by the help of these and a hundred other documents have identified the Holy Places of Buddhism. Then he was shown a mighty map, spotted and traced with yellow."[226] Here, in short, lay collected all the material detritus of the imperial archive, which "differentiates discourses in their multiple functioning," although it is so vast and amorphous that it "cannot be described in its totality."[227] As a physical realization of the past, the museum allows visitors to shape and mediate that past.

The sheer scale and breadth of this archive, the Lahore case representing only a small, local manifestation of an institution reproduced throughout the empire, as well as in metropolitan archetypes like the British Museum, suggests the comprehensive nature of imperial intelligence. On one hand, this enterprise may signify wild ambition and arrogance; and one is reminded of Joseph Goebbels' claim that, "*He who knows everything fears nothing.*"[228] Alternatively, the drive for all-encompassing knowledge may represent weakness and insecurity. Few circumstances allow the full weight of metropolitan force to be rapidly brought to bear against a given peripheral trouble spot; and however mighty an imperial power may be in absolute terms, it is almost everywhere liable to be at a relative disadvantage—in which case "overstretch" may be considered as a constitutive aspect of empire, rather than a modifier. In this situation, knowledge becomes a replacement for power, rather than its manifestation. "Replacement" here can be taken in a dual sense: knowledge is both a proxy—by facilitating control and influence where material means are lacking; and a mask—signifying the appearance of mastery where none tangibly exists. For the British:

> The truth, of course, is that it was much easier to unify an archive composed of texts than to unify an empire made of territory, and that is what they did—or at least tried to do, for most of the time they were unable to unify the knowledge they were collecting. It fell apart: ran off in many different directions like the hedgehogs

---

226 Ibid, 11-12.

227 Michel Foucault, *The Archaeology of Knowledge*, trans. A.M. Sheridan Smith, New York: Harper & Row, 1972, p. 129-130.

228 Cited in Paul Virilio, *The Information Bomb*, trans. Chris Turner, London and New York: Verso, 2000, p. 62.

in Alice's game of croquet, so much so that…I question whether the data they collected can even be called "knowledge."[229]

The comprehensive nature of such an archive, and the utility the British attributed to it, is indicated by the nature of the training undergone by its agents, in a regimen expanding far beyond "cultural awareness" briefings—or even the more extensive program undertaken by putative specialists like U.S. Foreign Area Officers. New officers of the East India Company, upon arrival in Calcutta, were expected to spend three years at the Fort William College—the "University of the East."

> They studied Hindu, Islamic, and English law; civil jurisprudence, political economy, general history, world geography, and mathematics. The rigorous curriculum also included natural history, botany, chemistry, astronomy, Latin, Greek, Sanskrit, Arabic, Persian, and modern European languages in addition to the culture and the six major languages of their South-Asian subjects (Hindustani, Bengali, Telagu, Marathi, Tamil and Kannada).[230]

The particulars of this program of instruction are historically specific and contingent; its *raison d'etre*, however, has more general applicability. Its purpose was not simply the practical one of passively facilitating interchange between rulers and ruled, in a kind of 19th Century version of today's Titan language contractor or Windows CE Phraselator. Rather, this suite of tools provided imperial administrators with the means for the positive construction of knowledge. For men like British adventurer and polyglot Richard Burton who was a product of this system: "All of his vast information about the Orient, which dots every page he wrote, reveals that he knew that the Orient in general and Islam in particular were systems of information, behavior and belief, that to be an Oriental or a Muslim was to know certain things in a certain way…" which his experience allowed him to merge with "the voice of Empire, which itself is a system of rules, codes and concrete epistemological habits."[231] Burton's contemporaries may have been more or less enthusiastic in mimicking his practical pursuit of cultural transvestism, but the intellectual project was the same.

---

229 Thomas Richards, *The Imperial Archive: Knowledge and the Fantasy of Empire*, London and New York: Verso, 1993, p. 4.

230 Kapil Raj, "Colonial Encounters and the Forging of New Knowledge and National Identities: Great Britain and India, 1760-1850," in *Nature and Empire: Science and the Colonial Enterprise*, ed. Roy MacLeod, Osiris, Vol. 15, 2000, p. 124.

231 Edward Said, *Orientalism*, New York: Vintage, 1979, p. 195-196.

In the course of such an endeavor, no particular variety of information was considered beneath notice. British officers collected and published folktales, songs, riddles and proverbs; they articulated this material into handbooks, caste schedules, and compendia.[232] In doing so, they followed Max Muller's dictum, which captures the double-edged nature of the whole affair: "Let us take the old saying, *Divide et impera*, and translate it somewhat freely by 'Classify and understand.'"[233] Even taking Muller's comments at their benign face value, such a project runs the risk that "such texts can *create* not only knowledge, but also the very reality they appear to describe."[234] Among the proliferation of gazetteers, language dictionaries, legal texts, and maps, many of which have quite obvious modern analogues, the knowledge production which I find most striking is the writing of history. India certainly did not lack for texts in and of the past, from religious and legal material in the *Puranas* and *Vedas* to epics like the Ramayana and Mahabharata, which the British set about energetically to translate and interpret. The very nature of the enterprise suggests the cautions we might still apply to well-meaning initiatives based on literal language learning. The word currently translated for history in Hindi is *itihasa*. For texts like the *Ramayana* and the *Mahabharata*, however, the concurrence is inexact. Even in its most postmodern, postcolonial, subaltern voice, history as genre is still initiated and given authority by the author. But *itihasa* is called into being by its audience, which demands a recitation from the narrator—who is explicitly not the author. Even the earliest versions of the *Mahabharata* begin by noting that the narrator heard this version from someone else.[235] When *ithasa* becomes history, it becomes something else.

The frontispiece from James Rennell's *Memoir of a Map of Hindoostan* shows imperial Britannia receiving from her subjects—not jewels or produce—but texts. In the course of interpretation however, they created "new" knowledge:

> If history, or more precisely the narrative articulation of the meaning and purpose of history, is an invention of the West, it becomes an invention designed to write the Western will triumphantly over the failure of backward civilizations to understand how perceiving the world has changed.[236]

232 Gloria Goodwin Raheja, "Caste, Colonialism and the Speech of the Colonized: Entextualization and Disciplinary Control in India, *American Ethnologist*, Vol. 23, No. 3 (August 1996), p. 495, 497.

233 Cited in Ronald Inden, *Imagining India*, Bloomington, IN: Indiana University, 2000, p. 35.

234 Said, Orientalism, p. 94.

235 Ranajit Guha, *History at the Limit of World History*, New York: Columbia University, 2002, p. 72.

236 Balachandra Rajan, *Under Western Eyes: India from Milton to Macaulay*, Durham and London: Duke University, 1999, p. 17.

This writing of the past, in accordance with the "voice of Empire" and its attendant concrete epistemological habits, did more than simply create knowledge where none had existed before, but rather constituted a substantive exercise of power on par with new modes of warfare, transport and communication that marked the physical landscape of the sub-continent.

> Europe's colonisation of India was not merely confined to some "territorial space" but went much further and deeper; it sought to colonise India's sense of time, its present being merely a corruption of the past; its past, though glorious, believed to be dead and gone. Thus arose the age-old romantic notion of India "speaking from the position in the remote past via its distorted present to [the] European present."[237]

In some cases, these twin spaces—in both space and time—were written over simultaneously. In the middle of the 19th Century, the British military officer Alexander Cunningham initiated a record of Buddhist monuments and archaeological sites, in a strategy ultimately to be institutionalized in the creation of the Archaeological Survey of India (ASI). His express purpose was to employ this physical material in demonstrating that Brahminism was a relatively recent religious invention, in a political world characterized by a cycle of fragmented petty chiefs repeatedly conquered by external invaders; and that only strong central government maintained the freedom and integrity of the sub-continent. In other words: there was ample space in the Indian tradition for the introduction of Christianity, the Raj was merely a natural consequence of Indian political history, and British rule was a positive benefit for its Indian subjects.[238] The justification for empire was thus found in the physical things and places of collective memory.

Continuing this trend of down-scoping—from archive, to text, to history— I find especially intriguing this particular aspect of time, as a site of knowledge, power and contest. Paul Virilio argues that we have collectively passed through the periods of the City-State and Nation-State, and their attendant *geo*-politics, into a new modern or postmodern period characterized by accelerating technology, which will be defined by chrono-politics.[239] I take exception to this periodization—much of what appears new and "postmodern" is only so when modernity is read exclusively in the context of the nation-state.

---

237 Nirmal Verma, "India and Europe: The Self and the Other," in *Perceiving India: Insight and Inquiry*, ed. Geeti Sen, New Delhi, Newbury Park and London: Sage, 1993, p. 142.

238 Dilip K. Chakrabarti, "The Development of Archaeology in the Indian Subcontinent," *World Archaeology* 13, no. 3 (February 1982), p. 332.

239 Paul Virilio and Sylvere Lotringer, *Pure War*, trans. Mark Polizzotti, New York: Semiotext(e), 1997, p. 13.

Outside the metropoles, however, chrono-politics may well describe a distinct imperial condition, with both past and current relevance.

In the context noted above, the geo-politics of British rule in the 19th Century were matched by a chrono-politics reaching far into the past. The nature of the caste system, the antecedents of contemporary social customs and religious injunctions, the relations between various confessional communities were all matters with immediate relevance for imperial administration, but they could only be confirmed or contested in the past. British operations in and on history constructed an India that was:

> ...a "living museum," where ancient customs, habits, and practices endured up to the present. Denied a history of their own, the peoples of India were defined by unchanging racial and cultural identities.[240]

Most modern military staffs have forward-looking operations/planning cells, with attendant intelligence support; a structure more-or-less mirrored in other government bureaucracies. Some may even have historians or archivists. The manifestation of British administration in India, however, suggests something altogether different—a kind of "past" operations/plans/intelligence cell to complement their "future" counterparts.

This problem of fighting in the past continues to endure in the erstwhile space of the British Empire. Culminating a campaign laden with religious symbolism, Hindu militants razed the 16th Century Babri Masjid Mosque in Ayodhya, India on 6 December 1992. Hundreds were killed in the run-up to this incident, while some 3,000 died in its aftermath; and a decade later, rioting in Gujarat, inspired by a clash with activists returning from the site, led to another roughly 1,000 deaths.[241] Riding the political momentum of the destruction, the right-wing Hindu nationalist *Bharatiya Janata Party* (BJP) came to power in Delhi, subsequently conducted India's first overt tests of a nuclear weapon, and brought the country to the brink of war with Pakistan in the spring and summer of 2002. While that particular tide has receded, the sequence of events and its possible consequences highlights the strategic relevance of information about the past. In another imperial theater, four years after the initial looting of the Baghdad Museum, stolen antiquities continued to flow out of the country. There is a direct cost associated with that information about the past, as it lends itself to portrayals of Americans as uncaring about any culture other than its own.[242] At a broader level, information about the

---

240 Metcalf, *Ideologies of the Raj*, p. 117.

241 Edward Luce, "The Saffron Revolution," *Financial Times* (4 May 2002), 1.

242 Matthew Bogdanos, "Fighting for Iraq's Culture," *New York Times*, 6 March 2007.

Battles in the present are fought in and over the past. Delhi's Gothic-style memorial to the 1857 "Indian Mutiny" (on which are still inscribed the British officers and other ranks who fell) is now the *Ajitgarh*, commemorating the Indian martyrs who died for freedom. *Source: photo by author.*

past—with meaning articulated in materials—takes on strategic significance as the very concept of certain states strains at the seams left by past empires: Is Iraq one nation or three? And Afghanistan…a half dozen or more?).

Time has another aspect in the British experience—as a component of speed, or the rate of movement in a specific direction. In the British articulation of history, as in other familiar imperial formations, time is moving in a specific progressive direction. Since the imperial power is naturally at the bow wave of this movement, other cultures must necessarily be behind—either stalled or moving at a slower rate. Rewriting that subject time, in both rate of change and direction, has potentially explosive effects if "interactivity is to information what radioactivity is to energy."[243] While some of the specific terms of reference employed by the British are no longer in vogue, the discourses of "modern" and "traditional" societies survive in strategic discussions. The general trend toward abandoning the First/Second/Third World nomenclature in favor of Developed, Developing and Lesser-Developed arranges the entire globe on a single continuum of time moving in a single direction. This organization of time presents a common feature of, and a challenge to, imperial thinking. From *imperium sine fine* (empire without end) to the "sun never sets," empires are always positioned at the end of time.[244] This makes thinking about the future rigorously and creatively a problem. While the blush of optimism surrounding ideas like Francis Fukuyama's *End of History* may have faded in a post-9/11 world, the basic assumptions remain. There may be bumps and trouble along the road, and while we may not be precisely at the end—we can see it from here. Aside from some concern about containing irruptions like religious fundamentalism or increasing Chinese military power, there is little, if any, serious discussion about a future world not principally defined by advanced technologies, more or less liberal capitalism, and its attendant political arrangements in an order which assumes sustained U.S. predominance. It's just possible that this is an accurate reflection of reality; but perhaps more plausible that it *seems* accurate principally because it is framed in imperial time, which can functionally envision no alternative future.

> From the impossibility of keeping true time in two longitudes and the inner incompatibility of empire and nation in the anomalous discourse of cultural progressivism, emerges an ambivalence that is neither the contestation of contradictories nor the antagonism of dialectical opposition.[245]

---

243 Virilio, *Information Bomb*, p. 134.

244 David Jablonsky, "Time's Arrow, Time's Cycle: Metaphors for a Period of Transition," *Parameters*, (Winter 1997-1998), p. 4-27. Writing before the commencement of the current Long War, Jablonsky provides a useful discussion of how perceptions of time influence security policy, concluding with a note on the inconclusiveness of "imperial" time, which strikes a modern chord.

245 Homi Bhabha, *The Location of Culture*, London and New York: Routledge, 1994, p. 131.

Although this is one of Homi Bhabha's less elegant phrases, it does high-light the challenge of operating in disjointed times—not the literal longitudes, but the actual chronological arrangements separating India from Britain in the 19th Century. Imagining alternative organizations of time is a perennial imperial problem. The Romans, at the end of time, lived in a chronological world utterly inimical to that of Christian eschatology, which was explicitly based on the conviction that the end was what came *next*. Modern strategic discourse is full of discussions about decision cycles and getting inside an op-ponent's OODA loop (Orient, Observe, Decide, Act).[246] Less well explored is how to get inside or engage another's time, as such, which may be moving at a different rate and in a different direction. When the U.S. commander in Iraq notes the problem of keeping true time in two longitudes, he is principally concerned about rate of change—the Washington clock is ticking faster than the Baghdad clock.[247] The presumption, however, is that the clocks are both ticking in the same direction. By way of contrast, after decades of war, time in Afghanistan does not proceed linearly, in a way which would dove-tail with invasion, regime change, elections, economic development, but is arranged in a series of repeating cycles (conflict, regime change, regime failure, resumed conflict), conditioned by the development of conflict memory.[248] Within that chrono-political space, no campaign would ever be "won" in 10 days or 100; rather roughly five years would be the critical point—both as a deadline for establishing a new order and for proving its sustained viability. Failure to synchronize with that construction of time—although it has not led to cata-strophic failure—has allowed the previous model to persist, leaving a host of attendant problems of allegiance and legitimacy in its wake.

Perhaps a more signal example of the costs associated with the failure to synchronize chrono-politics comes from 9 CE. Cassius Dio describes the situ-ation in Germany thus:

> [T]he barbarians were gradually re-shaping their habits in conformity with the Roman pattern, were becoming accustomed to hold markets and were meeting in peaceful assemblies.... So long as they were unlearning their customs little by little, by indirect means, so to speak, and were under careful surveillance, they did not object to the change in their manner of life, and were unconsciously altering their disposition. But when Quintilius Varus became governor of the province of Germany, and in the

---

246 David Fadok, *John Boyd and John Warden: Air Power's Quest for Strategic Paralysis*, Maxwell AFB, AL: Air University Press, 1995, p. 16.

247 Max Boot, "Can Petraeus Pull it Off?," *Weekly Standard*, 30 April 2007, p. 24.

248 Ali Jalali, "The Future of Afghanistan," *Parameters*, Spring 2006, p. 7.

exercise of his powers also came to handle the affairs of these people, he tried both to hasten and to widen the process of change.[249]

The narrative then describes the details leading up to the disaster of the Teutoberg Forest, the single most significant military failure of the Roman Empire. The tactical conduct, strategic import and intelligence failures associated with this event have been covered elsewhere many times over. For me, it is simply worth observing—and noting for others who may contemplate similar exercises of change—that this disjunction in time was ultimately resolved when "every soldier and every horse was cut down without resistance."[250] The way that time can fold and unfold is vividly manifest in the perfect way this description can be applied to events almost two millennia later, half a world away.

---

249 Cassius Dio, *The Roman History: The Reign of Augustus*, trans. Ian Scott-Kilvert, London: Penguin, 1987, 56: 18.

250 Ibid., 56:22.

Apocalypse: The Sepoy Revolt of 1857

> *...[T]his year, at midday on Monday 16th Ramzan, 1273 A.H., which corresponds to 11 May 1857...the gates and walls of the Fort and the battlements of Delhi were suddenly shaken. It was not an earthquake: on that inauspicious day a handful of ill-starred soldiers from Meerut, frenzied with malice, invaded the city—every man of them shameless and turbulent, and with murderous hate for his masters, thirsting for British blood.*

> Ghalib, *Dastambu*[251]

The events witnessed by the poet Ghalib, a resident of Delhi at the time, would soon bloom into what became variously known as the "Great Mutiny," "The Indian Rebellion," or "The First War of Independence." Each of these labels comes with its own ideological baggage, but for my purposes it is enough

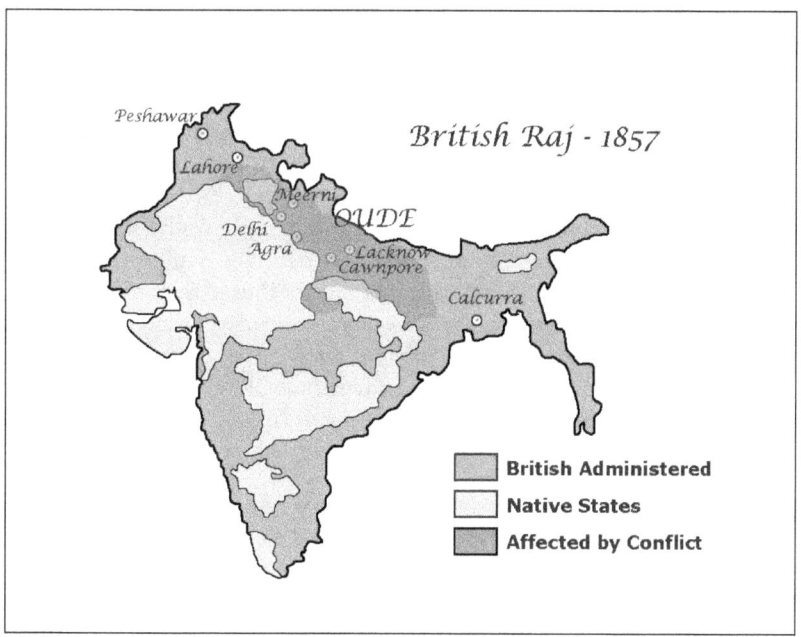

British imperial space "in the pink." *Source: Author's modification and distillation of various British maps.*

---

[251] Cited in Ralph Russell and Kurshidal Islam, *The Oxford India Ghalib: Life, Letters and Ghazals*, New Delhi: Oxford University, 2003, p. 117.

to accept the succinct description of the affair's official British historian, Sir John William Kaye: "The Indian Empire was in flames."[252]

Beginning on 10 May 1857 with the revolt of native Indian troops against their European officers in Meerut, a few miles north of Delhi, the rebellion spread over ensuing weeks to encompass much of northern India. While rumor was rife regarding what had happened, where and why, reliable information was hard to come by as British administration in the region collapsed. The letter of a British artillery officer stationed in Peshawar captures the anxiety repeated again and again in correspondence of the time:

> From Delhi and Meerut we hear strange accounts, all of which you will, of course, hear about in more detail than I can give, as, at present, we know nothing but what a short electric telegraph message could convey, the wires having been cut soon after, all communication is cut off.[253]

Beyond the mere technical problems of downed telegraph wires or interrupted mail carts, the British suffered more fundamentally from the disadvantages of language and culture which constrain any imperial power, and a lament on this account of a Civil Officer stationed in Lucknow strikes so many modern notes of relevance that it deserves to be quoted in full:

> If it be true, as has oft been asserted, that the enemy could always get information of our troops, while the country people were silent as to the movements of the mutineers, it must, I conceive, be attributed to other causes. The enemy was always ready to extort the required information by severities from which we would shrink. He would not hesitate to inflict death or mutilation, if information were with-held from him; we could not act thus. Again, the native is always better competent to gain information in India than the best-informed European. He has often connections, friends, clansmen, living on the spot. But with us, not only are such sources of information closed, but those are not unfrequently selected to procure intelligence, who possess little knowledge or experience of the native habits or character.[254]

The rebels, for their part, had anxieties of their own, assessing that the English were "low people like the shoemakers and spirit sellers, and have but

---

[252] John Kaye, *History of the Indian Mutiny of 1857-8*, Vol I., ed. George Malleson, Westport, CT: Greenwood Press, 1971 (First published 1897), p. 458.

[253] Fred Roberts, *Letters Written during the Indian Mutiny*, New Delhi: Lal Publishers, 1979, p.1.

[254] M.R. Gubbins, *The Mutinies in Oudh*, Patna: Janaki Prakashan, 1978 (First published 1858), p. 54.

a small body of troops, yet they get intelligence from every place."[255] Much of this tactical confusion can be attributed to the proverbial "fog of war," but more interesting to me is the problem of strategic information. Using the 1757 Battle of Plassey as a convenient benchmark, the British had been a major political power in the sub-continent for a century, consistently expanding their influence, participating in local networks of communication and constructing a whole body of knowledge about their newly conquered domains. Mutiny among locally recruited regiments was not unprecedented and had been dealt with before; yet when the storm came it nearly washed the British from Indian shores. The depth and breadth of unrest are described by the Reverend Alexander Duff:

> Never has the enemy been met without being routed, scattered, and his guns taken, but though constantly beaten he ever more rallies, and appears again ready for a fresh encounter. No sooner is one city taken or another relieved than some other one is threatened…. No sooner is one district pronounced safe through the influx of British troops, than another is disturbed and convulsed. No sooner is a highway opened between places of importance, than it is again closed and all communications are for a year cut off. No sooner are the mutineers and rebels scoured out of one locality than they reappear, with double or treble forces, in another. No sooner does a mobile column force its way through hostile ranks, than they reoccupy the territory behind it…. The passage of our brave little armies through these swarming myriads instead of leaving deep traces of a mighty ploughshare through a roughened field seems more to resemble that of an eagle through the elastic air, or a stately vessel through an unfurowed ocean.[256]

How did the imperial administration fail to see what was coming? The warning signs were certainly not secret, regardless of "how little knowledge or experience of native habits" those assigned to procure intelligence might have had. In fact, there was a surfeit of information available, with many words of caution expressed by everyone from military officers to the lowly district official who noted that "in the event of any insurrection occurring, we should find this great and consequential body, through whom we can alone hope to control and keep under the millions forming the rural classes, ranged against

255 Anonymous pamphlet, cited in Salim al-Din Quaraishi, *Cry for Freedom: Proclamations of Muslim Revolutionaries of 1857*, Lahore: Sang-e-Meel Publications, 1997, p. 115.

256 Alexander Duff, *The Indian Rebellion: Its Causes and Results in a Series of Letters*, New York: R. Carter, 1858, p. 233.

us on the side of the enemy.... My warnings were unheeded."[257] The failure was thus not lack of information, but incapacity to understand the information at hand. A key aspect of the British performance, and an enduring problem of imperial intelligence, I suggest, is not to correctly "know" foreign minds, but to read backward, and accurately perceive how those foreign minds come to understand the apparently familiar and domestic.

This failure to "know" in a contrary and unfamiliar way is highlighted in the case of one of the mutiny's critical precursor events: the annexation of the Kingdom of Oude. Located at the very heart of the British dominion in northern India, the stability of Oude was clearly central to the imperial enterprise both geographically and militarily—of the 200,000 Indians under British command in 1857, 40,000 hailed from the Kingdom.[258] In order to see imperial interests protected, a Treaty was signed in 1801 and Calcutta posted a British Resident to the capital at Lucknow. Despite the advice and counsel of this agent, the Kingdom's administration remained almost proverbially corrupt and inefficient, ultimately prompting the British to assert control in 1856. Although he was himself critical of annexation as policy, W.H. Sleeman (of Thuggee fame) made the case for this decision during his tour as resident:

> Our duties toward the sovereign of Oude, created by this and other treaties, have become incompatible with those created by the same treaties towards the people of Oude.... No security to life and property in any part of Oude; and the general impression is that, in supporting the government of Oude, the British Government neglects its duty towards its five millions of people.... The only alternative left appears to be to take the management upon ourselves, and give the surplus revenue to the sovereign and royal family of Oude.[259]

The British, then, had a duty to pursue a policy of "regime change" to rationalize the government of this sensitive but critical area, ostensibly in order to promote the welfare of its inhabitants. The nature of the transition is suggested in a letter from Lieutenant Colonel Herbert Edwards in Lucknow to his wife a month before the outbreak of unrest, noting: "Hitherto there seems to have been no sympathy for the native society, nothing but a rush of 'nukshas-nukshas,' to reduce the new Province as soon as possible to the Standard

---

257 William Edwards, *Personal Adventures During the Indian Rebellion in Rohilcund, Futtehghur and Oude*, Allahabad (India): Legend Publications, 1974 (First published 1858), p. 14.

258 Edward Hilton, *The Mutiny Records, Oudh and Lucknow* (1856-57), Lahore: Panco Press, 1975, p. 20.

259 William Sleeman, *Sleeman in Oudh: An Abridgement of W.H. Sleeman's A Journey Through the Kingdom of Oude in 1849-50*, ed. P.D. Reeves, Cambridge: Cambridge University, 1971, p. 41.

Plan."[260] Whether the intent was genuinely beneficent or not, the key issue was how the application of imperial rule was perceived, and in this regard the magnitude of power stood in almost completely inverse relationship to the knowledge required. Only the dramatic inversion of power relationships over the summer of 1857 would bring that equation back into balance, and in hindsight Kaye could observe:

> It was thought, as the work proceeded in quietude and in seeming prosperity, that it was a great success; and it gladdened the heart of the Government in Leadenhall-street, to think of the accomplishment of this peaceful revolution. But that the measure itself made a very bad impression on the minds of the people of India, is not to be doubted; not because of the deposition of a King who had abused his powers; not because of the introduction of a new system of administration for the benefit of the people; but because the humanity of the act was soiled by the profit which we derived from it; and to the comprehension of the multitude it appeared that the good of the people, which we had vaunted whilst serving ourselves, was nothing more than a pretext and a sham....[261]

While Kaye belatedly acknowledges the disjunction in perceived intentions that I wish to emphasize here, I believe his *mea culpa* only half right. Had the "humanity" of a new administration been free of commercial taint, in this formulation, all might yet have gone well. But insistence that such a policy was self-evidently for the "benefit of the people" suggests that Kaye remains within a domestically defined discourse about what, precisely constitutes a "benefit." If, as Peter Burke puts it, "when one inhabits a system, it generally looks like 'common sense,'"[262] Kaye has yet to find a way to see outside his system. A prime example of the problem, and one which continues to present itself today, is the issue of education—presumably one of the benefits of the new system.

The early decades of the 19th Century witnessed a development in the approach to education in the Raj driven by philosophical debates, British domestic politics, and the practical exigencies of imperial administration—all of which might be summed up in James Mill's observation: "The great end of Government should not be to teach Hindu or Mohammedan learning, but

---

260 *Letters of Sir Henry Montgomery Lawrence (Selections from the correspondence of Sir Henry Montgomery Lawrence (1806-1857) during the Siege of Lucknow from March to July, 1857),* ed. Sheo Bahadur Singh, New Delhi: Sagar Publications, 1978, p. 2.

261 Kaye, *History,* p. 110.

262 Peter Burke, *A Social History of Knowledge: From Gutenberg to Diderot,* Cambridge: Polity Press, 2000, p. 2.

useful learning."[263] Useful learning: a comparatively neutral phrase, not the sort of critical strategic intelligence issue to occupy grand councils of war; but thereby hangs a tale.

Shortly after seizing Delhi and nominally reinstating the rule of the functionally retired King Bahadur Shah II, the mutineers prepared a pamphlet—the "Proclamation Issued by the 'Royal Army of Delhi.'" More lengthy than the U.S. Declaration of Independence, this document serves a similar role in articulating the rebels' rationale for casting off the imperial yoke. After a brief preamble, the proclamation goes into an exhaustive—and often salacious—catalogue of British crimes, many having to do with the encouragement of "loose" conduct by both British and native women. The very first grievance, however, addresses education and the schools in which "the Hindu and Mussulman children began to be instructed in such books as after completing their education would inevitably lead them to renegades and lend to alienate their affection from our beloved prophet, his religion and his sect."[264] H.R. Gubbins, the Lucknow officer cited earlier, gave this issue similar priority, assigning the question greater relevance than all the other explanations then—and later—in vogue, including Russian intrigues, Muslim conspiracies, nascent nationalism, and anger over the Oudh annexation. He notes:

> I believe the native Hindoo mind to have been for some time previously alarmed on the subject of caste and religion. Many public measures had tended to this result; but perhaps none more so than the extreme rapidity with which educational measures had of late years been forced on.... All public servants were required to qualify themselves by literary requirements, for which examinations were instituted.[265]

There are two key issues formulated in this articulation. First, education attacks authority, both spiritual and temporal. A second aspect is speed, with echoes of Roman governor Varus in the German woods. Not only does the rapid replacement of "Hindu and Mohammedan learning" with "useful learning" undermine religious affiliation, but it also threatens to disenfranchise those traditional elites not educated in imperially "useful" ways. Literacy within a certain practical framework may in fact be useful and beneficial, but it also denigrates alternative ways of expressing truth and value through vision and voice:

---

263 Cited in Percival Spear, "Bentinck and Education," *Cambridge Historical Journal*, Vol. 6, No. 1 (1938), p. 83.

264 Quraishi, *Cry for Freedom: Proclamations of Muslim Revolutionaries of 1857, Lahore: Sang-e-meel Publications, 1997*, p. 3.

265 Gubbins, *Mutinies*, p. 77.

> Writing, in fact, can be seen as a *technology of power*, used and manipulated in different ways at different times depending on the specific historical context, but always with profound effects on the way people in the past (even the illiterate) lived their lives.[266]

As I have argued throughout this text, imperial intelligence is less a problem of determining the truth or falsehood of specific facts, and more an issue of negotiating how truth is constituted and what "knowing" means. These issues leap to the fore in the contest over education, which is fundamentally a fight to frame how meaning can and will be constituted in both the past and future. In this reading, it is no mere coincidence that Afghan insurgents go by an appellation meaning "students," nor that 2006 saw the burning of over one hundred schools and the closing of two hundred more in Afghanistan, nor that one of the most frequent refrains articulated in so-called Taliban night-letters reads: "Drop this business of teaching and the school or you will be responsible for your own death…. If you continue, you will have to wash your hands of your life."[267] In the study I prepared in Kabul regarding the Taliban, on "Why They Fight," after all the expected material about ideology, foreign influence, and the economy, I indulged in a single PowerPoint slide regarding just this issue. While this topic was greeted with skepticism in some quarters, when a version went before a senior Afghan officer—he immediately keyed in on this slide, saying "Yes, that's it."

Beyond the questions of understanding and perception in the lead-up to the revolt, similar contested readings of an information-rich environment played a key role in the conduct of the conflict. Then as now, the press, both foreign and domestic, played an important part in framing the meaning of what was happening, provoking a skeptical young engineer officer to observe: "And all this time we read sickening twaddle in the leaders from the *Times*, the *Examiner*, etc. where old women write their views on our great supremacy over our conquered subjects, our might never to be endangered, the Hindu element very strong, but no chance of a row as the Mohammedans are on our side (we are really fighting Cross versus Crescent now), and all such trash."[268] A more nuanced appraisal of the press, with attention to its promise and peril, is offered by the Chief Commissioner of Oudh during the siege of Lucknow, Sir Henry Lawrence, in a letter to Lord Canning:

> Whatever may be the danger of the Native press I look on it that the papers published in our own language are much the most

---

266 John Moreland, *Archaeology and Text*, London: Duckworth, 2001, p. 88.

267 Paul Watson, "Democracy in the Balance," *Los Angeles Times*, 3 December 2006.

268 Arthur Moffat Lang, *Lahore to Lucknow: The Indian Mutiny Journal of Arthur Moffatt Lang*, ed. David Blomfield, London: Leo Cooper, 1992, p. 51.

dangerous. Disaffected native Editors need only translate, as *they do*, with or without notes or words of admiration or exclamation, Editorials from the friend of India (on the duty of annexing Native States, on the imbecility if not wickedness of allowing a single Jagheer, and of preaching the Gospel even by Commanding Officers) to raise alarm and hatred in the minds of all religionists and all connected with native principalities and Jagheers.... I would not trouble any of them but, with your Lordship's permission, I think we might squash half the number by helping one or two of the cleverest with information, even with Editorials, and illustrations.... Of course, I would not appear and would use the present Editors—at any rate try to do so.[269]

As the war progressed, Lawrence continued to observe its conduct, and the information encoded in action, arguing that the key strategic objective was to retake Delhi, not because of its military value but due to its meaning: "Religion, fear, hatred, one and all have their influences, but there is still a reverence for the Company's Ikbal [honor, puissance]. When it is gone, we shall have few friends indeed."[270] As a military commentator, Karl Marx observed the same phenomenon, albeit with an interesting, if typical, contrarian twist:

As to the object of the war, it was beyond doubt the maintenance of English rule in India. To attain that object, Delhi was a point of no significance at all. Historical tradition, in truth, endowed it in the eyes of the natives with a superstitious importance, clashing with its real influence, and this was sufficient reason for the mutinous sepoys to single it out as their general place of rendezvous. But if instead of forming their military plans according to the native prejudices, the English had left Delhi alone and isolated it, they would have divested it of its fancied influence; by pitching their tents before it, running their heads against it, and concentrating upon it their main force and the attention of the world, they cut themselves off from even the chances of retreat, or rather gave to retreat all the effects of a signal defeat. They have thus simply played into the hands of the mutineers who wanted to make Delhi the object of the campaign.[271]

As Marx suggests, the mutineers were aware of the signs written in their actions and how this framed the meaning of the conflict. At Cawnpore, site

---

269 Henry Montgomery Lawrence, *Letters of Sir Henry Montgomery Lawrence,* ed. *Sheo Bahadur Singh, New Delhi: Sheo Bahadur Sagar Publications, 1978,* p. 7-9.

270 Lawrence, Ibid., p. 16-17

271 Karl Marx and Friedrich Engels, *The First Indian War of Independence, 1857-1859,* Moscow: Foreign Languages Publishing House, 1959, p. 101-102.

"Look, O Look!" Focusing attention on Delhi, and the pivotal fight for the still-scarred Kashmir Gate, shaped how the broader struggle was understood by both sides. *Source: photo by author.*

of the mutiny's most infamous atrocity among many, from the British perspective at least, the garrison and families defending the cantonments were lured from their entrenchments by promise of safe passage, only later to be butchered almost to a soul. The killing, however, did not take place all at once or in the same context, but was played out in two different registers. The first, as the garrison attempted to embark on boats for their escape, took place as soldiers waiting in ambush opened fire and brought down all of the men. This event took place with an almost festival air, to a cheering audience of locals in an obvious demonstration that the old order was being overturned. The second act, however, transpired weeks later, when the surviving women and children—who had been imprisoned in the interim—were killed indoors, literally behind closed doors, by a handful of men paid for the task when the sepoys refused the order, the bodies subsequently dumped and concealed in a nearby well. Information was transmitted in one context, concealed in another.[272]

As a sort of visual footnote, the subsequent history of the massacre re-enacts iteratively this problem of alternative coding and audiences in a particularly

---

[272] Rudrangshu Mukherjee, "'Satan Let Loose upon Earth': The Kanpur Massacres in India in the Revolt of 1857," *Past and Present*, No. 128 (Aug 1990), p. 108-114.

graphic way. The *Times* list of casualties published on 20 August 1857 follows the typical practice of specifying in order military officers, civil officers, medical establishments and other civilians across India—all "Killed" or "murdered"; but the victims of Cawnpore alone were "Butchered." Reflecting this special status, after the war the Cawnpore well was enshrined within an imposing imperial edifice and surrounding park, commemorating the British losses and justifying the subsequent equally gruesome retaliation; while after Indian independence, the memorial was removed, the well covered over with concrete and the park space rededicated to one of the leaders of the revolt, Nana Rao. One can still see the slender circle of brickwork marking the rim.

This context of performance suggests to me a critical intelligence challenge for imperial powers, in both the information they transmit through their own actions as well as what they seek to read in the actions of their sometime subjects/sometime antagonists. Understanding how performance encodes meaning requires on occasion deliberately abandoning "common sense," however viscerally difficult that might be. "Useful education" may be read as oppression, "atrocity" may be jubilation expressed. Reading that contrasting text is as much of a challenge, as much a "secret" in the streets of Mogadishu in 1993 or the Fallujah bridge in 2004 as it was in 1857, when a folk ballad ran thus:

> O come and look!
> In the bazaar of Meerut.
> The Feringi is waylaid and beaten!
> The whiteman is waylaid and beaten!
> In the open bazaar of Meerut.
> Look! O Look!
> He is beaten!
> His gun is snatched,
> His horse lies dead,
> His revolver is battered.
> In the open bazaar
> He is waylaid and beaten!
> Look! O look!
> The Feringi is waylaid and beaten
> In the bazaar of Meerut!
> Look! O look![273]

The desire to look—to see and observe—is a constant of the imperial encounter, while its complement, the desire to obscure—to conceal and deny observation—plays an equally insistent refrain.

---

[273] Cited in Henry Scholberg, *The Indian Literature of the Great Rebellion*, New Delhi: Promilla and Co., 1993, p. 115.

Masquerade: Agents and Actors

Daily Herald, January 5th 1929

LAWRENCE OF ARABIA
ARREST "ORDERED" BY AFGHAN AUTHORITIES
STARTLING REPORT

> *A sensational message reached London last night from Allahabad, stating that the Afghan authorities have ordered the arrest of Colonel Lawrence, known widely as Lawrence of Arabia, on the ground that he is believed to be assisting the rebels to cross the frontier. They describe Colonel Lawrence, says the B.U.P., as the arch-spy of the world.... For some time his movements as chronicled have been mysterious, and a few months ago it was stated that he was in Afghanistan on a secret mission, though earlier in the same week it had been reported that he was in Amritsar, posing as a Mohammedan saint.* [274]

Well. What is one to make of such a "sensational message?" The purported issues at hand certainly have contemporary relevance in the early 21st Century, as does the locale. When this press article was published, T.E. Lawrence was indeed stationed some 10 miles from the Afghan border, "in a brick and earth fort behind barbed wire complete with searchlights and machine-guns. Round us, a few miles off, in a ring are low bare porcelain-colored hills, with chipped edges and a broken-bottle skyline." [275] Even more strikingly, the letter was written from Miranshah—more recently infamous for its association with Taliban leader Jalaluddin Haqqani, who was believed to be assisting rebels crossing the frontier. [276] The accusations, while false, were public and embarrassing enough to compel British authorities to hustle Lawrence quickly out of the sub-continent, putting an abrupt end to his otherwise non-descript tour in India.

Nevertheless, the charges serve as fitting coda to Lawrence's public career, and as an opening bar to what I find most fascinating about him. According to the Daily Herald, Colonel Lawrence is an "arch-spy" and has recently been posing as a "Mohammedan saint." While the terms of imposture are false, their sense is correct—as Lawrence was in fact engaged in a deliberate masquerade, eschewing post-war notoriety to pursue a career as T.E. Shaw, enlisted mechanic

---

[274] Cited in *Letters of T.E. Lawrence*, ed. David Garnett, New York: Doubleday, Doran & Co., 1939, p. 632.

[275] T.E. Lawrence, *Letters*, p. 614.

[276] "Forces, Militants Headed for Truce," *Frontier Star*, 23 June 2006.

with the RAF. But of course, by this point, imposture was almost second nature for the erstwhile colonel, and his success in that enterprise was fundamental to the fame he claimed later to despise. Extraordinary though Lawrence may have been, this issue—and its personal ramifications—permeates the pursuit of imperial intelligence. If Gubbins, as cited earlier, was correct in noting that, "the native is always better competent to gain information in India than the best-informed European," then perhaps the answer is to make the European native—or, as Lawrence put it, "The leopard changes his spots to stripes, since the stripes are better protection in the local landscape."[277]

The problem posed continues to resonate, in regions not far removed from the porcelain-covered hills of Miranshah, as well as within regions closer to Lawrence's earlier theater of operations.

> Cultural awareness will not necessarily always enable us to pre-dict what the enemy and noncombatants will do, but it will help us better understand what motivates them, what is important to the host nation in which we serve, and how we can either elicit the support of the population or at least diminish their support and aid to the enemy.

> *Benjamin C. Freakley*
> *Commander, CJTF-76*
> *Afghanistan, 2006*[278]

> In accurately defining the contextual and cultural population of the task force battlespace it became rapidly apparent that we needed to develop a keen understanding of demographics as well as the cultural intricacies that drive the Iraqi population.

> *Peter W. Chiarelli*
> *Commander, 1st Cavalry Division*
> *Baghdad, 2004-2005*[279]

Responding to the challenge, the latter author notes that, "During the de-ployment to Baghdad, over 22,000 soldiers went through training on cultural awareness, which became an integral part of any operation. During the ramp-up to Ramadan, the division enacted a full-spectrum command information operations campaign to create understanding and empathy for the religious

---

277 Lawrence, *Letters*, p. 559.

278 Freakley, *Infantry* (March-April 2005), p. 2.

279 Peter Chiarelli and Patrick Michaelis, "Winning the Peace: the Requirement for Full-Spectrum Operations," *Military Review* (July-August 2005), p.5.

event."[280] More broadly, U.S. advisors in Iraq are urged to read T.E. Lawrence, an authority cited extensively in U.S. Army professional literature on counterinsurgency.[281] I first encountered Lawrence years ago in such a "professionally recommended" context, and as a second lieutenant stuck in the back of the Fire Direction Center HMMWV on night-watch, I was unsurprisingly drawn to the Peter O'Toole-style grandeur. What I perhaps deliberately neglected then, but am drawn to now, are the far more problematic aspects of the narrative. Take, for example, a passage which comes at the very outset of his magnum opus, the *Seven Pillars of Wisdom*:

> The public women of the rare settlements we encountered in our months of wandering would have been nothing to our numbers, even had their raddled meat been palatable to a man of healthy parts. In horror of such sordid commerce our youths began indifferently to slake one another's few needs in their own clean bodies—a cold convenience that, by comparison seemed sexless and even pure. Later some began to justify this sterile process, and swore that friends quivering together in the yielding sand with intimate hot limbs in supreme embrace, found there hidden in the darkness a sensual co-efficient of the mental passion which was welding our souls and spirits in one flaming effort. Several, thirsting to punish appetites they could not wholly prevent, took a savage pride in degrading the body, and offered themselves fiercely in any habit which promises physical pain or filth.[282]

This is a simply extraordinary piece of text, given the context, particularly as preface to the torture and rape scene at Deraa—referred to obliquely both in *Seven Pillars* and the famous film, but confessed more explicitly in later correspondence.[283] I would be extremely hard pressed to imagine a modern writer in an analogous position providing anything like a similar account—especially so explicitly and prominently. One presumes this material is not associated with the work's modern popularity as recommended professional reading, but I don't believe it is either prurient or irrelevant—and to disregard it is misleading.

---

280 Op cit, note 3.

281 Jim Michaels, "U.S. Advisors Find Joint Patrols with Iraqis Don't Go as Planned," *USA Today*, 5 February 2007.

282 T.E. Lawrence, *Seven Pillars of Wisdom: a Triumph*, Garden City, NY: Doubleday, Doran & Co., 1935, p. 30.

283 Jeffrey Meyers, "T.E. Lawrence in His Letters," *T.E. Lawrence: Soldier, Writer, Legend — New Essays*, ed. Jeffrey Meyers, London: Macmillan, 1989, p. 15.

Lawrence's visceral description of conflicted sexuality—echoed repeatedly throughout Seven Pillars and in his private letters—to me suggests something fundamental about the problem of acquiring, and communicating, information from within an unfamiliar cultural context: it is an intense, messy and profoundly personal affair for the agent involved. Should a modern Western imperial agent seek, as Lawrence did, "to stimulate the Orient into movement, to impose an essentially Western shape on that movement…to contain the new and aroused Orient in a personal vision…,"[284] it is unlikely to succeed primarily through sensitivity training or Human Terrain Systems and Human Terrain Teams, which as interlocutors facilitate talking about other contexts rather than within other contexts. Several years into a campaign which saw him living daily submerged in a foreign environment, Lawrence expressed to a friend in July 1918 a sense of the limited insight gained even from extraordinary efforts in identity assimilation:

> I have to try and hide my Frankish exterior, and be as little out of the Arab picture as I can. So it's a kind of foreign stage, on which one plays days and night, in a fancy dress, in a strange language, with the price of failure on one's head if the part is not well filled…and yet without in any way sharing their point of view, I think I can understand it enough to look at myself and other foreigners from their direction, and without condemning it. I know I'm a stranger to them and always will be…[285]

Lawrence was only able to manage this trick through a kind of self-fashioning and refashioning that would influence an entire life in which he would "only be able to define himself by extreme ambivalence."[286] As well-publicized as that life was, however, Lawrence was not unique, but rather fell last in a long line of British imperial officers who attempted this peculiar form of mimesis.

Lawrence's life, which through stage play became a kind of fiction, echoes that of English literature's seminal secret agent, Rudyard Kipling's Kim:

> The shop was full of all manner of dresses and turbans, and Kim was appareled variously as a young Mohammedan of good family, an oilman, and once—which was a joyful evening—as the son of an Oudh landholder in the fullest of full dress…a demon in Kim awoke and sang with joy as he put on the changing dresses, and changed speech and gesture forthwith.[287]

---

284 Edward Said, *Orientalism*, New York: Vintage Books, 1979, p. 241.

285 Lawrence, Letters, p. 244.

286 Kingsley Widmer, "The Intellectual as Soldier," *T.E. Lawrence: Soldier, Writer, Legend*, p. 32.

287 Rudyard Kipling, *Kim*, London: Macmillan, 1944, p. 226.

The same facility might also be attributed to Sir Richard Francis Burton, who in the second half of the 19th Century wandered the empire under various guises including religious mendicant, a Persian Shi'a dealer in fashion, and an Afghan merchant—reflecting, like Lawrence, a "reluctance to commit to a stable and readily identifiable identity."[288] Some of this fluid identity may have stemmed from Burton's marginal social status. While he was not, in Kim's terms, "a poor white of the very poorest," he spent most of his youth sojourning with his family in continental Europe among surroundings of genteel poverty, cut off from the mainstream of British society, a condition not unfamiliar to the bastard Lawrence.[289] This position in social space—neither quite in nor out—equipped Burton for his role in negotiating the fluid landscapes of imperial information.

Within seven years of his posting to India, Burton passed official examinations in "Hindostani, Guzaratee, Persian, Maharattee, Sindhee, Punjaubee, Arabic, Telagu, Pushtu (Afghan tongue), with Turkish and Armenian."[290] This aptitude for language, alongside liaisons with Indian women, ultimately established him as an expert in "manipulating the complexities of cultural exchange."[291] But Burton realized that all this knowledge about the communities which surrounded him was not the same as knowledge expressed within them, consequently determining that: "The first difficulty was to pass for an Oriental, and this was as necessary as it was difficult. The European official in India seldom, if ever, sees anything in its real light, so dense is the veil which the fearfulness, the duplicity, the prejudice and the superstitions of the natives hang before his eyes."[292]

And to what use, precisely, did Captain Burton put this extraordinary set of skills? Posted to the Sind Survey by General Napier, who "kept an eye on his promising young soldier," Burton could:

> …pass himself off as a mere officer of no special importance if he wished, as when he went to pay formal compliments to Ibrahim Khan and Hari Chand, or he could pose as a native servant in

---

288 Dane Kennedy, *The Highly Civilized Man: Richard Burton and the Victorian World*, Cambridge: Harvard University, 2005, p. 59.

289 Dane Kennedy, "'Captain Burton's Oriental Muck Heap': The Book of the Thousand Nights and the Uses of Orientalism," *The Journal of British Studies*, Vol. 39, No. 3 (July 2000), p. 322.

290 Isabel Burton, *The Life of Sir Richard F. Burton, K.C.M.G., F.R.G.S., by His Wife*, London: Chapman and Hall, 1893, p. 159.

291 Parama Roy, *Indian Traffic: Identities in Question in Postcolonial India*, Berkeley: University of California, 1998, p. 18.

292 H.T. Lambrick, "Editor's Introduction" in *Sindh, and the Races That Inhabit the Valley of the Indus*, by Richard Burton, Karachi: Oxford University, 1972, p. xiii.

Scott's entourage and slip out of the encampment to visit native quarters, or he could drop out completely from the Survey and wander around the countryside, into territory not only uncharted but hostile, where he could match nerve and wit against Baluchis, Sindhis, and Punjabis.[293]

Unfortunately, one of the missions allegedly assigned by General Napier included a survey of male brothels which were servicing both British and Indian troops. Burton's typically precise and detailed account ultimately passed to rather less clinically minded circles in Calcutta, with the result that he was very nearly expelled from India altogether and was certainly passed over for a key position in the 1848 campaign against the Sikhs—an assignment ultimately given to an officer incalculably less qualified linguistically and culturally, but also far less controversial.[294] How *practical* Burton's investigations were remains a point of controversy, but his interest in sexuality was clearly a core issue in his culture-crossing explorations of identity. While his "professional" works regarding India, Arabia and Africa are now generally confined to a specialist audience, his overtly erotic translations of the *Kamasutra* and The *Scented Garden* are widely available in recent reprints, as are various versions of his *Arabian Nights* (adorned with copious louche footnotes, often strikingly graphic). The issue here, as it was in the case of Lawrence, is that Burton's efforts to genuinely gain alternative perspectives were not simply staff exercises based on databases and memoranda, but involved viscerally immediate issues of personal, physical identity. Moreover, socially approved aims of cultural transgression were inseparable—for both Lawrence and Burton—from those boundary-crossing activities met with distaste, if not horror. Although the damage to Burton's fortunes was not irremediable—he was knighted, after all—he nevertheless failed to rise to the positions of authority his extraordinary abilities might have merited, passing the rest of his days in obscure consular posts not too dissimilar from the dusty airfield in Miranshah. Resembling as he did a character from fiction, it is perhaps appropriate that the apogee of his career, the post-Indian voyage to Mecca, was transplanted, with only slight alteration, into the history of another Victorian hero. Here Sherlock Holmes explains to Watson what he has been up to since disappearing over Reichenbach falls with Professor Moriarty:

> I traveled for two years in Tibet, therefore, and amused myself by visiting Lhassa, and spending some days with the head lama. You

293 Edward Rice, *Captain Sir Richard Francis Burton: The Secret Agent Who Made the Pilgrimage to Mecca, Discovered the Kamasutra, and Brought the Arabian Nights to the West*, New York: Charles Scribner's Sons, 1990, p. 120-121.

294 Rice, Ibid, p. 161-162.

may have read of the remarkable explorations of a Norwegian named Sigerson, but I am sure it never occurred to you that you were receiving news of your friend. I then passed through Persia, looked in at Mecca, and paid a short but interesting visit to the Khalifa at Khartoum, the results of which I communicated to the Foreign Office.[295]

Sherlock Holmes. Kim. Lawrence of Arabia. The Arabian Nights. There is more than a whiff of *Boy's Own Adventure* to these intrigues of the long 19th Century, but there was genuine information to be had, even when its interlocutors seemed to pass breezily between fact and fiction in a way likely to discomfit government bureaucracies. Outside the ranks of commissioned officers like Lawrence and Burton, however, there were equally problematic characters who could serve as a conduit to their formal imperial counterparts and who deserve at least brief mention. Two of the most noteworthy were Americans.

> I have not yet stated that my own traveling name was Arb Shah. I passed as a native of Arabia, and met very few in my travels who could speak Arabic. I explained my deficiency of knowledge of my native language by telling my interlocutor that I came from the opposite corner of Arabia to that with which he was acquainted, having previously taken care to worm this information out of him.[296]

So entered Alexander Gardner, originally from northern Wisconsin, upon the South Asian stage, already ensconced in fancy dress. Operating initially more or less as a freelance bandit, Gardner ultimately rose to command artillery units under Maharajah Ranjit Singh in the waning days of Sikh independence, an appointment earned through his ability to covertly read the English instructions hidden amongst a box of fuses accompanying field guns provided by the Indian Governor-General Bentinck. From his position at the heart of this key buffer state between the expanding British Empire and turbulent Afghanistan, Gardner was able to interact with a host of Europeans transiting the region. When the British position in Afghanistan turned sour with the massacre at Kabul and the disastrous retreat to Jalalabad in January 1842, Gardner was drawn into the tumult and "One day I heard that a sahib had come into camp, and seeing one or two persons under a tree, I went forward and found Lawrence dressed, not very successfully, as a Pathan."[297] Yet

---

295 Arthur Conan Doyle, "The Adventure of the Empty House," *The Complete Sherlock Holmes—Novels and Stories*, Vol. II, New Delhi: Classic Paperbacks, p. 218.

296 Alexander Gardner, *Soldier and Traveller: Memories of Alexander Gardner, Colonel of Artillery in the Service of Maharaja Ranjit Singh*, ed. Hugh Pearse, Jullundur City: Languages Department, Punjab, 1970 (First printing 1898), p. 37.

297 Gardner, Ibid., p. 243

another player in fancy dress, however unsuccessfully, this Lawrence (later Sir Henry Lawrence when he perished during the siege of Lucknow in 1857) was part of the ad hoc British response to the disaster. Arriving in the middle of confusion and haphazard communications at the Afghan frontier, Lawrence found an unexpected source of insight in "an American...He had married a native wife, given to him by Rajah Dhyan Singh out of his own house; and through her, and living always among the natives, he was behind the scenes, and heard a good deal of the intrigues that were on foot."[298] A second American, and another of Gardner's associates, was already inside Afghanistan, where he had remonstrated for some time against what he perceived to be, and as the facts bore out, profoundly misguided British policy.[299] Fortunately for him, the latter was away from Kabul at the time, in circumstances highlighting the extraordinarily fluid environment of identity and allegiance.

> We shall go to those parts and say to any King we find—"D'you want to vanquish your foes?" and we will show him how to drill men; for that we know better than anything else. Then we will subvert that King and seize his Throne and establish a Dy-nasty.[300]

> Those Hazarrah princes...invited me collectively into their mountain homes. Mohammed Refee secretly arranged a treaty with me, signing with the Koran and a guarantee of his *peer*. This treaty conveyed to me, under all the usual forms...the title of "Prince of Ghoree"...[301]

The first scenario is from Kipling, the second from the memoirs of a Pennsylvania Quaker, Josiah Harlan. These twin excerpts show a double mimesis—fiction mimicking history, just as the American mimics the Afghan. In the years running up to the Kabul disaster, Harlan had been a regular informant on local events to the British officer resident in Ludhiana on the Sikh frontier, as had yet another European in Kabul—Charles Masson, a British deserter under the guise of an American—and the regression proceeds further: British as American as Afghan.[302] Notably, all three "Americans" in their various guises survived the conflagration, in contrast to the official British agent, Alexander Burnes, who was butchered in his garden at the outset of unrest—

---

298 Herbert Edwardes and Herman Merivale, *Life of Sir Henry Lawrence*, London: Smith, Elder & Co., 1873, p. 224.

299 Ben MacIntyre, *The Man Who Would Be King: The First American in Afghanistan*, New York: Farrar, Straus, Giroux, 2004, p. 202-203.

300 Rudyard Kipling, "The Man Who Would Be King," *Kipling: A Selection of His Stories and Poems*, Vol. II, ed. John Beecroft, Garden City, NY: Doubleday, 1956, p. 121.

301 Josiah Harlan, *Central Asia: Personal Narrative of Josiah Harlan, 1823-1841*, ed. Frank Ross, London: Luzac & Co., 1939, p. 143-144.

302 MacIntyre, *Man Who Would Be King*, p. 192.

despite his fancy dress, and perhaps in consequence of his reputation as a Kabuli ladies' man.[303]

What strikes me in these brief biographical sketches of various imperial agents—both official and not—is the profound dislocation of physical and psychological identity required in order to genuinely serve as a conduit between the internal and external information spaces of empire. While there is clearly something of "play" in their activities, the stakes are deadly serious. Whether they decline into a career of irrelevance (Burton), spiral into psychic disintegration (Lawrence), lose their homeland forever (Gardner) or are murdered outright (Burnes)—none of these boundary crossers succeeded in ultimately profiting from their extraordinary endeavors. For imperial powers seeking to acquire understanding that is more than acronym-deep, the costs and consequences are worth sober consideration. Lawrence's writing should indeed remain required reading, but perhaps for insights other than those most commonly cited:

> In my case, the effort for these years to live in the dress of Arabs, and to imitate their mental foundation, quitted me of my English self, and let me look at the West and its conventions with new eyes: they destroyed it all for me.... Sometimes these selves would converse in the void; and then madness was very near, as I believe it would be near the man who could see things through the veils at once of two customs, two educations, two environments.[304]

Despite the obvious dash and romance associated with these colorful figures, it is unclear whether their experiments in identity transgression actually had any substantive impact. For each, I think, a case could be made in their specific respective contexts. More intriguing to me, however, is the loss and anxiety they represent at a broader level, symptoms of self-imposed information denial. Gautam Chakravarty notes that fictional cultural imposters like Kim—Burton and Lawrence are, after all pseudo-fictions—became hugely popular in the wake of the 1857 revolt:

> At once a sign of mastery and anxiety, of lack and promise, the fantasy of surveillance projected back from the 1890s on to the 1850s is important for at least two related reasons. Though there were many Indian spies, harkaras (messengers) and double agents who operated behind the lines in 1857-9, and like the *maulvi* Rajab Ali at Delhi provided valuable intelligence to the army of reconquest, there are no records of ethnic British spies.

303 James Lunt, *Bokhara Burnes*, London: Faber and Faber, 1969, p. 185.
304 Lawrence, *Seven Pillars*, p. 31-32.

Read against that historical absence, the novels revise the Mutiny archives with insertions that construct masterful knowledge and control, and their obverse, the transparency of native society. The demand for knowledge and transparency is significant when read alongside the concerns of the last three decades of the century, when the British state in India, faced with internal "disaffection," sectarian conflict, border skirmishing and the Russian threat, set about reorganizing and extending its intelligence apparatus.[305]

Recall "Look. Look, O look" the refrain of victory in the folk-songs of the mutineers. The aspect of seeing here is the fundamental refrain, and represents the exact counter-point to the British enterprise of seeing and being seen as presented by Captain Geoffrey Birch in 1819: "[I have undertaken this journey] to acquaint the people who they are subject to, for as I suspected they were not properly informed of it and seem only to have heard of our existence from conquering the Goorkah and from having seen a few Europeans passing thro' on horseback." As Gayatri Spivak reads it:

> Birch on horseback passing through the country sees himself as a representative image. By his sight and utterance rumor is being replaced by information, the figure of the European on the hills is being reinscribed from stranger to Master, to the sovereign as Subject with a capital S, even as the native shrinks into the consolidating subjected subject in the lower case. The truth value of the stranger is being established as the reference point for the true (insertion into) history of these wild regions.[306]

Long mythologized in the romantic distance, the exotic East had now become an immediate object of observation—indirectly to the metropole and directly to the growing number of imperial agents on site. They experienced a "[t]elescoping of the near and far, the world's expanse suddenly becoming thin, 'infra-thin,' thanks to the capacity for *optical magnification* of the appearances of the human environment."[307] Here they were brought into more instant contact with the imperial Other, and as they became more familiar, with less time to reflect and process, they withdrew into increasing segregation and separation.[308] Acceleration and the attendant telescoping of distance

305 Gautam Chakravarty, *The Indian Mutiny and the British Imagination*, Cambridge: Cambridge University, 2005, p. 157.

306 Spivak, *Critique of Postcolonial Reason*, p. 23. Also in Spivak, "The Rani of Sirmur: An Essay in Reading the Archives," *History and Theory*, Vol. 24, No. 3 (1985), p. 254.

307 Paul Virilio, *A Landscape of Events*, trans. Julie Rose, Cambridge: MIT, 2000, p. 48.

308 Sudipta Sen, *Distant Sovereignty: National Imperialism and the Origins of British India*, New York and London: Routledge, 2002, p. 121.

Empire's hybrid identity drives places, as well as people, to masquerade. A Christian church re-imagined as a mosque in the Hagia Sophia; Classical columns take on Mughal décor in Lutyens' Delhi. *Source: photos by author.*

created anxiety as rapidly delivered information threatened to undermine identity and consequently to inspire the reification of difference. In this context, Mikhail Bakhtin's words of assurance become ones of menace:

> To be means to be for the other, and through him, for oneself. Man has no internal sovereign territory; he is all and always on the boundary; looking within himself, he looks *in the eyes of the other*.... I cannot do without the other; I cannot become myself without the other; I must find myself in the other, finding the other in me.[309]

This intimacy and the threat it represented drove a century-long recoil, manufacturing difference and social space, with a consequent loss of insight. It is precisely this growing blindness which inspired the popularity of cultural masquerade, a popularity which underscored a series of withdrawals that resulted in a growing distance between the "official mind" and social world of Anglo-India on the one hand, and Indian public opinion on the other. In this light, Lawrence's claim that he can understand the natives, while he remains a stranger to them, is an admission of anxiety rather than a boast of prowess (one might read related themes into the claim of a U.S. Air Force pilot in the first Gulf War, "We could reach out and touch him, but he could not touch us").[310]

In an earlier era, masquerade was unnecessary as both British and Indians could see and be seen by each other in the most intimate domestic way. At the end of the 18th century, one in three wills prepared by East India Company servants in Bengal included bequests to an Indian wife, companion or natural child.[311] Such relations provided practical insight into language and culture, as well as facilitating access to broader female information networks similar to those noted earlier in the Ottoman context. British involvement in the domestic world consequently extended into the most veiled sector of the Indian courts. An observer of the period notes the sometimes "blue" nature of such intelligence:

> Until recently the British Government installed akhbar-nuwees (news-writers) at each of the native courts of Rajasthan who were employed to give regular intelligence of all that occurred worth recording to the Resident. A great deal of trash and nonsense

---

309 Cited in James Der Derian, *Anti-Diplomacy: Spies, Terror, Speed, and War*, Cambridge: Blackwell, 1992, p. 165.

310 Shapiro, *Violent Cartographies*, p. 93.

311 William Dalrymple, *White Mughals: Love and Betrayal in Eighteenth Century India*, New Delhi: Viking, 2002, p. 34.

was mixed up with their details—they often infringed on delicacy and sometime suppressed information at the suggestion of the ministers of state—but these servants were on the whole useful…[also employed were] female domestics or slaves of the seraglio who collect a daily budget of tittle-tattle not always of a description fit to be given to the world.[312]

This extraordinary access was slowly but surely and deliberately ceded by British authorities, both for reasons of the British evolving domestic mores as well as from anxiety over the two-way transmission of information such associations permitted[313]—a constitutive aspect of empire. The retreat from windows may have preserved the British from Indian view, but it blinded them as well—a loss as visceral as the appeal of characters, in both life and fiction, who promise to undo it. However, even when these windows remain open, when agents of one social space rewrite themselves entirely to fit another, tensions remain. One particularly well-documented case of such an individual appears centuries earlier, in the spaces that would one day become closely associated with Lawrence of Arabia and the myth of masquerade.

---

312 Westamacott Papers, Oriental and India Office Collections, Eur. MSS. C39.
313 Bayly, *Empire and Information*, p. 94-95.

Josephus: The "Hellenizing" Glass

So, for a conclusion, the nine offered their necks to the executioner, and he who was the last of all took a view of all the other bodies, lest perchance some or other among so many that were slain should want his assistance to be quite dispatched; and when he perceived that they were all slain, he set fire to the palace, and with the great force of his hands ran his sword entirely through himself, and fell down dead near to his own relations. So these people died with this intention, that they would leave not so much as one soul among them all alive to be subject to the Romans.[314]

This moving image from Masada continues to echo from the First Century CE into modern times. Judaean Governor Lucius Flavius Silva is able to bring the overwhelming physical power of the Roman Empire to bear upon its opponents; and yet, for all that power, is unable to make those opponents speak. Silence is the principal, and profoundly unnerving, element which greets the legionaries mounting the Masada plateau.[315]

While this silence may represent a discourse of its own, it remains irretrievable and incomprehensible to the imperial power.[316] As such, it marks an act of resistance to imperial knowing, to the drive to understand reasons and causes—the proper work of intelligence—rather than simple surface effects obvious to the observer.[317] If the compulsion to speak opens up avenues of control and domination, the refusal to speak closes those avenues off, with suicide marking the most dramatic technique of closure—the ultimate retention of the "secret." Yet, at Masada, the closure was not complete:

> Yet there was an ancient woman, and another who was of kin to Eleazar, and superior to most women in prudence and learning, with five children, who had concealed themselves in caverns underground, and had carried water thither for their drink, and were hidden there when the rest were intent upon the slaughter of one another...[the women] came out of their underground

---

314 Flavius Josephus, *The Wars of the Jews*, *The Works of Flavius Josephus*, trans. William Whiston., Auburn and Buffalo: John E. Beardsley. 1895, VII: 397-398.

315 Ibid., VII: 403, 406.

316 Pramesh Lalu, "The Grammar of Domination and the Subjection of Agency: Colonial Texts and Modes of Evidence," *History and Theory*, Vol. 39 No. 4 (December 2000), p. 68.

317 N.J.E. Austin and N.B. Rankov, *Exploratio: Military and Political Intelligence in the Roman World from the Second Punic War to the Battle of Adrianople*, New York: Routledge, 1995, p. 69.

Counter-insurgency, law enforcement or war? Strictly speaking, the Jewish Revolt was an irruption of non-state violence, but political considerations elevated it to a "War," meriting commemoration on the Arch of Titus. *Source: photo by author.*

cavern, and informed the Romans what had been done, as it was done, and the second of them clearly described all both what was said and what was done, and the manner of it...[318]

Like the women at Masada, the author of this text survived the conflagration of the Jewish War, writing to tell both Roman and Jew "what was said and what was done, and the manner of it." Josephus ben Matthias, another of our cast of characters moving across cultural boundaries, was an upper-class Jew with ties to the high priesthood and the monarchy, later a rebel general in the early years of the insurrection. Prefiguring the fate of the Masada narrators, Josephus too took refuge in a cave in the face of a Roman siege at Jotapata, avoided an earlier version of the mass suicide pact, and subsequently surrendered, serving out the war as confidant and companion of the Roman commander.[319] After the war, Josephus moved to Rome—enjoying the patronage of that same commander, Vespasian, when he shortly afterward became emperor—and set about writing a variety of texts concerning the recent conflict and the broader history of the Roman-Jewish encounter. As he transitioned through these multiple guises, Josephus embodied the potential and

318 Josephus, *Wars of the Jews*, VII: 399, 404.
319 Josephus, *Wars of the Jews*, III: 387-408.

the problems facing "marginal actors" who serve as an intermediary between imperial powers and their subjects.

With the terms of Roman governors and procurators averaging roughly only three years, "native" intermediaries like Josephus could provide an obvious source of insight and ready-made understanding for Imperial officials with only superficial experience in a specific region.[320] Not only would a man like Josephus speak the language and be familiar with the geography, but he would also be able to translate cultural sensitivities with potential repercussions for imperial policy—e.g. Jewish traditional objections to both the census and Roman legal patterns of land entitlement.[321] Nevertheless, "native" belongs in quotations, since Josephus, and those like him, would also have been atypical in their own contexts—by virtue of their elite status, linguistic capacity and cosmopolitan outlook. Enmeshed in local power disparities, these agents were already outsiders after a fashion within their own communities, and their engagement with more obvious imperial outsiders would often have served then to create a doubly-opaque veil of foreignness and prejudice, rather than simply reflecting an unvarnished "ground truth."

That Josephus served as such an intermediary is clear from the trajectory of his career, beginning with his service as part of a Jewish delegation to Rome in 64 CE to negotiate the release of certain prisoners, a mission which highlights his domestic social standing, linguistic capacity and connections to the transnational elite.[322] That same social position paved the way for his reluctant assignment as a rebel general upon the outbreak of rebellion in 66 CE, charged with the defense of Galilee. Despite his later betrayal and long subsequent association with the Flavian emperors—Josephus ben Matthias later became *Flavius Josephus*—financially (in Rome, he occupied Vespasian's former residence) and literarily (his *Wars of the Jews, Bellum Judaicum*, enjoyed the official imperial imprimatur)—Josephus nevertheless remained embedded in his original social matrix. His later works, especially his *Life* and *Against Apion*, represent a concerted apologia both for his own conduct in the war (written for his peers in the Jewish diaspora) and for the Jewish nation as a whole (written for an audience still developing policy for his homeland).[323] In this brief biographical arc, we see a man who clearly was, and remained, a Jew, a subject of empire, and an active leader of armed resistance to imperial

---

[320] Austin and Rankov, 143.

[321] Shimon Applebaum, "Zealots: The Case for Revaluation," *The Journal of Roman Studies*, Vol. 61(1971), p.162.

[322] Tessa Rajak, *Josephus*, 2d ed., London: Gerald Duckworth and Co., 2002, p. 39-43.

[323] Shay J.D. Cohen, "History and Historiography in *Against Apion*," *History and Theory*, Vol. 27 No. 4 (1988), p. 1.

power. However, the same tokens noted above just as clearly indicate a Roman and an imperial agent. Josephus may have been unique in his exceptionally high place in both contexts, and was certainly so in the degree of documentation of the experience; and given the nature of empire, his position as intermediary must have been oft replicated, although on a more subdued scale. What do the surviving texts tell us regarding the nature of this intermediary role, and how imperial intelligence might be shaped by the nature of the imperial encounter?

Not surprisingly, Josephus is principally remembered as a historian, albeit one of dubious reliability. G.A. Williamson introduces his 1959 translation of the *The Jewish War* by noting, "From one who boasted so proudly of his own achievements in the art of deception we should hardly expect a high standard of objectivity." Nevertheless, we can detect traces of his more or less formal role as an intelligence agent at the point of contact during the war. By Josephus' own account, we are told that he was the "constant companion" of the soon-to-be emperor on campaign, he served at least a translator's role—acting as an interlocutor with the defending rebels and encouraging deserters from the Jewish cause.[324] The extraordinary benefits bestowed upon him in the immediate aftermath of the conflict suggest that such efforts, while only vaguely alluded to, were highly regarded by his new masters. Although Josephus, still defending his reputation two decades later, is appropriately discreet regarding the specific transactions that took place between "constant companions," the nature of his later works indicate some of the problems involved in imperial translations.

Let us imagine Josephus on the day after the Battle of Jotapata, day one of his new career. He has come out of subterranean concealment in the caves, he has declined the silence of the suicides left behind and yet to come. He has chosen to speak. But how shall he speak and of what? Clearly not in Hebrew or Aramaic, the language of the imperial subjects; but most likely in Greek, the "second language" of both the empire and Judaea. Despite his later protestations that he was compelled to study Greek extensively before writing his histories, Josephus' social placement in Palestine and his earlier ambassadorial service suggest at least a rudimentary familiarity. Using this already "intermediary" language, Josephus might have proceeded to provide an insider's account of the rebellion. As a senior military official, he would have been privy to strategic aims which, as articulated by the movement's leaders, were constructed around religiously inspired resistance to imperial forms of rule.[325]

---

[324] Josephus, *Wars of the Jews*, V: 109, 362-420.
[325] Applebaum, p.169-170.

To whom are you speaking, are you an insider or outsider? Different spaces, different voices, different truths—the open, public platform of the Rostra against the backdrop of the cloistered Senate Chamber. *Source: photo by author.*

Josephus would have been admirably suited to such an explanation, grounded as he was by his own religious training.[326] The latter histories, autobiography and apologia all suggest that Josephus continued to see the world through a matrix of divine action, with the narrative arc of his accounts marked by the recurring theme of sin and punishment.[327] He certainly took recourse in supernatural narratives when, shortly after his surrender, Josephus claimed to have received a vision foretelling, accurately as it turns out, that Vespasian would ultimately be named emperor—a sign Josephus employs as explanation for his decision to switch to the "divinely favored" side. Nevertheless, flattery aside, it is unlikely that Josephus—likely speaking in Greek, the standard language of imperial history—provided the consumers of his intelligence with a vision of the world distinctively alternative to their own. Noting a distinct lack of appreciation for non-rational popular ideologies in Graeco-Roman historiography, Tessa Rajak observes:

---

326 Rajak, 29-33.
327 Ibid, 95-97.

Beyond this, there is the fact that, these ideas had dangerous political implications built into them. So Josephus had every reason to eschew mention of that other world of thought and vision.[328]

To explore how Josephus might have framed his intelligence in light of such historiographical prejudices, we might profitably turn to the histories proper, delayed though they may have been by years in their composition. The disjunction in time, I contend, is not necessarily a disjunction in genre. First, because the discipline of history writing per se was not always so distinct from other forms of information transmittal, and was formerly considered the preserve of those who—like Josephus—had been witnesses, or could interview living witnesses to events.[329] The great historians of antiquity like Thucydides, Herodotus, and Polybius wrote about near-contemporary events, more akin to modern in-depth journalism than strictly academic writing. Second, because I wish to introduce here briefly a theme to which I shall return on various occasions, i.e. that "intelligence," considered as a packet of information about the world which influences policy decisions, is only haphazardly a formal text prepared by a bureaucracy. As a newly assigned analyst to the Combined Forces Command headquarters in Afghanistan, not once did I hear anyone recommend that I orient myself to the situation by reviewing Rand study *X* or National Intelligence Assessment *Y*—but everyone considered Steve Coll's *Ghost Wars* a must read, a pattern which I frankly followed later with my own replacement. While discussing Chinese nuclear capability at the Indian Defense Services Staff College, rarely did I hear a fellow officer refer to any assessment or analytical publication of the Indian government; but virtually everyone was talking about *Dragonfire*, the fictional account of an Indo-China nuclear confrontation by former BBC reporter Humphrey Hawksley, perhaps because a copy was noted in the possession of one of the Directing Staff. Beyond personal anecdotes, one might consider how much the British campaign against Thuggee was fuelled by Queen Victoria's enthusiasm for a novel on the topic: not content to wait for publishing, she insisted on reading the chapter drafts as author Meadows Taylor submitted them. Whether in the first millennium or the third, "intelligence" comes in many forms.

Leaving those reflections aside for the moment, let us return to Josephus and his histories. Like any writer or historian Josephus wishes to be heard, his words given credibility. Like any informant, particularly one who has just betrayed his own side, establishing such credibility is an almost existential

---

328 Ibid, 89.

329 Arnaldo Momigliano, "Tradition and the Classical Historian," *History and Theory* Vol. 11 No. 3 (1972), p. 280-281.

challenge. One route to surmounting this obstacle is to frame the informant's narrative in a structure instantly recognizable to the audience, preferably a structure with inherent credibility. This Josephus sets out to do, openly claiming to follow the conventions of traditional Greek historiography which has no place for a personal god as an explanatory element in the course of human events,[330] while making pointed jabs at his Greek contemporaries who had fallen from methodological grace.[331] As noted above, God does slip into Josephus' story, highlighting the narrative tension in this intermediary text, but the author struggles throughout to keep the divine safely compartmentalized in such a way that it not discomfit the imperial audience.

One way Josephus achieves this end is to construct his religious discussions around criticism of the insurgents—*they* are the defilers of the Temple, the sowers of domestic discord, and thus the just recipients of divine vengeance. The God of the Jews can then enter the narrative as a more or less benign assistant to Roman imperial aims. Of course, this requires that the same divine power not be in league with the people of Israel, and it is this problem which most fully engages Josephus' creativity. At the broadest level, Josephus resolves the issue by denying that the rebels even are Jewish, in any fundamental sense, or even legitimate combatants. Repeatedly throughout the text, the rebels are described as bandits, lumped into the classificatory hold-all in which the Romans—as noted earlier—collect the various and sundry contestants to their rule. More critically, in stories of growing internecine strife, the rebels are contrasted with, in Josephus' description, relatively moderate leaders who might have been amenable to conciliation with Rome.

This narrative of civil strife serves Josephus' aims in several ways. First, this theme serves to exonerate many of the senior traditional leaders still in nominal revolt, among whom number some of Josephus' friends and family members, and who more accurately represent the sentiments of the general population, whom Josephus seeks to defend before broader imperial policy. Second, the theme of stasis employed here explicitly follows the narrative arc set down by Thucydides in his Corcyrean excursus.[332] This train of events, familiar to Josephus' audience, simultaneously provides a readily comprehensible frame to the story, safely strips out uncomfortable religious elements, and shields the narrator from criticisms of partisanship, obvious though they

---

[330] Josephus, Wars of the Jews, I: 13-16.

[331] *Momigliano*, 284.

[332] Gottfried Mader, *Josephus and the Politics of Historiography: Apologetic and Impression Management in the Bellum Judaicum*, Leiden, Boston, Koln: Brill, 2000, p. 61.

are. This represents the fatal flaw alleged in contemporary evaluations of historiography.[333] Gottfried Mader's study identifies case after case where classical topoi—traditional literary motifs or conventions—are deployed both to establish narrative credibility and to drain away the religious and "foreign" aspects of the story for a Roman audience, replacing them with rationalist psychological and political explanations for the insurgents' conduct.

As noted above, Josephus is fundamentally operating from a religious perspective, but feels compelled to refract this world view through a "Hellenizing" glass for his audience.[334] While the project and its articulation are more polished and complete in the formal and post facto composition, the same pressures would have operated during his personal interactions with Roman officials on the battlefield. In the camp, as well as in the study, Josephus would likely have attempted to both mask and couch uncomfortable elements—the "real" inside story—in comfortable and familiar frames. What is perhaps most striking, and instructive for the more general problems of imperial intelligence, is precisely where these frames were brought into play. Classical topoi would have been available throughout Josephus' enterprise, in the structure of the chapters, discussions of tactics, descriptions of terrain, etc.—all relatively neutral in content (a competent Roman tribune might have done the same); but he deploys them most energetically just when the most profound tensions of understanding threaten to erupt, just when it is only the local informant who can explain what is really happening. Josephus the informant becomes most distinctively Roman precisely where his unique insight is most distinctively Jewish. The phenomenon suggests a fundamental principle of *caveat lector* for the imperial consumer of intelligence—when the reporting looks most familiar, the divide between text and reality is at its broadest.

While the British voices we have examined highlight the tensions involved with imperial agents seeking to pass into sub-altern social space—and the Roman experience portrays the hazards of sub-alterns moving into imperial social space—an Ottoman agent provides a counter-subject alternative. The example which follows paints a figure clearly imperial in his social status, but of hybrid identity with respect to his association with the imperial state.

---

[333] T.J. Luce, "Ancient Views on the Cause of Bias in Historical Writing," *Classical Philology*, Vol. 84, No. 1(Jan 1989), p. 17-18.

[334] Dilip K. Chakrabarti, *"The Development of Archaeology in the Indian Subcontinent,"* *World Archaeology 13*, no. 3 (February 1982), p. 332.

Dérive and Drift: Evliya Celebi, an Ottoman Situationist

He had brought a large map representing the sea,
  Without the least vestige of land:
And the crew were much pleased when they found it to be
  A map they could all understand…a perfect and absolute blank! [335]

Ottoman sailors were fortunately not so ill-served as Carroll's hapless crew in their hunt for the elusive Snark. Practical charts for marine navigation were well developed, incorporating both European and Islamic historical models, with works like that of Muhyiddin Piri Re'is justly famous for their quality and sophistication. Depicting the "empire" proper, however, was another affair, lacking even a specific vocabulary; and in contrast to the particular terminology referencing marine cartography, terrestrial maps were consigned to the more general baskets of "pictures" (*resm*) or "images" (*suret*).[336] Consequently, the vast majority of imperial information was preserved and communicated as texts—even material with an obvious geographic aspect like the *defter* surveys or legal decisions over land disputes remained bound by the written word.[337] As noted earlier however, most of this voluminous material was spare and statistical in nature, although augmented on occasion by apparently directed studies like the *Nizamname*.

This collection of data leaves obvious blanks in the "imperial topography," which if filled in might prove useful, if not vital, for policy makers; that is, What is the status of local and regional infrastructure? Military fortifications and administrative facilities? What are the dispositions, cultural leanings and languages of the population? Despite these apparent blank spaces, as I suggested by the introduction of rhizomatic models here, both substantive information and information transmission networks were rich throughout the empire. The real problem, both then and now, is in managing to tap into these dispersed and sometimes hidden lattices. The Ottoman authorities did dispatch official agents of surveillance, principally through the janissary corps, who would monitor chatter in the coffee-houses, practices in the bazaar and

---

335 Ranajit Guha, *History at the Limit of World History*, New York: Columbia University, 2002, p. 72.

336 Balachandra Rajan, *Under Western Eyes: India from Milton to Macaulay*, Durham and London: Duke University, 1999, p. 17.

337 Nirmal Verma, "India and Europe: The Self and the Other," in *Perceiving India: Insight and Inquiry*, ed. Geeti Sen, New Delhi, Newbury Park and London: Sage, 1993, p. 142.

Rotations within rotations, the "whirling" of the dervishes acts out the mobile, always changing network of Sufi societies—a living counterpoint to the static, linear way of knowing embodied in the imperial court. *Source: photo by author.*

reports of immoral behavior.[338] I am interested in one individual in particular who successfully pursued these alternate networks without resort to British masquerade—Evliya Celebi, an Ottoman author whom I find intriguing as much for his methods as for the substance of his work.

Born in 1611 CE to Dervish Mohammed, a Sufi identity he maintained throughout his life, Evliya Celebi was introduced to the Sultan's palace through the *ghulam* system as a page and intimate of the living quarters or seraglio, a process which provided his education and initiated his life-long affiliation with the imperial elite. Abjuring the normal ladder of career advancement open to a man in his position, he left the palace on the eve of his thirtieth birthday for a brief spell of truancy. That experience ignited a passion for travel which he almost immediately began to feed with a longer expedition in the company of an imperial patron. Evliya Celebi would subsequently spend the next forty years of his life drifting about the empire, sometimes in an official capacity and sometimes essentially as a tourist.[339] His official posts

338 Dilip K. Chakrabarti, "The Development of Archaeology in the Indian Subcontinent," *World Archaeology* 13, no. 3 (February 1982), p. 332.

339 Paul Virilio and Sylvere Lotringer, *Pure War*, trans. Mark Polizzotti, New York: Semiotext(e), 1997, p. 13.

included the roles of military officer, diplomat, muezzin caller and sometime sympathizer of insurgents (the appellations *Celebi* or *Efendi* represent a generic honorific rather than a specific function). In referring to himself, however, Evliya most often used terms suggesting a wandering Sufi dervish, or the self-coined title, "World Traveler and Boon-Companion to Mankind."[340]

Evliya combined the journals from his various travels into a monumental opus, the *Seyahatname*, ultimately composed and edited during the years of his retirement in Cairo. In this final form, the text resembles the more-or-less familiar travelogue genre, combining actual observations, second-hand tales, and autobiographical discursions. Instructive as his encyclopedic insights might be to modern historians of the Ottoman milieu, Evliya's work also suggests how information moved around the empire and in what forms. From his own accounts, Evliya seems rarely to have been associated with officially directed document production like the *Nizamname*, and was almost certainly innocent of the more pedestrian imperial statistical accounting. Nevertheless, his observations on everything from the status of religious shrines to local sexual practices reached a very high-level audience. Whenever his perambulations brought him back into the cosmopolitan centers of imperial power, Evliya regularly found himself sharing his insights with generals, governors, sultans and grand viziers.[341] The heterogeneous nature of these insights might be suggested by an excerpt from a discussion of walks around the Goksu River area:

> A river resembling the spring of life, which flows from mount 'Alem-tagh, is adorned on both banks with gardens and mills. It is crossed by a wooden bridge, under which pass the boats of lovers, who come here to enjoy the delicious meadows; it is a place very well worth seeing. Cans, cups, and pots, are made and sold, of a reddish clay found here. The jurisdiction of this place belongs to the Molla of Scutari. The executive power is divided between the Subashi and Bostanji-bashi.[342]

This piece is perhaps uncharacteristically terse for Evliya—his entire *Seyahatname* is a prodigious mass of narrative, constituting ten full books. Nevertheless, it concisely captures the range of his interests, and in just a few lines we find information on geography, geology, transport infrastructure, local economy, sociology, religious authority and political arrangements in a style

---

340 Dankoff, *An Ottoman mentality: The World of Evliya Celebi*, p. 9, 117.
341 Ibid, p. 185-187.
342 Evliya Efendi, *Narrative of Travels*, Vol. 1, Part II, p. 76.

which envisions these disparate lines of inquiry holistically. Evliya's exceptional access to elites suggests that just this sort of information appealed most to the policy-making audience. It is designed for laymen—as senior decision makers tend to be—rather than the technocrats who presumably labored over the painfully dry defter rolls. That distinction in style and substance finds its modern corollary in the *Seyahatname's* enduring appeal as a work of literature—in contrast to imperial archival material, of interest principally to academic specialists.

The problems of identity and objectivity addressed by Classical writers resonate with Postmodern inquiry, with both probing an information environment rather than a temporal era. The *Seyahatname's* device of assembling data through apparently near-random movement throughout the imperial space prefigures postmodern visions of cognitive mapping, which:

> ...enable a situational representation on the part of the individual subject to that vaster and properly unrepresentable totality which is the ensemble of society's structure as a whole.[343]

Specifically, Evliya's apparently well-received methodology parallels the "psychogeography" of the Situationist International.[344] Arguing that there are connections in any given space as experienced, rather than as represented, the situationists proposed a method of drift (or *dérive*) for exploring those spaces. This approach drew from the literary wanderings of Baudelaire and the artistic experiments of the Surrealists to provide an alternative way of articulating the meaning of a particular environment.[345] My application of the concept here to imperial information ordering is a deliberate act of *détournement*—a strategy the situationists frequently employed to radically divert or misappropriate society's "pre-existing aesthetic elements" to support their radical anti-imperialist program.[346] Such an ironic embezzlement seems nevertheless appropriate, as *dérive* and like themes were in turn drawn from military inspiration.[347] Mirroring Evliya Celebi's physical wandering and idiosyncratic musing, such methods offer a way to address a geography, which widely respected but anarchist 19th Century French cultural geographer Elisée

---

343 Fredric Jameson, *Postmodernism, or, the Cultural Logic of Late Capitalism.* Durham: Duke University, 1991, p. 51.

344 A small-scale, international political and artistic movement of the 1960s with roots in Marxism and early 20th century avant-gardes, intending to reawaken the radical political potential of surrealism.

345 Simon Ford, *The Situationist International: A User's Guide*, London: Black Dog, 2005, p. 34-35.

346 Simon Sadler, *The Situationist City*, Cambridge: MIT, 1998, p. 17.

347 Michel de Certeau, *The Practice of Everyday Life*, trans. Steven Randall, Berkeley: University of California, 1984, p. 36-37.

Reclus early recognized as "nothing but history in space .... Geography is not an immutable thing. It is made, it is remade every day; at each instant, it is modified by men's actions."[348]

For Evliya Celebi, as for the situationists, this geography is first and foremost about cities. Reflecting the commonplace that Islamic civilization has been principally an urban one, Evliya generally neglects rural areas and the *Seyahatname's* table of contents frequently reads like a list of cities and towns.[349] This principle of organization highlights the key unit of analysis—the city, rather than the province, the "nation" or the empire more generally—and suggests that for this particular imperial space, urban areas could be considered the apartments, or residential units of empire. As German cultural critic Walter Benjamin would have it, "The city was the 'interior' of the collective, its home."[350]

Guy Debord, godfather and most vocal proponent of the situationist movement, attempted to put this argument into practice with the 1957 presentation of a psychogeographic map titled *Naked City*.[351] This work, one of a series, begins by taking a typical tourist *Plan de Paris* and cutting it into fragments—reorienting the resulting images and arranging them to reflect the connections and affinities "discovered" by Debord and his associates. By nature partisan and particular, the consequent "map" is more useful to those with a radical political bent and a social inclination toward alcohol than, say, to electrical engineers attempting to overhaul the city grid. Nevertheless, it provides a method for drawing out otherwise unnoted rhizomes, a graphic correlate of Evliya's texts. Moreover, the *Seyahatname* shares a common function with psychogeographic maps: "That is, both maps are figured as narratives rather than as tools of 'universal knowledge.' The users of these

---

348 Elisée Reclus, *L'Homme et la terre*, vol. V (Paris: 1905-08), p. 335, cited in Kristin Ross, *The Emergence of Social Space: Rimbaud and the Paris Commune*, Minneapolis: University of Minnesota, 1988, p. 91. The peripatetic Reclus, a member of the French National Guard and supporter of the Paris Commune in 1871, was recognized by 20th century situationists as the inventor of "social geography." Reclus wrote of the individual's "experience" of places, and of movement, real or imagined, to understand our environmental whole. In one of his principal works translated into English, he remarks of the apparent immutability of the earth itself, that given our ability to imagine and vicariously experience the deep past through geological interpretation, we can see that "[i]n the universe, everything is changing and every thing is in motion, for motion itself is the first condition of vitality," p. 567 of *The Earth: A Descriptive History of the Phenomena of the Life of the Globe*, trans. B.B. Woodward, ed. Henry Woodward, New York: Harper and Brothers, 1872.

349 Dankoff, p. 48, 56.

350 Cited in Christel Hollevoet, "Wandering in the City Flanerie to Dérive and After: The Cognitive Mapping of Urban Space," *The Power of the City/The City of Power*, New York: Whitney Museum of American Art, 1992, p. 28-29.

351 See Simon Sadler, *The Situationist City*, and illustration and commentary at http://mypages.surrey.ac.uk/pss1su/lecturenotes/documents/nakedcity.html

maps were asked to choose a directionality and to overcome obstacles"; there was no one "proper" reading.[352]

None of these products would suitably respond to any conceivable state information request, and certainly would not fit into the almost infinitely replicated "intelligence cycle" model, but they might well answer information *requirements*. The rhizomatic nature of information, particularly in an imperial environment, indicates that there will nearly always be connections and contexts not immediately evident to any decision-maker posing specific questions. However, such techniques provide a means for portraying the hidden and the unsuspected—the "secrets" that are more impenetrable than any deliberate concealment or cryptographic expression. Better still, they are quite obvious in what they leave out, and in this are less deceptive than traditional maps.[353] Considering both the temptations and risks of aerial photographs as alternatives to more partisan projections like the *Naked City*, Thomas McDonough argues:

> The elevation provided by "the overflight at high altitude" transforms the sociologist [or intelligence analyst] into a voyeur of sorts, who not only enjoys the erotics of seeing all from his hidden vantage point, but who also enjoys the erotics of knowing all. The scopic and epistemophilic drives unite in mutually seeking pleasure in the totality of the city as seen in the "vue verticale" of the aerial photograph (or of the *Plan de Paris* for that matter).
> But this whole is imaginary, a fiction...[354]

This fiction—rather than illuminating any "truth" beyond the merely topographical—then creates another obstacle for the analyst to overcome, a net to escape, before returning to rewrite the complex web of human behaviors and interactions which give the city meaning. A more recent analog presents itself in Saul Steinberg's *A View from 9th Avenue*. Famously reproduced as a cover for the *New Yorker*,[355] this work is only slightly tongue-in-cheek in its representation of how the world looks from downtown Manhattan, with individual street details vanishing beyond the Jersey border to a narrow strip of non-descript countryside bounded by the Pacific Ocean. This vision echoes my own experience as an undergraduate at Georgetown, when I literally had to explain to graduates of prep schools like Deerfield and Choate just where Detroit might be—beyond simply "west of the Hudson".

---

352 Thomas McDonough, "Situationist Space," *October*, No. 67 (Winter 1994), p. 61. Thomas McDonough, "Situationist Space," *October*, No. 67 (Winter 1994), p. 61.

353 Louis Marin, *Utopics: Spatial Play*, trans. Robert Vollrath, New Jersey: Humanities Press, 1984, p. 202.

354 McDonough, "Situationist Space," p. 70.

355 Published 29 March 1976.

Imagine, if you will, how a similar *View from the Green Zone* (U.S. administrative area of Baghdad) might look, and then contrast this with a View from Sadr City (a host-nation enclave of Baghdad). Both might prove instructive (particularly in their disjunctions), though neither would much resemble a View from the American Enterprise Institute. While "drifting" around Baghdad, á la Guy Debord or Evliya Celebi, might prove hazardous (at least in 2006-2008), the value of such psychogeographic experiments persists. Attempting to plot a line of escape from the more apocalyptic implications of Samuel Huntington's "Clash of Civilizations" thesis, Dominque Moisi argues:

> Yet what has not been recognized sufficiently is that today the world faces what might be called a "clash of emotions" as well. The Western world displays a culture of fear, the Arab and Muslim worlds are trapped in a culture of humiliation, and much of Asia displays a culture of hope.[356]

A representation of this condition (not unique to modern empires, I suspect) is difficult, though not impossible. The "situationist" approach of Evliya Celebi suggests at least one method for carrying out such a project. However, even the most enlightened government bureaucracy, quixotically seeking to "institutionalize creativity" is unlikely to support dispatching its agents to simply wander, in hopes of potentially netting something useful. In this regard, ancillary organizations come into their own. Much ink has been spilt over the unprecedented rise of the media and how it has fundamentally transformed the information environment, but I suspect the change is principally one of form rather than substance. Evliya Celebi and others like him—within the guilds, the Sufi tarrikats and the umma—spread information throughout the Ottoman imperial space with little regard for the expressed interests of the state, as did Roman authors and cult orders. That same rhizomatic sprawl continues in the guise of CNN or the BBC, augmented by pseudo-official think-tanks and consultants. The fundamental lesson of Evliya Celebi and the situationists is that these alternative information orders are at their most valuable not when they support or mimic the organs of the state, however desirable that might seem, but rather precisely at the point of most profound aggravation. By providing those perspectives which are most radically alien, rather than simply politically opposed, these alternative orders provide access to what would otherwise be "properly unrepresentable."

---

[356] Dominique Moisi, "The Clash of Emotions: Fear, Humiliation, Hope and the New World Order," *Foreign Affairs*, Vol. 86, No. 1 (January/February 2007), p. 8.

Boukoloi: Historicizing Fiction/ Fictionalizing History

Still in Ottoman space, but back in time, we turn to Egypt under the Roman Empire in 171/2 CE. First, we have some intense reporting on the case of the *Boukoloi* (herdsmen-bandits) in Egypt. Our interlocutor is Cassius Dio, and as the account is a brief one, it may be set out in full:

> The people called the Bucoli began a disturbance in Egypt and under the leadership of one Isidorus, a priest, caused the rest of the Egyptians to revolt. At first, arrayed in women's garments, they had deceived the Roman centurion, causing him to believe that they were women of the Bucoli and were going to give him gold as ransom for their husbands, and had then struck down when he approached them. They also sacrificed his companion, and after swearing an oath over his entrails, they devoured them. Isidorus surpassed all his contemporaries in bravery. Next, having conquered the Romans in Egypt in a pitched battle, they came near capturing Alexandria, too, and would have succeeded, had not Cassius been sent against them from Syria. He contrived to destroy their mutual accord and to separate them from one another (for because of their desperation as well as of their numbers he had not ventured to attack them while they were united), and thus, when they fell to quarrelling, he subdued them.[357]

Though lurid with bloody detail, this entry is tantalizingly brief for a revolt which threatened the potential loss of a major province, particularly in contrast to the material which survives regarding similar events in Palestine and Britain. However, Josephus and Tacitus may have been writing out of their personal interest in these earlier affairs, whereas here Dio observes the injunction for Roman writers not to draw out their histories with "petty details."[358] While too serious to gloss over entirely, disturbances such as that of the Bucoli might be minimized by this slight and dismissive treatment; however, at the very least these disturbances belie the claims of an earlier generation, that:

---

[357] Cassius Dio, *Roman History*, Vol. IX, Loeb Classical Library, trans. Earnest Cary, Cambridge: Harvard, 1927, 72:4.

[358] Ammianus Marcellinus, *Roman History*, trans. C.D. Yonge, London: Bohn, 1862, XXVII:2:11.

The *Pax Augusta*, which has spread to the regions of the east and of the west and to the bounds of the north and of the south, preserves every corner of the world safe from the fear of brigandage.[359]

As noted earlier, the Romans took great pains to erase such contests and contestants from their mental map despite their repeated irruption, although frequent reiteration of claims to power and stability highlight just how contested the situation really was.[360] Novelists, by contrast, were not so entirely constrained in their subject matter. Egyptian herdsmen hiding in the marshes of the Nile Delta and striking out in a variety of rebellious or criminal activities appear to move the plot along in *Daphnis and Chloe, Phoinikika, Ephesiaka, Aithiopika*, and *Cleitophon and Leucippe*—any or all of which may have drawn on earlier indigenous Egyptian narrative traditions.[361] The last is perhaps the most interesting for my purposes, as it is roughly contemporary with Dio's account. The marsh bandits play a vital and recurring role in Achilles Tatius' romance, highlighting the threat they posed to the region in general, while the apparent fate of the heroine (captured here by bandits led by an Egyptian priest) mirrors in detail that of the centurion's companion in Dio:

> Then he took his sword and plunged it below her heart; twisting it downwards he ruptured her belly. Her innards leaped out at once. Tearing them out with his hands he placed them upon the altar. When they were roasted, each man cut off a portion and ate it.[362]

Traditional scholarship presumed that Tatius was simply drawing on history to flesh out his fable, achieving the desired rhetorical effect of *enargeia*—making the story "feel true." More recent consideration, however, suggests that the reverse was the case, and although *something* surely happened in late 2nd Century Egypt, the details provided by Cassius Dio are in fact drawn from fiction.[363] In this case, the historian achieves an *enargeia* effect of his own by drawing on the currency of popular romance.

Less important than the pathways such transmissions might have followed are the conditions under which they *could* have done so, with no appreciable

359 Velleius Paterculus, *Roman History*, Loeb Classical Library, trans. Frederick W. Shipley, Cambridge: Harvard, 1924, II: 126: 249.

360 Thomas Grunewald, *Bandits in the Roman Empire: Myth and Reality*, trans, John Drinkwater, London and New York: Routledge, 1999, p. 32.

361 Ian Rutherford, "The Genealogy of the Boukoloi: How Greek Literature Appropriated an Egyptian Narrative-Motif," *The Journal of Hellenic Studies*, Vol. 120 (2000), p. 106-108.

362 Achilles Tatius, *Leucippe and Clitophon*, trans. Tim Whitmarsh, Oxford and New York: Oxford University, 2002, 3:15.

363 Jack Winkler, "Lollianos and the Desperadoes," *The Journal of Hellenic Studies*, Vol. 100 (1980), p. 175.

damage to either genre of text, for the Principate saw an explosion of such literary interventions with fiction and history actively cannibalizing one another.[364] In addition to new fictions, the literary world of the early empire saw wholesale rewriting of both established "secular" history as well as the more mythologized past, and growing popularity of the exotic and fantastic in travel literature, blending truth and romance irremediably both for the contemporary consumer as well as the modern historian. What particularly intrigues me about such a dissonant information environment is the possibility that it might be a distinctly, although not uniquely, imperial phenomenon. [I suspect today's readers will view the Internet as a site where fiction and history cannibalize each other]. The imperial situation engenders new forms of information, as well as new information producers and consumers, as the imperial *episteme* (its way of knowing) attempts to incorporate both the hegemonic visions of Rome's armchair historian Velleius Paterculus and the gritty realities of combatants like Boudica. The Roman Empire, for all its universalist claims, was not, as noted earlier, a bounded and identifiable polity. Rather, it more closely resembled W.J.T. Mitchell's critique of the modern articulation of the West, which is "a half truth, a premature generalization, an impression."[365] The dissonance of these two realities, imagined and encountered, amplified the problems of identity in a polity managing the transition between Republic and Empire—a kind of social schizophrenia which manifested itself through increasingly formalized narratives, which proliferated despite stiff resistance from more traditional defenders of the *mos maiorum*.[366] The satirist Lucian embodied this atmosphere, generating insights into such "real" issues as Greek treaty protocols and the conduct of athletic games through a travelogue which took him to, among other locales, the moon and the Isle of the Damned. His introduction to the *True History*, commenting on his predecessors in the genre, captures the status of such truths:

> I do not much mind his lying; the practice is much too well established for that, even with professed philosophers; I am only surprised at his expecting to escape detection. Now I am myself vain enough to cherish the hope of bequeathing something to posterity; I see no reason for resigning my right to that inventive freedom which others enjoy; and, as I have no truth to put on record,

---

364 G.W. Bowersock, *Fiction as History: Nero to Julian*, Berkley, Los Angeles and London: University of California, 1994, p. 7-9.

365 W.J.T. Mitchell, "Postcolonial Culture, Postimperial Criticism," *Transition*, 56 (1992), p. 15.

366 Vasily Rudich, *Dissidence and Literature Under Nero: The Price of Rhetoricization*, London and New York, Routledge, 1997, p. 6-10. Mos Maiorum: literally "the ways of our ancestors," encompassing traditional standards of conduct in personal, martial, legal and governmental affairs – a vague ultimate authority for defining what was "proper."

having lived a very humdrum life, I fall back on falsehood—but falsehood of a more consistent variety; for I now make the only true statement you are to expect—that I am a liar.[367]

I am inclined to wonder whether Cassius Dio took this advice to heart as well. In any event, I have quoted above from an imperial historian, a novelist and a satirist principally because they feel so familiar. Their relationship to, and articulation of, their material would not feel out of place in a 20th Century Thomas Pynchon novel or the meticulously footnoted Flashman novels, in their 19th Century setting. As they attempt to make sense of their imperial world, Dio, Tatius and Lucian are all engaged with processes which are "producing increased cultural fragmentation, changes in the experience of space and time, and new modes of experience, subjectivity and culture."[368] In a word, they are *postmodern*: I use the term in a deliberately ironic sense to suggest that the most salient features associated with "postmodernism" are not in fact bound to a specific chronological period. For these Roman writers, as for Jean Baudrillard, high priest of 20th Century postmodernism, the world seems to have passed "a curve in the road, a turning point. Somewhere, the real scene has been lost, the scene where you had rules for the game and some solid stakes that everybody could rely on."[369]

I propose that the current anxiety over what constitutes legitimate information (is the "Daily Show" news? Is Wikipedia a reliable reference?) signifies the multiplying and contested sources of identity inherent to an imperial condition, rather than the mechanical effluvia of cable TV or the Internet. To the many already-hotly contested readings of postmodernism, I would add "imperialism" both as a social condition and a way of knowing.

In one regard, this ludic and almost playful approach to truth can open up new ways of knowing, or as Nietszche would have it "the *more* affects we allow to speak about one thing, the *more* eyes, different eyes, we can use to observe one thing, the more complete will our 'concept' of this thing, our 'objectivity' be."[370] But such free-play always has limits, and even deliberately "open" information architectures must ultimately institute frames of authority

---

367 Lucian, *The True History, The Works of Lucian of Samosata*, Vol. II, trans. H.W. Fowler and F.G. Fowler, Oxford: Clarendon, 1905, Introduction, p. 137.

368 Steven Best and Douglas Kellner, *Postmodern Theory: Critical Interrogations*, New York: Guilford, 1991, p.3.

369 Jean Baudrillard, *Forget Foucault*, New York: Semiotext(e), 1987, p. 69.

370 Friedrich Nietzsche, *On the Genealogy of Morals*, trans. Walter Kaufmann and R.J. Holligndale, New York: Vintage Books, 1989, 3.12.

to prevent contamination by unauthorized voices.[371] The tensions noted in Josephus suggest that what is excised is precisely that which is most unique in the unauthorized voice, a mutilation necessary since, if I accept a text as a form of art, it:

> ...requires not merely a creator but also an audience who will receive the work, and who will thereby allow it *to work*. The work of art is an inherently social happening. Hence, it is not sufficient merely to concentrate on who is producing it, or on what is "in" it.[372]

So too must the authors describing bandits in North Africa shape their work to fit the audience; but, again echoing Josephus, their accounts from the margins permit polyvalent readings by multiple audiences[373]—suggesting once more that interrogation precisely at the points of greatest apparent familiarity holds the possibility of opening up the strange. The relative facility with which these writers can adapt to the imperial idiom, which structurally conceals as much as it reveals, returns to a theme I introduced earlier—i.e. a key problem of imperial intelligence is that empires, in effect, shed information. The language and image of empire is universally visible and available to its nominal subjects, while the reverse is not usually the case. Josephus, a Jewish priest, can write a generally acceptable history and enter the informal canon of Roman literature. Moreover, discounting divine inspiration, his prophecy of Vespasian's ascension suggests a savvy understanding of Roman politics. It is far less likely, were the attempt ever undertaken, that a Roman noble could enter the discourse of the *Midrashim* (various collections of Jewish commentary on Scripture, especially prevalent in the 2d Century CE). Similarly, Osama bin Laden and his ilk are far more ready and able to post videos to the Internet—to enter the imperial discourse—than are U.S. interlocutors suited to interact with restive tribes in Pakistan's North West Frontier Province via Urdu poetry. Even more benign attempts at communication, such as Al Jazeera English broadcasts, are reformatted for their audience with recognizable modern studios and recycled BBC, CNN or even ABC hosts.

Christine Sylvester captures the problem in her review of an Australian Defence White Paper which seeks to understand the regional challenges fac-

---

[371] Wikipedia, "John Seigenthaler Sr. Wikipedia Biography Controversy," accessed 20 Nov 2006 at: *http://en.wikipedia.org/wiki/John_R._Seigenthaler_Sr._Wikipedia_biography_controversy.*

[372] Steve Garlick, "Distinctly Feminine: On the Relationship between Men and Art," *Berkeley Journal of Sociology*, 48 (2004), p. 123.

[373] Daniel Selden, "The Genre of Genre," *The Search for the Ancient Novel*, ed. James Tatum, Baltimore: Johns Hopkins, 1994, p. 49-50.

ing Canberra: "They are also reminders that it is easier for the colonized to world-travel to Australia than it is for the Australian to world travel the other way to knowledge."[374] The cognitive structures inherent in the imperial relationship act as a screen, rather than a window, falling short of Lao Tzu's dictum:

> It is precisely where there's no substance, that we find the usefulness of clay pots. We chisel out doors and windows; It is precisely in these empty spaces, that we find usefulness of the room.[375]

Despite its questionable reliability, Cassius Dio's account of the Boukoloi nevertheless preserves traces highlighting precisely this quandary. The principal imperial actor in his brief scene is a Roman centurion, apparently acting as the custodian of unspecified associates among the bandits. As such, he is specifically a soldier conducting a police function. More generally, the district centurions of this period were conducting a host of extra-military functions including assisting tax collectors, adjudicating local grievances and passing information on more serious issues to higher authority.[376] While not described as one of the *frumentarii* discussed earlier, he was—like them—translating imperial information from a position of double geographic and cultural displacement. The displacement triples when we take into account his role as a soldier, principally relaying "civilian" information. From the opposite end of the imperial spectrum, one author attributes British military intelligence failures in WWI to an overlong association with colonial concerns.[377] Finally, the centurion's role is simply to be seen, to serve as a visible presence and reminder of imperial power.[378]

The Boukoloi, by contrast, are concealed in multiple layers. In both the romances noted earlier and in "proper" history, these troublesome herdsmen occupy swamps and fenlands around the Nile Delta,[379] places which are "noisome" and "pestilential." Remote and difficult to penetrate, they are not unlike the Masada plateau, the torch-lit shores of Anglesey, or the current

---

374 Christine Sylvester, *Feminist International Relations: An Unfinished Journey*, Cambridge and New York: Cambridge University, 2002, p. 120.

375 Lao-Tzu, *Te-Tao Ching*, Part I, Chapter 11, trans. Robert Henricks, New York: Modern Library, 1993, p. 65.

376 Richard Alston, *Soldier and Society in Roman Egypt: A Social History*, New York: Routledge, 1995, p. 87-93.

377 Jennifer Siegal, "Training Thieves: The Instruction of 'Efficient Intelligence Officers' in Pre-1914 Britain," *Intelligence and Statecraft: The Use and Limits of Intelligence in International Society*, eds. Peter Jackson and Jennifer Siegal, Westport, CT and London: Praeger, 2005, p. 127.

378 Alston, p.95.

379 Strabo, *Geography*, Vol. VIII, Loeb Classical Library, trans. Horace Leonard Jones, Cambridge: Harvard, 1932, XVII: 6:36.

Looking out on empire: a view of the Palatine from the Coliseum. A window is only useful by its absence—for what it is not. *Source: photo by author.*

favorite—the "caves" of Al Q'aida's senior leaders. This remoteness—while it may reflect a geographic reality—serves a rhetorical purpose of depicting the concealed, accentuated by other aspects of Dio's story. Most obviously, the bandits deliberately conceal themselves in disguise; amplified by their feminine mask, providing yet another degree of remove; and finally supplemented by a lie. In these few terse phrases, Cassius Dio graphically captures the imperial information deficit, between who is seen and who is concealed—here the Panopticon is reversed. More importantly, however, the historian's flirtation with fictitious detail to address this deficit highlights the temptation to fill the blank spaces in the narrative with something—anything, really—which will conceal the gap.

In both Britain and Palestine, we saw attempts to rationalize the conduct of contestants to imperial power, and to push the strange and unfamiliar away, to the other side of the hill. But here is a revolt clearly from the inside, well within the established space of the empire—however imagined—and consequently all the more worrisome. The response is a dramatic one, whether the lurid images arise from the historian or the novelist. Human sacrifice was already established as a Roman marker of barbarism, conventionally applied to "foreign" spaces and past times (outside), but here it appears (inside) with the additional gruesome detail of cannibalism.[380] As we have seen, the unstable boundary between foreign and domestic space is a key feature of the imperial episteme, and that instability engenders unique and urgent anxieties. A Roman might reasonably understand why, say, a Parthian might resist Roman power, but for a resident of the empire to do so undermines the fundamental assertions of the *Pax Augusta*—this disruption of identity requires an "othering" of the most dramatic kind to push the offending element away—to outside in space, backward in time.

As a more recent example, the work of Adda Bozeman makes liberal use of the "other" concept which entered modern discourses principally in the post-colonial context.[381] Yet throughout her essays, collectively published just as the Cold War sputtered to an end, a fascinating historical artifact appears. Bozeman continually and forcefully places Marxism-Leninism in the camp of the "other," opposed to the West and consequently more in tune with the Rest, despite the fact that the formal ideology of Marxism was, and remains, quite clearly a product of the West. Ongoing debates after the Cold War thaw within post-colonial, sub-altern and feminist studies over the validity of Marxism highlight how closely this is associated with the Western episteme. Precisely that aspect of familiarity may lie at the root of Bozeman's profound antipathy. Observing this tendency, modern analysis might do well to tread cautiously as it seeks to understand the most recent revolt against a universalist perspective, which dissociates the observer from the "other." Passionate efforts to displace the threat, to relocate what it represents, whether to the 1930s or the 11th Century, may conceal more intimate connections.

---

380 J. Rives, "Human Sacrifice among Pagans and Christians," The Journal of Roman Studies, Vol. 85 (1995), p. 70-71.

381 Adda Bozeman, Strategic Intelligence and Statecraft: Selected Essays, London: Brassey's, 1992.

Ekphrasis: Showing or Telling?

Beyond the gruesome vignettes cited above, Achilles Tatius and his peers filled their narratives of northern Egypt with various asides and excursions of geographical, cultural and biographical description—in many cases drawing on images that would have been familiar to readers through mosaics and sculpture—attesting to the popularity of these other visually apprehensible media at the time.[382]

Ekphrasis, the literary description of objects produced by the plastic arts or their real world referents, was not an innovation, but rather an established practice of rhetoric which gained particular popularity under the Principate.[383] This device is particularly interesting to me as a technique for engaging the blank spaces and polyvalent meanings which confront the consumer of imperial information, and variants of its employment highlight a number of fields where information producers attempt to negotiate these hazards.

Art mirrors life mirrors art. Depictions in fiction and mosaic shaped what could be known and said about "real" life in the Nile Delta. *Source: photo by author, with permission of the National Museum of Rome.*

382 Shadi Bartsch, *Decoding the Ancient Novel: The Reader and the Role of Description in Heliodorus and Achilles Tatius*, Princeton, NJ: Princeton Univ., 1989, p. 166.

383 Eleanor Winsor Leach, *The Rhetoric of Space: Literary and Artistic Representations of Landscape in Republican and Augustan Rome*, Princeton, NJ: Princeton Univ., 1988, p. 44.

Ekphrasis, as technique, is particularly attractive for the *enargeia* effect it produces—creating an "eyewitness experience" at second hand; as the Chinese proverb has it, the picture is worth 1,000 (or 10,000, actually) words. Edward Tufte renders the issue as follows:

> Visual displays of information encourage a diversity of individual viewer styles and rates of editing, personalizing, reasoning and understanding. Unlike speech, visual displays are simultaneously a wideband and perceiver controllable channel.[384]

Tufte's paean to the visual provides additional clues to the appeal of *ekphrasis*. While appearing to offer the clarity and comprehensiveness of vision, the text contains both more and less than the image. The primary "value-added" content of a textual manifestation of spatial phenomena is in the format of text itself. Text provides narrative, direction and structure—it harnesses and guides the "diversity of individual viewer styles." In doing so, it introduces into the ungoverned space of the image tools for ordering and classification, for expressing the overarching obsession of antique rhetoric.[385] Less is provided insofar as narrative text—a string of unbroken words, phrases and sentences—viscerally offers no gaps; the paragraph conceals the empty spaces that are incorporated into an image or map. Negative information, but information all the same, is lost in the unity and completeness of text.

Similar to the conflation of understandings between fact and fiction noted earlier, this theme raises another enduring problem of imperial intelligence for distinguishing (or not) between "showing" and "telling." While my modern references are always in danger of being outpaced by events, in a brief moment of pessimism I feel confident that the modern manifestation of this phenomenon will be relevant long after my writing—i.e. PowerPoint, or variants thereof. Anyone familiar with decision-making processes in a large, modern organization, and especially the U.S. military and civilian government, will be familiar with the issue. Far beyond the pedestrian dangers of "death-by-PowerPoint," this mode of information transmission risks serious epistemological confusions of the kind I am exploring through traces from two millennia ago. These slides, or computer screens, are practically the apotheosis of this conflating technique. They look and feel like pictures, and are often liberally sprinkled with actual images of one kind or another—practically, they are "seen" before (if ever) they are "read." Yet in a performative sleight-of-hand, they are also texts of a particularly rigid, narrative and hierarchical type, reflecting the nature of the organizations

---

[384] Edward Tufte, *Envisioning Information*, Cheshire, CT: Graphics Press, 1990, p. 31.

[385] Roland Barthes, *The Semiotic Challenge*, trans. Richard Howard, New York: Hill and Wang, 1988, p. 47.

where those performances take place.[386] Despite the almost universal opprobrium in which this technique is held, however, it remains, and will regretfully likely remain, ubiquitous and persistent because its very defects fulfill the dual functions of addition and deletion stemming from imperial information needs.

Ekphrasis, in my broader reading, is then a way of transfiguring a vision of the world—with all its apparent objectivity and openness to multiple readings—into a structured discourse. Once so constituted, this discourse takes on a logocentric character, classifying the polyvalent possibilities of the image into a series of binary sets—same/different, domestic/foreign, interior/exterior, male/female—where one element is more or less self-contained, while the other is inferior, opposite or affected,[387] forestalling the interpenetration of identity which genuinely characterizes the imperial encounter more accurately than the concepts of "conquest" or "colonization."[388] It also thereby conceals potentially fruitful sources of information, intelligence which cannot be assimilated because it simply doesn't "fit."

If, as Derrida would have it, "there is no outside to the text,"[389] the imperial information producer is straitjacketed from the outset. Julia Kristeva would multiply these constraints, noting that "every text is from the outset under the jurisdiction of other discourses which impose a universe on it."[390] These other discourses, and their intertextual relations, however, may offer escape routes from the normalizing rhetoric of narrative, providing alternative glimpses of the image beyond the *ekphrasis*.

I addressed Roman history earlier specifically to consider how the social position of various writers interacted with the literary *topoi* (motifs) available to them. As a strictly intelligence problem, the topic invites a re-addressal in this context. First, because as imperial powers strive to understand those over whom they hold sway, history is of fundamental importance, as in many ways

---

386 Tufte, *The Cognitive Style of Power Point: Pitching Out Corrupts Within*, Cheshire, CT: Graphics Press, 2006, p. 4.

387 Jonathon Culler, *On Deconstruction: Theory and Criticism after Structuralism*, Ithaca, NY: Cornell Univ., 1982, p. 94.

388 William E. Connolly, "Identity and Difference in Global Politics," *International/Intertextual Relations:Postmodern Readings of World Politics*, eds. James Der Derian and Michael Shapiro, Lexington, MA: Lexington Books, 1989, p. 323.

389 Jacques Derrida, *Of Grammatology*, trans. Gayatri Spivak, Baltimore: Johns Hopkins, 1976, p. 158.

390 Julia Kristeva, *Revolution in Poetics*, trans. Margaret Waller, New York: Columbia Univ., 1984, p. 146.

societies are *their* history, however that may be constituted.[391] Moreover, in the forecasting role of intelligence:

> "Thought about the past" is an important element in social creativity because it is part of the information which people use in making decisions which affect the future.[392]

But what kinds of societal identities and "thoughts about the future" are available to the producer of imperial information? Earlier citations from Josephus, Cassius Dio and Tacitus demonstrate what kinds of histories these agents *produce*. While clearly products of their time, they are nevertheless recognizable to the modern Western reader of "history," and their collective mode of depicting the world remains a part of the formal discourse of security and intelligence officers—Thucydides' *Peloponnesian Wars* is on the current U.S. Army Chief of Staff professional reading list, illustrating the position it has long enjoyed in similar "canonical" collections.[393]

While the material they had to draw on, beyond personal experience, may not be recoverable, consideration of "alternative" histories drawn from subsequent eras may suggest the nature of the challenge.

	[CE] Annals of Saint Gall
What are we to make of the blank spaces?	709. Hard winter. Duke Gottfried died. 710. Hard year deficient in crops. 711. 712. Flood everywhere. 713. Pippin, mayor of the palace, died. 715. 716. 717. 718. Charles devastated the Saxon with great destruction.[394]

---

391 Jose Ortega y Gasset, *History as a System, and Other Essays Toward a Philosophy of History,* New York: Norton, 1961, p. 210.

392 John Davis, "History and the People Without Europe," in *Other Histories,* ed. Kirsten Hastrup, London and New York: Routledge, 1992, p. 25.

393 Army Chief of Staff professional reading list, accessed 30 Nov 2006 at: http://www.army.mil/cmh/reference/CSAList/list4.htm

394 Hayden White, *The Content of the Form,* Baltimore and London: Johns Hopkins, 1987, p. 6-7.

The Year 1262 [approximately 1845 CE]

In the month of Rabi' I a large star fell from west to east,
bathing the earth in light stronger than the moon, beams
of it being red and beams white. It crashed into the
ground toward the east in about the time it takes to read
the *surah of* Fidelity. As it went over there was a powerful
noise like thunder. After this, in those same months there
were heavy rains and fearful strikes of lightning which
destroyed many people. There were big hailstorms, each
hailstone like an ostrich egg, which smashed houses and
ripped through the roofs to destroy everyone inside except those whom God wished to spare.

What kind of
"history"
is this? What
is it about?

In the month of Rajab in this year, one of the Sharifs of
Mecca whose name was Sayyid Isma'il, set off toward
lower Yemen, always calling on people to support the *jihad* and to expel the Franks from Aden. A mass of people
answered him. Then he arrived near Aden, about a far-
sakh away, and besieged the place until he was poisoned
and died. Those warriors in God's cause who were in his
company dispersed.[395]

A Herodotus or a Polybius might feel free, or more likely be required,
to reorder the material, to fill in the blank spaces (both in the original and
my rendering here) which create a sense of anxiety, of something amiss; but
it is precisely that sense of strangeness which offers opportunities for new
ways of knowing, because it is so different in the ways that matter most.
"Information consists of *differences that make a difference.*"[396]

In Palestine, Britain and Egypt, the Empire was caught repeatedly unaware
by major wide-scale social upheaval and violence. With no 9/11 Commis-
sion to explain who should have known what and when, it is interesting to
note that women, in various guises, emerge at precisely these points of anxiety
in the histories where they rarely play a prominent role. *Women* arise from
concealment in the caves beneath Masada to reveal "what was said and what
was done." *Women* stand guard in supernatural frenzy around the last Druid
redoubt, concealed in remote Anglesey. A *woman*, femininity concealed in
masculine characteristics, explains and leads the rebellious Celts. Bandits,
concealed as women (though perhaps Dio was doing some concealment

---

395 Al Wasi'i, cited in Paul Dresch, Tribes, *Government and History in Yemen*, Oxford:
Clarendon, 1989, p. 174-175.

396 Tufte, *Envisioning Information*, p. 65.

of his own), initiate the Boukoloi revolt. So many concealed women at key points, explaining massive intelligence failures, lead one to wonder whether this might be an outbreak of the "transvestism" Baudrillard associates with the postmodern condition. After all, these are the women who are by nature weak-minded and thus not fit for public roles, as Cato is made to complain in Livy:

> As things are now our liberty of action, which has been checked and rendered powerless by female despotism at home, is actually crushed and trampled on here in the Forum.... I should have said, "What is this habit you have formed of running abroad and blocking the streets and accosting men who are strangers to you? Could you not each of you put the very same question to your husbands at home? Surely you do not make yourselves more attractive in public than in private, to other women's husbands more than to your own?"[397]

The point here is manifold. First, that women as women might have unique insights that are rarely appreciated in public issues, unless they play masculine roles in the vein of Margaret Thatcher's "Iron Lady." Women rarely enter the modern discourse of the War on Terror except as oppressed burka bearers in Afghanistan, or as particularly frightening curiosities like Chechnya's Black Widows. On several occasions I have heard senior flag officers comment on or critique the intelligence they receive by noting, to paraphrase "I don't need to know what's going on out there—I can read the news; I need to know what's going on inside his mind, what he's thinking." This critical intelligence requirement is explicitly one about interiors, about domesticity and private realms: one is reminded of Osama Bin Laden's reputed 10 or 11 wives. The requirement is one which can primarily be addressed by the feminine in terms of associative space and gender, rather than biology. This reading of the feminine, reflected in our imperial authors, suggests other avenues of information. From the feminine space, from the domestic and interior, comes precisely the intelligence required by Dio, Tacitus and others to explain these apparently foreign eruptions within the body of the empire—suggesting that many of the answers about events on the outside can be approached from the inside, blurring logocentric dichotomies. Finally, these women indicate that the feminine as a role can achieve a unique status of knowing. While official actors in today's conflicts (those with money, technology and violence at their disposal—those who rule in an identifiably masculine role) in up-armored vehicles and Kevlar, struggle to unearth "actionable" intelligence, Non-Governmental Organizations (those without guns and armor—those who

---

397 Livy, History of Rome, Vol. 5, *Everyman's Library*, trans. Canon Roberts, New York: E.P. Dutton, 1912, 34:2.

Although the Roman residence of the Vestal Virgins represents the precise opposite of the Ottoman harem, it too was a space of physical seclusion at the center of female information networks. *Source: photo by author.*

minister to and care for others through an identifiably feminine role) interact with people at every level of a society, frequently in the most intimate ways. While NGOs in practice may establish their own boundaries and "othering" practices in regard to agents of the state, their insights and perspectives suggest potentially valuable alternative ways of knowing.

The penultimate argument above highlights another enduring opportunity and dilemma, that of law—considered in a practical and explicit fashion, to include its attention to issues of personal intimacy. Often stationed for long periods overseas, U.S. soldiers in earlier times would often enter those cultures on a personal as well as professional level, building families which bridged the seas of deployments, and depending on the unit of assignment a soldier could expect to encounter German chit-chat in the barracks, or kimchi at the 4th of July picnic. For all its attendant troubles, this phenomenon did create a reservoir of linguistic and cultural awareness similar to that enjoyed by early British endeavors in India (only to subsequently be lost, as noted earlier); but the current cycle of engagement and its attendant imposed separations is unlikely to result in a future where Pashto floats through the commissary or Arabic is shouted across post housing playgrounds. The Roman attitude displayed a similarly schizophrenic approach to the acquisition and deployment of affective knowledge developed over the course of long affiliation. Policy discouraged the repeat posting of officers to the same province,[398] for the same reasons and with the same implications as the Ottoman assignment rotation. At the individual level, although informal marriages and liaisons may have flourished, Roman citizens (including soldiers) were banned from forming legally valid marriages with *peregrine* (non-citizens), with implications for inheritance and property.[399] The crossing of social and sexual boundaries was thus possible among individual bodies, but the line stopped where those bodies entered the space of law—i.e. with property.[400] This legal elaboration at the most intimate and bodily level constitutes another kind of ekphrasis—textually describing a world "seen" in a legal way.

I noted earlier the peculiar problem of the *latrones*—they are not *hostes* (enemies, proper) nor simple law-breakers. They are outside the law altogether, and cannot even be fixed with a clear legal label. The Greek and Latin roots suggest a man of violence not in the explicit employ of the state—analogous

---

[398] Cassius Dio, *Augustus*, 52.23.

[399] Judith Evans Grubb, *Women and the Law in the Roman Empire: A Sourcebook on Marriage, Divorce and Widowhood*, London and New York: Routledge, 2002, p. 154.

[400] Brian Campbell, "The Marriage of Soldiers under the Empire," *The Journal of Roman Studies*, Vol. 68 (1978), p. 153-4.

Law has always been a space of contested value and identity. Even on the high culture steps of the imperial courts, low culture could pass the time with inscribed game boards. *Source: photo by author.*

perhaps to the awkward "illegal combatant."[401] Perhaps this contributes to the extreme punishments to which they were subject, and the ontological tension in attempts to identify and address the problem. Such interstitial identities constituted a direct challenge to a world enveloped in law as power and politics, even if created from within the society rather than imposed by government.[402] However, in an imperial world, Roman law for Romans would be insufficient; rather, for *imperium sine fine*, law would have to be equally without limits. Constructing this legal world is a performative act in which "jurisprudence as a discursive practice is a self-perpetuating way of producing a truth,"[403] but whether for British courts trying to reconcile confessional and common law, or for the Ottomans balancing *Shari'a* and *kanun*, it is not strictly a one-way affair. Local practice and the way subject people engage with and in the imperial court system can also shape this "truth production." Through necessities of commerce, Roman law was compelled to

---

401 Shaw, "Bandits in the Roman Empire," 28-29.

402 Alan Watson, *Roman Law and Comparative Law*, Athens and London: University of Georgia, 1991, p. 97-98.

403 Douglas Litowitz, *Postmodern Philosophy of Law*, Lawrence, KS: University of Kansas, 1997, p. 86.

identify certain practices and agreements that would be acceptable to non-Romans among themselves, a basis for what would presumably be acceptable to *peregrine* when dealing with citizens.[404]

The distinction between the law of the Romans and the law of the *peregrines* would ultimately become moot with the extension of Roman citizenship to virtually all of the free inhabitants of the Empire with the Edict of Caracalla in 212 CE, but the route of development is noteworthy. Through a specifically legal way of knowing, the Romans were able to successfully identify widely acceptable principles of "outside" which gradually began to shape the principles of "inside"—and universal law become Roman quite as much as the reverse. This way of creating knowledge addresses the intelligence problems confronting an entity seeking to understand and co-opt alternate visions of the world, both historically in the articulation of custom, and in the function of projection. For while history may have something of the future implicitly contained within it, addressal of the future is explicit in law. In its imagination of likely cases and their appropriate resolution, the formulation of law is a kind of writing about the future, using historical methods to build scenarios.[405] The survival of Roman law in many present incarnations suggests the profit in this approach, and the danger in attempts to proceed along an opposite route, establishing law via (in order): Islamic principles, international standards, the rule of law, and Afghan local traditions.[406]

My intent in juxtaposing these discourses—images of history, gender and law rendered into text—is to highlight the mixed danger and opportunity in both rupture and over-determination. Kristeva and Derrida may be right that we are wrapped in discourse of our own, but if we seek to grasp the "real" secrets of thought and belief, we can invite intertexts of our own devising. We *can* create spaces for the feminine to speak via NGOs or other "women's" agencies which deal with private and domestic spaces where thoughts and beliefs reside. We *can* imagine histories beyond what "We have been taught inside the classroom and outside of it, that there exists an entity called the West, and that one can think of this West as a society and civilization independent of and in opposition to other societies and civilizations;"[407] and we can consider

---

404 Ramsay MacMullen, "Provincial Languages in the Roman Empire," *The American Journal of Philology*, Vol. 87, No. 1 (1966), p. 2.

405 David Staley, "A History of the Future," *History and Theory*, Theme Issue 42 (Dec 2002), p. 73.

406 Bonn Agreement on Provisional Arrangements in Afghanistan, II.2, German Foreign Office, 2001.

407 Eric Wolf, *Europe and the People without History*, Berkeley and Los Angeles: University of California, 1982, p.5.

that alternative imaginings of the past do open space for alternative imaginings of the future. We *can* articulate and address non-state violence as an internal symptom of globalization, rather than rhetorically extruding it into the space of the irremediably other.[408] Roman haphazard success in various experiments along all these routes suggests how wide the field of possibility may be; and while some or all of these alternative others may fail, we *can* try (but probably not successfully in PowerPoint.)

---

[408] Connolly, "Identity and Difference in Global Politics," p. 334.

Boudica: "A Terrible Disaster"

Just as the imperial east began its descent into the conflagration described in Josephus' *Bellum Judaicum*, the uttermost fringes of the northwest exploded into an even gorier—if more rapidly contained—orgy of bloodletting with the revolt led by the female warrior Boudica in Britain. These paired rebellions of 60 C.E. highlight both the contested nature of empire, always lived more insecurely than recounted in hindsight, and the gaps in understanding which exacerbate such insecurity. While in the case of Josephus I focused on the problems facing intelligence producers—those seeking to translate the experience and outlook of a subject community for an imperial audience—I now wish to turn to problems within that audience which constrain what the imperial consumer of intelligence can absorb.

By the time of the revolt, variously argued in scholarly literature as dating to 59, 60 or 61CE, Britain was by no means *terra incognita*. Julius Caesar first invaded the island (twice) in 55 and 54 BCE, and despite a pause in military incursions for over a century, growing Roman activity in Gaul would have included interaction with cross-channel communities. After a proper invasion in 43 CE, the emperor Claudius formally received the submission of "a part of the island."[409] Two decades later, Britain would host three major Roman population centers: a colony of military veterans at Camulodunum, the municipality of relatively Romanized Britons at Verulamnium, and the commercial center at Londinium.[410] While these three centers of imperial influence—each within about fifty miles of one another—integrated themselves into the British landscape around the Thames estuary, they were protected by four legions, and an ongoing campaign in the west of the island aimed to stamp out residual resistance. Although this overt, military resistance was spirited and prolonged—prompting Nero briefly to consider simply abandoning the island[411]—success was steady, and on the very eve of the revolt, which erupted only a few miles north of Camulodunum, the legions apparently had reduced the last bastion of rebellion to the Isle of Anglesey. Despite this impression, within weeks all three Roman towns would lie in ruins, with tens of thousands killed, in one of the empire's most stunning setbacks. Clearly the

---

[409] Suetonius. *Claudius*, xvii.

[410] Tacitus, *Annals*, XIV 31, 33.

[411] Graham Webster, *Boudica: the British Revolt Against Rome AD 60*, Totowa, NJ: Rowman and Littlefield, 1978, p. 84.

Romans missed key indicators, having been caught unaware by a disaster of such magnitude; what is less clear is whether they would have been capable of seeing the indicators in the first place, or were they constrained by the very nature of imperial knowing? A brief sketch of the main actions, drawn principally from Tacitus and Cassius Dio, will set the stage for this discussion.[412]

Suetonius Paulinus—a general whose extraordinary renown was won principally during campaigns in the mountains of North Africa—was assigned as the Governor of Britain, with the chief aim of bringing unrest there to an end. Despite the invasion of 43 CE and subsequent establishment of a permanent Roman presence, various tribes and confederacies had continued to resist in a decades-long withdrawal, taking ultimate refuge in the mountains of Wales— a terrain for which Paulinus' background made him especially suited. While the Governor prosecuted this frontier war, administration of now- "domestic" imperial space fell to the Procurator, Catus Decianus. Decianus' charter was principally fiscal, and encompassed the management of taxes, property and loans among associated client-kings as well as formal Roman communities. The ruler of the Iceni, in modern Norwich, was one such client-king, and when he died the disposition of his property fell to the Procurator. King Prasutagas had hoped to protect his posterity by declaring the Emperor Nero and his daughters as joint heirs in his will; but on his passing, the Procurator proceeded as if the "client" relationship had now come to an end and began to enslave and dispose of Iceni bodies and property at will. Tacitus additionally offers images of Romans flogging Prasutagas' wife, Boudica, and raping his two daughters.

Cassius Dio differs from Tacitus in claiming Decianus was calling in vast loans; but both chroniclers provide similar images of contested property as background for what came next. Boudica rallied the Iceni and neighboring tribes with tales of Roman outrage, both to her body and her community, and they rose in massive revolt. Dio claims 120,000 joined the entourage, moving quickly to destroy the essentially undefended colony at Camulodunum. At the same time, Suetonius Paulinus had achieved the climax of his Welsh campaign, which involved between one-half and two-thirds of the Roman military resources in the island, with the invasion of Anglesey and the destruction there of a Druid sanctuary. The Governor, along with the bulk of the forces at his command, was over two hundred miles away when he learned of events at Camulodunum. Unable to redeploy his combat power quickly over such

---

412 Cassius Dio, *Roman History*, Vol. VIII, Loeb Classics Edition, trans. Earnest Cary, Cambridge: Harvard, 1925, LXII: 1-12; Tacitus, *The Annals and the Histories*, Modern Library Edition, trans. Alfred Church and William Brodribb, New York: Random House, 2003, XIV:29 - XIV:38.

"Regions Caesar Never Knew Thy Posterity Shall Sway." Two millennia after Boudica led a blood-soaked revolt against imperial power, her statue now stands as a symbol of imperial identity. *Source: photo by author.*

distances, and unwilling to risk defeat in piecemeal battles, he deliberately sacrificed the Roman centers at Londinium and Verulamnium (where archaeological evidence of the First Century conflagration still emerges during modern construction) to the British tide while he marshaled his forces. Ultimately Paulinus, along with some 10,000 troops, managed to defy the odds and destroy Boudica's host in battle. A victory, of sorts, but at enormous cost.

This then is the basic story—a series of people, places, and events—a picture full of gruesome details in the account of Tacitus, who had at least second-hand knowledge via his father-in-law Gnaeus Julius Agricola, a member of Paulinus' staff during the revolt. Those images, like that of Masada recounted earlier, have been re-imagined through the years, losing little of their visceral appeal. In a singular irony, this statue of Boudica—the principal architect of a bloody revolt against imperial rule—now holds a place of honor, only a stone's throw from another center of imperial power in Whitehall. More interesting than those images and stories, however, are the blank spaces and silences in between—an emptiness that highlights the problems of receiving, rather than generating, imperial intelligence.

Senatus Populusque Romanus, the Senate and People of Rome, SPQR became the ubiquitous sign of Roman dominion. This inscription on the Temple of Saturn captures the Roman idea of empire—not in space or military power—but in the identity of people. *Source: photo by author.*

At first blush, Suetonius Paulinus appears to have blundered badly. The vast majority of his forces were devoted to a threat which was marginal at worst, hundreds of miles from the regions he sought to protect. While the armed rebels and Druid orders in the Welsh mountains might give support and inspiration to other malcontents, they were in no position whatsoever to wreak the havoc brought by the Iceni and their allies—tribes which had broken into open revolt as recently as 47 CE over the attempt by a previous governor to disarm them. A veteran of guerrilla campaigns in North Africa, and successful at first in a similar British environment, Seutonius' military experience ought to have alerted him to threats in depth. But precisely that experience may have proven his most significant handicap. Suetonius was a soldier, a gifted one at that, and his approach was shaped by that identity.

The Roman empire, like many others, was largely military in character, particularly in the course of its expansion. This condition shaped the nature of the intelligence it gathered, in both process and substance. As noted earlier, Roman intelligence arose from the purely military aspects of reconnaissance and scouting and evolved into the more sophisticated networks of the *frumentarii* and the *agentes in rebus*, the successor organization to the *frumentarii* after these were disbanded. But even these later developments were still essentially military in character, and were manned by military officials. The evolving nature of the imperial enterprise, based in military action, privileged this military outlook. Moreover, the rise of imperial power creates the demand for a whole host of new government functions and institutions, which cannot be created, except with great difficulty and foresight, *ex nihilo*. Far easier, and more common, is to simply adapt existing institutions to new roles; and the military with its established bureaucracies, processes, and experience in the imperial effort is frequently among the institutions most at hand. Substantively, although particularly prescient generals like Julius Caesar may interest themselves in a whole host of topics, the most pressing concerns are about the enemy and what lies on the "other side of the hill," in Wellington's phrase. It is an outward perspective well suited to combat, but less so to government. Suetonius Paulinus' apparent blind spot highlights the risk associated with the transition from military conquest to civilian rule—his success in Wales suggests that he was well informed about the enemy on the other side of the hill, but ignorant of events within the spaces he was charged to govern. While various political systems face similar competing information demands, this is a particularly critical imperial problem as the status of various places and peoples can shift rapidly from outside to inside, and frequently continues to fluctuate long after empire arrives. Paulinus, in this regard, was less a bungler than the prisoner of an imperial episteme.

And what of the procurator Catus Decianus? As the proximate cause of the issues which inspired the revolt, he might more readily be accused of deliberate malfeasance, in contrast with the Governor-general's more benign misfeasance. But here, too, are traces of problems in imperial *ways* of knowing, rather than in simple technically correct or incorrect information. Tacitus laces his story of material expropriation with sexually charged details of rapine and abuse, but a key element of this rhetorical device is to highlight how the expropriation was mishandled, rather than fundamentally critiquing the practice as such—making this episode part of his broader critique of imperial management. Had the transition of power been properly arranged, no revolt would have been necessary.[413] Providing a lurid pretext for rebellion conceals the possibility that the revolt might have been against Roman domination *per se*, rather than its specific form of imposition, which allows Tacitus to implicitly validate Decianus even while he criticizes him—both men would understand this subjugation as an essentially natural development. In this, they would not be outside the mainstream of Roman perception. Despite the

---

413 Alain Gowing, "Tacitus and the Client Kings," *Journal of the American Philological Association* (1974), Vol. 120, 1990, p. 327.

various categories of client-kings, friends and allies, the Romans conceived of their domain as composed of people—specifically the *populus Romanus* (people of Rome) and the *socii et amici* (allies and friends) united in contributing to Roman power.[414] Consequently, the supposition by the Iceni and others that their privileges might be sustained, their property disposed of by themselves, was simply a misapprehension. The tension between just policy and unjust execution—and the Iceni response—emphasizes the disjunction between understandings of the world which are particular and universal. This latter is distinctly imperial, and is echoed more broadly in the Roman concept of the Ottoman world tree and the British maps depicted earlier, implying a pink girdle around the globe on which "the sun never sets." The error implied in this way of knowing need not be restricted to formal empires, and suggests caution, given the world view described by Adda Bozeman:

> Modern Americans have come to believe that the norms and values encapsulated in their form of government and their ways of conducting foreign relations are the birthright and open options for men everywhere. In accordance with this persuasion there simply can be no "others."[415]

This last point echoes the dilemma raised as part of Suetonius' military perspective—i.e. who is the "other" in an imperial world with universalizing claims? In a traditional military or nationalist perspective the issue is relatively simple, although the consequences are frequently less than benign. The space of the other is "out there," across the border or on the other side of the hill; but inside and outside rapidly become blurred in the imperial context. The problem is akin to that confronted by feminist theory, which attempts to "…shift the political, interrogating the opposition between the public and private spheres."[416] One response is simply to make the contested spaces disappear by either eliminating them or covering them over, as in the cartographic examples discussed earlier. Another technique is to refashion or bifurcate the other in order to make it fit with imperial foreign/domestic, public/private boundaries by filling in the spaces.

This latter technique both Tacitus and Cassius Dio follow in their creation of speeches for Boudica, both in the original incitement to revolt and in preparation for the final battle. Technically, the device is a conventional one, common across ancient historians to provide flavor to their narratives,

---

414 Andrew Lintott, "What Was the 'Imperium Romanum,' " *Greece & Rome*, 2nd Ser. Vol. 28, No. 1, 1981, p. 53.

415 Bozeman, *Strategic Intelligence and Statecraft: Selected Essays*, p. 158-159.

416 Diane Elam, *Feminism and Deconstruction*, New York and London: Routledge, p.94.

and the authors take similar imaginative liberties with Paulinus. In the case of Boudica, however, they are attempting to speak for the other (and a woman, in the bargain); and the result tells us more about how the Romans need to see the world than about what the Iceni might have been thinking, and this quite explicitly so, as "others" were a useful device for giving voice to a whole tradition of imperial self-critique. Let us turn to Cassius Dio; while Tacitus raises similar themes, he is stingier in his prose):

> For what treatment is there of the most shameful or grievous sort that we have not suffered ever since these men made their appearance in Britain? Have we not been robbed entirely of most of our possessions, and those the greatest, while for those that remain we pay taxes? Besides pasturing and tilling for them all our other possessions, do we not pay a yearly tribute for our very bodies? How much better it would be to have been sold to masters once for all than, possessing empty titles of freedom, to have to ransom ourselves every year! How much better to have been slain and to have perished than to go about with a tax on our heads! Yet why do I mention death? For even dying is not free of cost with them; nay, you know what fees we deposit even for our dead. Among the rest of mankind death frees even those who are in slavery to others; only in the case of the Romans do the very dead remain alive for their profit.[417]

The themes are not especially surprising to the modern reader, no more than presumably to his Roman counterpart. Like the crimes Tacitus associates with Decianus, this list of grievances is a reasonable, secularized critique of Roman administration. There is no "other" here. In some respects this is likely a case similar to that of Josephus, where the author structures his content to the expectations of the audience. But additional aspects of the story suggest something else is at work. The Iceni, till recently loyal under a client king and living cheek-by-jowl with the colony at Camulodunum, are clearly not on the other side of the hill—they are not "outside." Just as clearly, however, they are not "inside" either. They occupy something like that indeterminate space left by the itineraries, the space of latrones, but the discourse here domesticizes them. Compare this with a description of Britons, also in revolt, who are indeed over the hill, or in this case across the straits of Menai as Suetonius prepares to invade Anglesey (Tacitus is more loquacious this time):

> On the shore stood the opposing army with its dense array of armed warriors, while between the ranks dashed women, in black attire like the Furies, with hair disheveled, waving brands.

---

417 Cassius Dio, *Roman History*, LXII:3; also see Tacitus' version in Annals, XIV: 35.

All around, the Druids, lifting up their hands to heaven, and pouring forth dreadful imprecations, scared our soldiers by the unfamiliar sight, so that, as if their limbs were paralysed, they stood motionless, and exposed to wounds. Then urged by their general's appeals and mutual encouragements not to quail before a troop of frenzied women, they bore the standards onwards, smote down all resistance, and wrapped the foe in the flames of his own brands. A force was next set over the conquered, and their groves, devoted to inhuman superstitions, were destroyed. They deemed it indeed a duty to cover their altars with the blood of captives and to consult their deities through human entrails.[418]

Here, the "other" appears with a vengeance—the weird and fantastic and supernatural—but all safely outside imperial space. As an imperial power attempts to understand those over whom it holds sway, how does it construct and negotiate between the "other" and the "same?" While Cassius Dio and Tacitus are writing well after the events, their struggle to make sense of them speaks to a wider dilemma, one which their occupation as historians highlights.

Even in the most efficiently managed satellite/Predator-fueled real-time environment, all intelligence is fundamentally historicized. For a general negotiating the deserts of Southwest Asia in either the First Century or the Twenty First, new information—in order to make sense—must fit into a narrative, a history, and this history amplifies the problem of the other/same dichotomy.

As distinct from the present, the past is alien, exotic, or strange; as continuous with it, this past is familiar, recognizable and potentially fully knowable.[419]

As such, the past must be imagined in much the same way Tacitus imagines Boudica's motivations, subject to the same constraints of narrative "fit." Moreover, intelligence must frequently be narrativized—i.e. imagined—twice. Not only must it find a place in a constructed scheme of past events, but as an influence on decisions yet to be taken it must fit in with a future still becoming—it must be a signifier for which there is no extant referent. I do not think I generalize too broadly for others who have been involved in the field when I recall that the single most frequent and nettlesome question from a decision maker

---

418 Tacitus, *Annals*, 14:30.

419 Hayden White, *The Content of the Form*, Baltimore and London: Johns Hopkins, 1987, p. 89.

upon being delivered some intelligence item is "So What?" Or, "What next," "And then?" etc. The answers to these questions must be constructed in this space I am attempting to describe, one peculiarly though not uniquely "imperial" in nature. To borrow a phrase from Diane Elam, this phenomenon gives rise to the "future anterior tense."[420] Through the structures of its encompassing narrative, imperial intelligence answers neither "what was" or "what is," but "what will have been."

---

420 Elam, *Feminism and Deconstruction*, p. 41.

Lessons Learned (or rather... observed)

At the thought of statistics, the Collector, walking through the chaotic Residency garden, felt his heart quicken with joy.... For what were Statistics but the ordering of a chaotic universe? Statistics were the leg-irons to be clapped on the thugs of ignorance and superstition which strangled Truth in lonely byways.[421]

Any reader who has hung on this long will recognize, I am sure, that I am generally disinclined to provide set resolutions to the problems of imperial intelligence. By design, I have not even provided a single, uncontested definition of empire or intelligence to which these problems, and any potential resolution, might be assigned. Nevertheless, I do not believe the labor of writing this work—or the labor of reading it—constitutes time wasted. Particularly for those actively involved in the enterprise of U.S. intelligence gathering and analysis at the beginning of the 21st Century (and ideally for other interested parties), the challenges and pitfalls I have sketched above will resonate, regardless of any overtly drawn parallels. Whether America is or is not an empire will likely not be resolved till long after the fact. It has been widely observed that Rome had an empire long before it *became* an empire; and Queen Victoria wasn't crowned Empress of India until 1877, more than a century

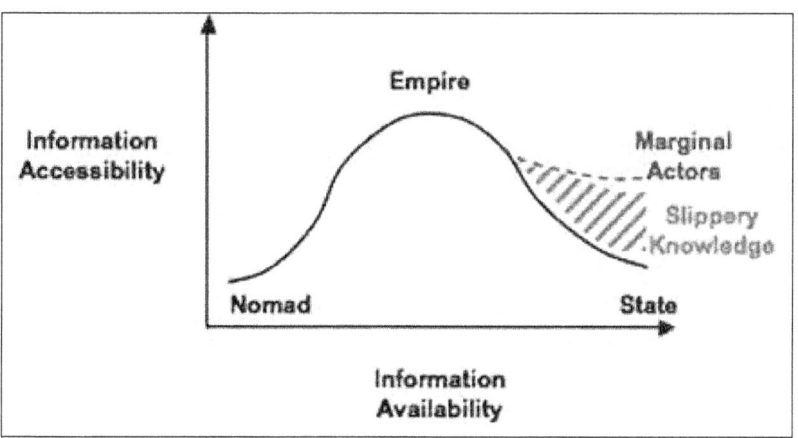

A model of information and power relationships attending the imperial way of knowing. *Source: created by author.*

---

[421] J.G. Farrell, *The Siege of Krishnapur*, New York: New York Review Books Classics, 2004, p. 186.

after Britain took on a political role in the sub-continent. For my purposes, it is sufficient to recognize that the kinds of knowledge required and produced about people, places and meaning by these historical empires bear considerable familiarity with our enterprise in the 21st Century—far more so than the intelligence of the 20th Century, involving the counting of tank divisions and calculating missile throw weights. This ring of familiarity indicates to me the relevance of the historical examples I have considered.

As I indicated at the outset, I sought to explore three major issues that flow from the question I set out to explore. The central question concerns the nature of the intelligence of empire; that is, the nature of information gathering and use to promote the survival of an empire and its polity. The three issues are: How do power and knowledge interact? How do marginal actors and slippery knowledge mediate this interaction? And is there a distinctly imperial way of knowing? The chart on the previous page captures in rough snapshot my answer to these three issues.

A few notes of explanation: This formulation makes two major distinctions—between information availability and accessibility as functions, and between nomad and state as information-manipulating social organizations. As to the first, a distinction of my own devising, I largely hold this truth to be self-evident, that the availability of information and the capacity of any given consumer to access that information do not progress in a direct relationship. Rather, three primary, possible conditions present themselves. Where information is scarce and the means of accessing it are Spartan—we have ignorance. Where information is rich, and open to interpretation through sophisticated and polyvalent reading—we have knowledge. Where information grows and expands with organic profligacy while institutions of understanding grow increasingly formal and rigid—we have information overload, the Tower of Babel. Similarly, my second distinction, drawn from Deleuze and Guattari, allows for three conditions. In the nomad world, space and social organization are smooth and undergoing constant, rapid change. In the state, space and society have become fully striated and increasingly resistant to change. Empire, appropriately enough, occupies a marginal position of its own somewhere between these two extremes.

Thus defined, this chart tells the story of empire and knowledge in this way: As imperial formations and associated political power expand from the inchoate and fractured nomad condition, information availability increases with more of the world entering a single social space. It also becomes increasingly accessible as communities merge and morph, and individuals are able to circulate and contest definitions of identity. In short, power and knowledge grow together; they are mutually enhancing. At the apogee of imperial power, this hybrid and experimental condition begins to take on more of the formal attributes of the state. Information availability continues to increase, but it becomes progressively less accessible as only one frame of reference defines legitimacy, only one perspective constitutes truth, and only one network of transmission seeks to control the passage of information. In short, from this point on, power increasingly inhibits knowledge. A distinctly imperial way of knowing then lies at precisely this transition point, and by definition success-ful empires are the ones that most effectively prolong this inevitable transition. This is the task marginal actors seem best positioned to perform, as they man-age to retain access to alternate frames of knowledge which become increas-ingly inaccessible as state power grows. By their very nature, such marginal actors cannot be intentionally produced. Rather, successful empires appear to be those blessed by fortune with rich alternative formations—and the key task of imperial policy is to recognize and cultivate these formations rather than to exclude, eliminate or co-opt them.

This is briefly the story I have attempted to tell, but of course there are other possible stories. Since this project was by design an "alternative" approach, the chief alternative to this would naturally be the conventional wisdom—that knowledge and power are essentially equivalent without caveat. To know all is to have power over all. This seems to me the implied perspective behind recent intelligence initiatives like Total Information Awareness, or the proposed Sentient World Simulation, with billions of software nodes representing every human being on Earth—accompanied by virtual financial institutions, utilities, media outlets and corner shops—programmed to play out responses to any designed policy or event.[422] Such alternatives require no particular advocacy from me.

Another plausible, although disturbing, possibility emerged in my discus-sions with those more knowledgeable than I—that knowledge is simply irrele-vant, and power alone succeeds or fails simply on the merits of brute strength. Pursuing an Occam's Razor approach to the nuanced, complex, shifting and contested varieties of knowing I have associated with growing imperial pow-er, one might simply dismiss them. The Romans didn't make detailed maps simply because they didn't need them while their armies were sufficiently powerful. The British only began to experiment with sophisticated ways of understanding once raw might began to flag in the face of overwhelming re-quirements of imperial control. Read this way, increasing knowledge marks the tombstone, rather than the ensign, of power.

---

[422] Mark Baard, "Sentient World," The Register, 23 June 2007.

My particular approach has been to avoid a perspective that follows intentional government policies and organizations, looking instead at interstices, gaps and contested spaces in the imperial information space. Nevertheless, the work remains metropole-centric—i.e. intelligence flourishes or fails depending on how imperial powers negotiate these spaces. A more radical possibility is to shift the focus even further, and examine whether "imperial knowing" is itself irrelevant, as if the information networks subordinate to and outside government essentially constitute reality independently of some nominal imperial "viewer." This would mirror some academic efforts in sub-altern historiography, that have the stated aim of re-writing colonial history in order to "provincialize Europe." While intriguing to me, this program has proven problematic in historiographical practice due to a paucity of sources—how does one recover the vast historical information space occupied and negotiated by communities which did not leave written records, or that was overwritten by state texts? The modern proliferation of communications technology, often wildly outside the control of states or civil elites, might prove a fruitful arena for pursuing this argument in our current context.

All three of these alternatives have their own merits, advocates and traditions of investigation, but the fruits of the project at hand suggest to me that some of its major themes merit further investigation, perhaps in other imperial fields.

> By one Chinese view of time, the future is behind you, above you, where you cannot see it. The past is before you, where you can examine it. Man's position in time is that of a person sitting beside a river, facing always downstream as he watches the water flow past.[423]

This conception of time, radically dissimilar from the Western experience, suggests an East Asian locale for case studies on how experiences and framing of time can change the meaning of nominally objective facts. For example, during the Ming-Qing transition, the accepted world order, with Confucian culture and political power centered in China, was upset by the ascending rule of "barbarians," the effects rippling out across Chinese imperial space. Korean elites were compelled to revisit history in an effort to make sense of their position in this new world. One faction, the *Soin*, chose to remember the Ming period as the apex of Confucian culture, which Korea needed simply to maintain; while another party, the *Namin*, leapfrogged backward over the entire Ming period, seeking authority in classical Confucian texts, which it was

---

[423] Graham Peck, *Two Kinds of Time*, 2d Edition, Revised and Abridged, Boston: Houghton Mifflin, 1967, p. 7.

then the Korean mission to revive.[424] In the contemporary world, both Christian and Muslim religious traditions are engaged in a similar struggle to reconcile their identities with the experience of globalization through redrawing the flow of time and the channels through which it passes—an enterprise far more sophisticated than simply trying to "go back to the 11th Century (or 1st, or 14th, etc.). Analysis which seeks to understand these movements, as either productive or threatening, must find a way to engage this temporal manipulation. Chinese imperial history may provide an arena to explore these issues, with less ideological baggage than doing so in an overtly modern context. A recent assessment concurs that:

> Analysts of Eurasian commonalities and interconnections have focused on geography, institutions, and culture, but we need to broaden the scope of comparison. Control of time mattered as much as the standardization of space and culture. Temporal control was closely linked to mastery of space.[425]

Additionally, the Chinese imperial experience provides another site for exploring alternative ways of knowing, particularly in the relational, rather than unilateral, sense which I have tried to emphasize. Early imperial texts on homosociality emphasized "knowing" as normally operating in a downward hierarchical direction, in which a superior subject must know subordinate objects in order to control them—not so different from the Benthamite unilateral perspective. By the late Han and Wei-Jin period, however, the discourse changes to define "knowing" as a condition of mutual intelligibility—particularly in homosocial relations and more widely as a metaphor for "knowability" in general.[426]

These temporal and epistemological issues played out in a political space honeycombed by secret societies that often constituted states within the state—whether benevolent, criminal or revolutionary—giving rise to threat perceptions that seem at first blush to verge on conspiracy paranoia.[427] However, the problems of understanding posed by such communities map closely to those

---

[424] Ja Hyun Kim Haboush, "Contesting Chinese Time, Nationalizing Temporal Space: Temporal Inscription in Late Choson Korea," in *Time, Temporality, and Imperial Transition: East Asia from Ming to Qing*, Ed. Lynn Strive, Honolulu: University of Hawaii and the Association for Asian Studies, 2005, p. 121-122.

[425] Peter Perdue, "The Qing Empire in Eurasian Time and Space: Lessons from the Galdan Campaigns," in *The Qing Formation in World Historical Time*, Cambridge and London: Harvard, 2004, p. 84.

[426] Christopher Leigh Connery, *The Empire of the Text: Writing Authority in Early Imperial China*, New York: Rowman and Littlefield, 1998, p. 116.

[427] Bozeman, *Strategic Intelligence*, p. 170.

I have generally assigned to imperial intelligence sui generis—i.e. the enemy, as such, is not clearly "out there" as a foreign threat, nor is it simply a problem of domestic resistance, but rather it interpenetrates the imperial world. The grounds for further research in this arena are twofold. First, research from a modern intelligence perspective into these organizations provides a choice of substantive alternate models into how information networks operate in extra- or anti-state communities beyond the Soviet/Maoist cell model that continues to dominate much current analysis, in a kind of lingering Cold War hangover. At a more esoteric level, conspiracy thinking as such provides a model for considering alternative ways of imagining the world. Too often, analysts dismiss the kinds of conspiracy theories that populate much of the non-Western press (for example, the Israeli role in September 11th, or the building of secret U.S. bases in Nepal). While the theories themselves may be of little worth, the vision of reality that nurtures them has a logic of its own that may be instructive in efforts to see the world through the eyes of others. To take a particular case in point, after the tsunami of December 2004, theories flew around the Indian Ocean basin attributing the disaster to U.S. nuclear or meteorological experiments which had either gone awry, or had been specifically designed to disrupt the region to facilitate an increased U.S. role and presence. Rather than being considered irrational, such thinking may instead be associated with a kind of "hyper-rationality" which seeks to assign order and meaning to the chaotic chance of the natural world. In other contexts, similar themes may be expressed in religious terms, but the underlying perspective remains the same—ironically enough, a position which assigns more weight to rationality than the Western perspectives which dismiss it. As an aside, it is perhaps worth noting the distinction between these kinds of problems and those which occupy the Chinese intelligence services today. Chinese institutions working the U.S. target set overwhelmingly focus on three priorities: commercial activities and information, U.S. policies and actions toward China, and Chinese dissidents abroad—a narrow array of topics far removed from the kinds of imperial questions which preoccupied, say, the Ming dynasty or U.S. intelligence consumers today.[428]

Finally, beyond these clandestine networks, the striated political space of the Chinese empire was underwritten by the smooth space of other connections linking disparate communities both intra- and inter-empire in much the same way as those examined in this study. Indeed, the Sufi networks seen in an Ottoman context were prominent in Central Asia as well, which along with

---

[428] Nicholas Eftimiades, *Chinese Intelligence Operations*, Annapolis, MD: Naval Institute Press, 1994, p., 27, 35, 38.

perambulatory Christian missionaries and the Tibetan Dge-lugs-pa made up one of the "parallelisms" that characterized the years between 1500 and 1800 across Eurasia.[429] These three groups in particular present themselves as potentially rich veins of research along the lines I have proposed. So too do the Freemasons spun across the British Empire. While freemasonry as a topic of research is only slightly more respectable than UFOs or Noah's Ark, the phenomenon makes a suitable topic for examining how connections bleed across private and public spaces. Masonic lodges, especially those associated with military units, could travel the globe, sprouting civil counterparts in their wake. Lodge No. 227, affiliated with the 46th Regiment of Foot, makes for a particularly vivid example of the phenomenon. During the Seven Years War, 227 met in Halifax, Nova Scotia and the West Indies. The American Revolution found 227 in Massachusetts, where the chest of the lodge was captured, but returned under guard of honor by Brother George Washington, after which it returned to the Caribbean and then to Ireland. During the subsequent wars against France, the lodge traveled back to the Caribbean, then to southern India and finally to Montreal.[430]

Despite its almost mythical connections to formal power and influence, the Freemason phenomenon did operate within a worldview sometimes distinctly at odds with its associated host regimes. Despite hardening racial identities in 19th Century British India, lodges there remained far more inclusive than the official British organs. Research here might identify how tensions were negotiated and information passed through the permeable spaces surrounding the imperial state in more practical, specific ways than I have done. Similar possibilities suggest themselves from the Spanish imperial enterprise. Particularly within South America, imperial power was maintained both through the formal bureaucracy of the state and the Catholic Church, each with different goals, worldviews and networks of information acquisition, processing and analysis.[431] Within the latter social space, the Jesuits operated at even further remove from institutional authority, asserting independence in their assignments, missions and allocation of resources from both civil authorities and bishops of the Church.[432] Despite a generally clear evangelical purpose, the

429 James Millward, "The Qing Formation, the Mongol Legacy and the 'End of History' in Early Modern Central Eurasia," *The Qing Formation in World Historical Time*, p. 103.

430 Jessica Harland-Jacobs, *Builders of Empire: Freemasons and British Imperialism, 1717-1927*, Chapel Hill, NC: University of North Carolina, 2007, p. 34-35.

431 John Leddy Phelan, "Authority and Flexibility in the Spanish Imperial Bureaucracy," in *Administrators of Empire*, ed. Mark Burkholder, Brookfield, VT and Aldershot, UK: Ashgate, 1998, p. 2, 16-17.

432 William Bangert, *A History of the Society of Jesus*, St. Louis: Institute of Jesuit Sources, 1972, p. 170-1.

Jesuits operated a wide variety of institutional projects, requiring an equally diverse set of skills and perspectives.

> To support their evangelical projects, early Jesuits invested in the silk trade in Japan, served as diplomats in Portugal, and grew sugar on slave plantations in Brazil and tobacco in colonial Virginia.[433]

These kinds of experiences underpin the imperial identity manifested in slogans associated with Jesuit missions along themes like—*Unus Non Sufficit Orbis* (One world is not big enough for them).[434] More to the point for my purposes, the Jesuit experience, particularly in its relationship to the Spanish imperial state and the Catholic Church proper, provides a case study for exploring more carefully the specific kinds of institutional arrangements a successful imperial regime can pursue in order to incorporate the knowledge gathered by non-state entities—a question I have not yet answered to my own satisfaction. Additionally, Jesuit internal administration provides a distinct site for considering how a hierarchical institution with clear prejudices and social discipline can nevertheless encourage and develop alternate perspectives and ways of knowing—enshrining in doctrine a kind of relativism and opportunism in what its members study, how they pursue their mission and how they comport themselves.[435] While my project here has dealt primarily with identifying this problem in imperial practice, the Jesuit experience might be mined for solution strategies.

In the paragraphs above, I have attempted to capture my principal findings, identify shortcomings and alternative explanations, and suggest additional imperial environments to pursue these questions further. Beyond these specific issues, the substantive material I have covered also prompts consideration of a few broader implications, which some may see as theoretical propositions.

Disorder is deliverance. The most profound challenge confronting imperial knowing is the potential for wildly divergent constructions of meaning. How is time experienced in rural Lashkar Gah? What constitutes individual identity in Fallujah? How does history work in Mindanao? When we ask these questions with the presumption that time, identity and history are fixed categories our answers will inevitably go awry. The messy experience of imperial contact, not only "out there," but within our own organizations, provides op-

---

[433] Gerald McKevitt, *Brokers of Culture: Italian Jesuits in the American West 1848-1919*, Stanford: Stanford University Press, 2007, p. 5.

[434] Bangert, *History*, p. 92.

[435] George Ganss, trans., *The Constitution of the Society of Jesus*, St. Louis: Institute of Jesuit Sources, 1970, p. 187-88, 204.

portunities to disrupt those fixed presumptions. America, in particular, is especially well-suited to this interpenetration by virtue of steady immigration, at least, so far. Workplace diversity in this regard gains practical utility beyond the imperatives of domestic policy, as a practical instrument for incorporating alternative perspectives. The principal issue will be to resist the temptation to reduce discord through organizational "norming." The problems associated with pursuing gender equality—particularly within the military—suggest the steepness of the challenge. While assigning particular roles, values and attributes to a given individual based solely on their biological equipment may be an error, attempting to erase gender altogether for the sake of amity presents risks of its own. In our encounters with other cultural orders, we are quite proud of the fact that U.S. women need adopt nothing like the veil. The mechanism for this, however, is principally through divorcing female bodies from attributes previously considered "feminine." Participation in the public sphere and the acquisition of social status principally through financially rewarded labor are good things, as is the (attempt at) removal of sexual harassment. What has been lost, however, for bodies of all assortments is the virtue of the private and interior, the intuitive, of value not tied to a market transaction, of sexual identity and difference. These qualities—call them feminine if you like, or anything else—provide access to alternate perspectives and frames of meaning; but they remain as firmly in *purdah* as any of the Sultan's concubines.[436]

The accidents of history may come into play here, at least for the near term. With a generational shift overtaking many of the state's intelligence agencies, a new cohort arriving in disproportionate numbers may create a climate which resists the collective socialization which descends upon isolated individuals entering during a normal period of steady departure and replacement. Moreover, the oft-noted career expectations of Generation Y, with multiple job/career changes the presumed norm, suggests a greater resistance to institutional pressure. Within the military as well, the pressure to conform during the zero-defect mentality of drawdown years will likely remain in abeyance so long as a volunteer force is actively engaged in conflicts across the globe. Both the practical demands of operations and the demographic demand of sustaining end-strength will reduce the costs associated with articulating alternative perspectives. While individuals may be increasingly able to generate the chaos that breeds creativity, the broader institutional level is the arena that

---

436 While purdah translates literally as "curtain" or "veil," the term captures the whole spectrum of practices—from headscarves and burqas to covered carriages and special women's quarters—employed to conceal the female world from the gaze of outsiders.

harbors the greatest risk. The drive to streamline, coordinate and consolidate, however laudable, will always threaten to silence dissent. While an alphabet soup of acronym agencies is always a recipe for cacophony, it's reassuring that in most recent assessments of "intelligence failures" someone, somewhere did get it right. Whether that particular voice was heard or synchronized with other institutional priorities is a separate issue. The drive toward a single agency "position," and ultimately a single community position will inevitably reduce the opportunities to get it right. It is worth noting in this regard a U.S. Army training motto, to the effect that "We teach how to think, not what to think." Although laudable, this goal requires at least one caveat. As much of the discussion above has illustrated, I hope, those two aspects are not entirely discrete. Particularly in a cross-cultural, counter-terrorist, or in my case, imperial, context—specifying and thus limiting *how* we think may be just as critical in constraining insight as any imposition regarding *what* to think.

Empires thrive despite, rather than because of, their information institutions. Laplace's Demon and Borges' Map embody the temptations of imperial institutions to know everything, preferably in real-time, sub-national granularity, temptations that crowd out all other endeavors or paradoxically lead to ever-increasing margins of error. Posed against these threats are the Sufi brotherhoods, the Mithraic cults and early Christian churches, the harem relations and village news-writers. Empires thrive and grow amid such disparate constellations of information, and then decline as these are inexorably subsumed or over-written by the imperial state. It is during this period of decline that the principles of imperial error, identified in my historical discussions, tend to accumulate and compound one another. The insatiable appetite of LaPlace's Demon creates an ever-wider and more indiscriminate demand for information, especially for information of a certain type, i.e.—that couched in the frame of reason, science and history (a la Sleeman) and in the idiom of imperial power (a la Josephus). When these three factors assemble, the possibility of strategic level error escalates dramatically.

My own recent experience during the Nepal elections on 10 April 2008 provides a suitable snapshot of how these principles can apply in practice. Faced with a volatile and unpredictable political situation, American officials in Nepal (as well as Indian officials, UN officials, NGOs, etc.) reached out for all the information they could garner in the run-up to 10 April, with data collection and analysis steadily proliferating. Of course, LaPlace's Demon is never satisfied, but we collectively certainly tried. Various Nepali interlocutors and experts, many of them with extensive education and experience in the West, provided detailed assessments, statistics and historical argument to buttress predictions—often in English better than my own and employing political theories and models so *au courant* in the U.S. that I was unfamiliar with them. Almost without exception, the collective assessment was sure and certain that the prevailing constellations of power would prevail, albeit with minor tweaking. Then we woke up on 11 April, and found ourselves stunningly in the wrong as the erstwhile Maoist insurgents piled up electoral victory after victory. This wasn't a case of successful deception by an enemy—no Pearl Harbor or Normandy—but rather of a reality we couldn't see because of the very principles upon which our information architecture operated. Reflecting on all the erroneous texts I had read (and authored), I was reminded of a Nepali artist's observation that the history of the powerful is found in texts, the history of the weak in songs. Success requires listening to songs as well as reading texts.

Alternatively, these negative principles might be articulated in a positive way. Despite the pressure to generate literally endless streams of data, value may often be found in the telling detail—no less useful for its obvious limits—which produce in the consumer the appropriate cautions which might be lost when confronted with statistical "fact." Similarly, one can productively seek out new voices and modes of communication (e.g. songs rather than texts) which apparently abrogate consensus views of what constitutes normative constructions of reality (e.g. conspiracy theories). In these realms, here again we may be the happy beneficiaries of historical chance. The current explosion of alternate and often antagonistic voices, from YouTube to Al Jazeera, seems highly unlikely to come under harness any time soon.

During the course of my research, it was striking to read the rather dire predictions of imminent total information control predicted by authors seeking lessons from the media-genic first Gulf War; while concurrently scanning through BBC stories about frantic attempts to constrain jihadi web-sites, control soldiers blogging from the field, and compete for Internet attention through officially sanctioned video-clips. The key issue for those working in this field is to recognize that this is largely a healthy thing, even if occasionally uncomfortable. *The Washington Post* or *New York Times* can afford to pay a Steve Coll or Thomas Friedman to wander around and find surprising connections, the *Atlantic* can support a Robert Kaplan—all valuable functions virtually impossible for government institutions. It's even okay if your boss gets his news from a Rendon Alert e-mailed to his Blackberry rather than from his morning intelligence briefing. Organizations that thrive will likely not be those that seek information dominance (a chimera if ever there was one), but those that provide innovative perspectives and connections. In practice, this means there is a place in strategic intelligence analysis for topics as apparently irrelevant as women's literacy rates and rural access to irrigation systems. These kinds of threads may prove more valuable in mapping the recruitment patterns and ultimate intentions of extremists in the developing world than more traditional, technological initiatives like mapping cell phone towers or bomb-making techniques. Within the U.S. Intelligence Community, an environment populated by sixteen different agencies with countless subordinate entities, relatively robust resources might wisely be allocated to the former set of issues, rather than dozens of reporting streams overlapping on the latter set.

The real secrets are the things we aren't looking for. On a number of occasions, I have heard representatives from one U.S. agency or another repeat the phrase, "Our job is stealing the enemy's secrets." It's catchy and kind of sexy, and lexically illuminating in perhaps unintentional ways. First, the focus on "secrets" highlights the problem I have discussed earlier regarding the overvaluation of information based on its degree of protection. Applying the information economy template, this is like according value to a commodity based on its dearness to the seller, rather than to the purchaser—generally not a sound practice. You might think your 1972 *Superman* comic is worth $200, but I won't pay that unless it holds similar value for me. Nevertheless, modern intelligence analysis tends to attribute undue value to information obtained via "sensitive sources and methods"—i.e. the value of its degree of protection, its dearness to the seller—rather than information which meets purchaser requirements. Moves to embracing Open Source information in recent years have ameliorated this problem somewhat, but the unclassified realm remains something of an analytical and professional ghetto, and the technical compartmentalization of systems and workspaces continues to reinforce these barriers. Similarly, the emphasis on "stealing" speaks about the kinds of things intelligence collection tends to value—i.e. discrete factotums, previously identified in some kind of tasking order or plan, which can be retrieved from one context and reassembled in another. This is something like an old school archaeologist or tomb raider attempting to snatch a golden idol concealed within the Temple of the Chachapoyan Warriors. He may well succeed, but in doing so entirely miss the less obvious or less well protected pollen spores and ceramic fragments scattered about the site, which hold far more value as repositories of information regarding the age of the find, the diet of the Chachapoya, clues to climate change which may have influenced their history, etc.

The earlier stages of the imperial experience provide a greater opportunity for stumbling upon the unexpected and apparently unimportant—the spores rather than the idol—largely because the information environment remains so unstructured. This idea suggests an alternate reading for the now-established aphorism: there are known knowns, known unknowns, and unknown unknowns—a series progressively ordered by increasingly dangerous categories of information. In early days, say just after you have sacked Carthage or defeated the Nawab of Bengal, you might know very little, but you also know what you don't know, i.e. basically everything. This makes the "known unknowns" a very large category, but also makes the more dangerous "unknown unknowns" very small. As imperial experience progresses, as administrators learn the languages and jurists incorporate local legal principles, the "known known" flourishes in a rhizomatic way. Empire can read, without yet over-writing, the text of multiple information systems, which remain independent despite their imperial connections (e.g. British residents can functionally adjudicate local disputes, but there is not yet a casebook of Anglo-Indian law). Ironically, while improving routine efficiency, this trend increases the possibility of catastrophic error. For as "known unknown" shrinks with every census and cartographic survey, the "unknown unknown" consequently expands proportionately. While the analogy may be inexact, imperial power becomes more expert over time, and consequently more subject to the patterning and heuristic biases associated with the "Paradox of Expertise."[437] With the increasing presumption of knowledge, both the desire and capacity to learn appear to decline, a trend amplified by imperial policy choices.

The Romans and Ottomans deliberately abjured accumulating too much local experience in a given region, while the British cut themselves off from Indian society and edited out the texts which didn't fit their own narrative frames. A general imperial ailment is not an incapacity to know, but a choice not to know. We choose deliberately to make foreign personal associations a significant handicap to security clearances, as if seeking to ensure that those charged with understanding and assessing alternate views, activities and intentions are the least qualified to do. This is not a glib remark, as I recognize there are associated risks (just as there were behind the British, Roman and Ottoman choices); but there is far too little weight given to the opportunity cost of this risk management. My general assessment has been that empires

---

437 Rob Johnston, "Reducing Analytic Error: Integrating Methodologists into Teams of Substantive Experts," *Studies in Intelligence*, Vol. 47, No. 1, 2003, p. 64-66. Accessed online, 15 April 2008 at *http://www.au.af.mil/au/awc/awcgate/cia/reducing_analytic_error.htm*.

are always at an information deficit—telling more than they hear—and the deficit over time becomes associated with a lost capacity to listen. That quality of listening is key to generating truly alternative analysis, if as we might guess it takes surprising approaches to anticipate surprise. Alternative analysis is not a matter of offering $x + y$ could $= c$, as well as $x + y = b$, but rather wondering whether $x + y$ might not be irrelevant and looking at $d + n$. I would love, for example, to read a Red Cell paper on jihadi activity genuinely proceeding on the assumption that there really is a God active in human affairs. I'm not really concerned which side the authors put him on, but the fact that this would be so uncomfortable and foreign, although so completely integral to the issue at hand, is what makes it intriguing. The spiritual, the sexual, the aesthetic and the emotional are whole realms of human experience that condition the meaning, reception and transmission of knowledge, but are utterly barred from intelligence analysis except in the most clinical and dismissive fashion. Our imperial predecessors, particularly in their more successful enterprises, managed to participate at least for a time in these spaces. A Richard Burton, a Josephus or an Evliya Celebi was a human intelligence collector in the fullest sense of the term. They believed, they felt, tasted and touched—the kinds of things that human beings do, the kinds of things that matter—and it shows in the texts and insights they produced. They were certainly not carbon-based collection platforms, or bi-pedal signals and imagery systems reporting back simply what they had seen and heard. A perspective which presumes the role of an objective machine loses twice over by deliberately abjuring to assimilate the specifically human factors that only humans can collect, while making inevitable bias more difficult to detect in bureaucratically neutral discourse.

Perhaps the most fundamental principle of all is *the absolute necessity to question and question ourselves again*. Intelligence is not purely, or perhaps even mainly, about what is actually out there. Virtually every single aspect of the frame, language, and context we deploy shapes the information we receive—and by interrogating the world through these qualities we shape what we find there and what we leave behind. Consequently, we must remain vigilant if we are to distinguish what we find from what we have imposed—a distinction which works in two ways. Our preferred forms of reasoning and communicating are always at risk of altering the unfamiliar in order to make it familiar; conversely, the power relationship between the subject and object of interrogation may impose illegitimate differences and distinctions, making the familiar unfamiliar and consequently "other," with all the political and moral latitude that status entails. Taking these aspects for granted at best leaves us open to misdirection and blindness, and at worst can materially injure a world we engage with even the best of intentions. When we think of empire's legacy, the things which most rapidly come to mind are the physical artifacts—the roads and railways, mosques and arches. But the things which truly endure, the features we in many cases still live with, are artifacts of the imagination. From Roman Law to Indian caste quotas, for both good and ill, these aspects of lived experience were constructed and reinforced by the questions past empires asked of the world. I was once asked quite bluntly during my research interviews whether I believed there could be any such thing as an ethical empire. For me the jury is still out, but I have no doubt the answer is inextricably bound up with these problems of imperial intelligence.

> Don't be too proud of this technological terror you've constructed. The ability to destroy a planet is insignificant next to the power of the Force.
>
> Darth Vader
> Star Wars, 1977

Although a recurring theme in my research has been the way popular media historically both reflects and shapes a given information environment, I have so far largely resisted the temptation to pursue the same theme in my contemporary points of reference. Here at the end, however, I think it is worth reflecting on what is certainly the most widely communicated modern vision of Empire, and perhaps also the defining myth for many of my generation, prompting my confidence in its enduring relevance. While the story of *Star Wars* may be read in a variety of ways, with heroism, tragedy, sin and redemption, technological wizardry, or simply popcorn fun taking center stage, at the broadest level it is about the rise and fall of Empire, clearly a story related to that I have attempted to tell. Even more critically, this particular empire primarily rises and falls based on the ability of its leaders to "know" in sometimes uncomfortable and undervalued ways.

During the declining years of the Republic, the Jedi knights become increasingly blind to developments in the world around them, crippling their efforts to defend a particular political order. "The Dark Side clouds all," as Yoda would have it. This Dark Side of the Force is a near-perfect identification of knowledge with power—the same capacity that can strangle an opponent without a touch can also descry events half a galaxy away. However, Yoda's complaint does not mean that the Dark Side actually conceals anything. Rather, the "darkness" reflects a deliberate choice by the Jedi not to see the world in a particular way—they reject and denigrate those who do adopt this alternative perspective, and consequently fail utterly to anticipate or disrupt the plans of those who oppose them. As the future emperor explains to his apprentice, there are a great many alternative insights to be gained about the world, but they can't be learned from a Jedi.

Of course, in time the newly ascendant guardians of the Empire make precisely the same error. Their own experience of the Force is as lopsided as that of the Jedi, a handicap enhanced by their growing manifest power—as they enter the downward slope of my bell-curve chart. Despite Darth Vader's admonition regarding the relative value of the Force and technological prowess, the imperial perspective becomes increasingly technological (as does Vader's physical person) in how it can physically perceive the world, and consequently how it orders and values those perceptions. Eventually, the Empire fails and collapses, not because it is brought down by a band of cinematically ill-conceived teddy bears, but because its leaders deliberately chose not to recognize alternative ways of understanding the world around them. In the films, as in the worlds I have explored, the role of choice is fundamental. While the imperial condition creates both opportunities and constraints to knowing the world, imperial actors finally choose their destinies by choosing the ways they are willing to know. With this in mind, it is perhaps fitting to conclude with the words which greet Luke Skywalker's ultimate choice, and bring the end of empire. So be it, Jedi.

BIBLIOGRAPHY

Achilles Tatius, *Leucippe and Clitophon,* trans. Tim Whitmarsh, Oxford and New York: Oxford University, 2002.

Adonis. *Sufism and Surrealism*, trans. Judith Cumberbatch, London: Saqi, 2005.

Agoston, Gabor. "Information, Ideology, and Limits of Imperial Policy: Ottoman Grand Strategy in the Context of Ottoman-Hapsburg Rivalry," *The Early Modern Ottomans*, pre-publication draft.

Aksan, Virgina. "Ottoman Political Writing, 1768-1808," *International Journal of Middle East Studies*, Vol. 25, No. 1 (Feb. 1993).

Al-Qattan, Najwa. "Dhimmis in the Muslim Court: Legal Autonomy and Religious Discrimination," *International Journal of Middle East Studies*, Vol. 31, No. 3 (Aug 1999).

Alston, Richard. *Soldier and Society in Roman Egypt: A Social History*, New York: Routledge, 1995.

Ammianus Marcellinus, *Roman History*, trans. C.D. Yonge, London: Bohn, 1862.

Anderson, J.N.D. "Law as a Social Force in Islamic Culture and History," *Bulletin of the School of Oriental and African Studies, University of London*, Vol. 20, No. 1/3, Studies in Honour of Sir Ralph Turner, Director of the School of Oriental and African Studies, 1937-57 (1957).

Appadurai, Arjun. *Modernity at Large: Cultural Dimensions of Globalization*, Minneapolis and London: University of Minnesota, 1996.

Applebaum, Shimon. "Zealots: The Case for Revaluation," *The Journal of Roman Studies*, Vol. 61(1971).

Armstrong, David. "Law, Justice and the Idea of a World Society," *International Affairs (Royal Institute of International Affairs, 1944-)*, Vol. 75, No. 3 (Jul 1999).

Austin, N.J.E. and N.B. Rankov. *Exploratio: Military and Political Intelligence in the Roman World from the Second Punic War to the Battle of Adrianople*, New York: Routledge, 1995.

Baard, Mark. "Sentient World," *The Register*, 23 June 2007.

Bach, Johann Sebastian. *Fugue No. 2 in C minor, BWV 847, The Well-Tempered Clavier, Book 1,* Bach-Gesellschaft Ausgabe, 1866.

Bacharach, Jere L. "Administrative Complexes, Palaces and Citadels; Changes in the Loci of Medieval Muslim Rule," *The Ottoman City and Its Parts: Urban Structure and Social Order,* eds. Irene Bierman, Rifa'at Abou-El-Haj, and Donald Preziosi, New Rochelle, NY: Aristide D. Caratzas, 1991.

Bacon, Francis. "Of Heresies," *Meditationes Sacrae, in The Works of Francis Bacon,* Vol. 2, Boston: Houghton, Mifflin and Company, 1897.

Baer, Gabriel. "The Administrative, Economic and Social Functions of Turkish Guilds," *International Journal of Middle East Studies,* Vol. 1, No. 1 (Jan 1970).

Baker, James A., III and Lee Hamilton, Co-Chairs. *The Iraq Study Group Report,* New York: Vintage Books, 2006.

Bangert, William. *A History of the Society of Jesus,* St. Louis: Institute of Jesuit Sources, 1972.

Barkey, Karen. "In Different Times: Scheduling and Social Control in the Ottoman Empire, 1550 to 1650," *Comparative Studies in Society and History,* Vol. 38, No. 3 (July 1996).

Barnes, John Robert. "The Dervish Orders in the Ottoman Empire," *The Dervish Lodge: Architecture, Art and Sufism in Ottoman Turkey,* ed. Raymond Lifchez, Berkeley and Los Angeles: University of California, 1992.

Barthes, Roland. *The Semiotic Challenge,* trans. Richard Howard, New York: Hill and Wang, 1988.

Bartsch, Shadi. *Decoding the Ancient Novel: The Reader and the Role of Description in Heliodorus and Achilles Tatius,* Princeton, NJ: Princeton Univ., 1989.

Baudrillard, Jean. *Forget Foucault,* New York: Semiotext(e), 1987.

_____. *The Intelligence of Evil or the Lucidity Pact, trans.* Chris Turner, Oxford and New York: Berg, 2005.

Bayly, C.A. *Empire and Information: Intelligence Gathering and Social Communication in India, 1780-1870*, Cambridge and New York: Cambridge University, 1996.

Behar, Cem. *A Neighborhood in Ottoman Istanbul: Fruit Vendors and Civil Servants in the Kasap Ilyas Mahalle*, Albany: State University of New York, 2003.

Bentham, Jeremy. *Panopticon* in *The Works of Jeremy Bentham*, Vol. 4, ed. John Bowring, New York: Russell and Russell, 1962.

Best, Steven and Douglas Kellner. *Postmodern Theory: Critical Interrogations*, New York: Guilford, 1991.

Bhabha, Homi. *The Location of Culture*, London and New York: Routledge, 1994.

Bhatia, Michael. "Fighting Words: Naming Terrorists, Bandits, Rebels and other Violent Actors," *Third World Quarterly*, Vol. 26, No. 1 (2005).

Bodnar, John. *Warning Analysis for the Information Age: Rethinking the Intelligence Process*, Washington, D.C.: Joint Military Intelligence College, 2003.

Bogdanos, Matthew. "Fighting for Iraq's Culture," *New York Times*, 6 March 2007.

Bon, Ottavio. *The Sultan's Seraglio: An Intimate Portrait of Life at the Ottoman Court [from the Seventeenth Century Edition of John Withers]*, London: Saqi Books, 1996.

Bonn Agreement on Provisional Arrangements in Afghanistan, II.2, German Foreign Office, 2001.

Boot, Max. "Can Petraeus Pull it Off?," *Weekly Standard*, 30 April 2007

Borges, Jorge Luis. *A Universal History of Infamy*, Trans. Norman Thomas di Giovanni, New York: E.P. Dutton, 1972.

Bowersock, G.W. *Fiction as History: Nero to Julian*, Berkley, Los Angeles and London: University of California, 1994.

BIBLIOGRAPHY (Continued)

Bozeman, Adda. *Politics and Culture in International History: From the Ancient Near East to the Opening of the Modern Age*, 2d Ed., New Brunswick and London: Transaction Publishers, 1994.

_____. *Strategic Intelligence and Statecraft*: Selected Essays, London: Brassey's, 1992.

Bruce, George. *The Stranglers: The Cult of Thuggee and Its Overthrow in British India*, New York: Harcourt Brace, 1968.

Burke, Peter. *A Social History of Knowledge: From Gutenberg to Diderot*, Cambridge: Polity Press, 2000.

Burton, Isabel. *The Life of Sir Richard F. Burton, K.C.M.G., F.R.G.S., by His Wife*, London: Chapman and Hall, 1893.

Cambone, Stephen. *Statement for the Record by Dr. Stephen A. Cambone Under Secretary of Defense for Intelligence before the Senate Armed Services Committee Strategic Forces Subcommittee*, 7 April 2004.

Campbell, Brian. "The Marriage of Soldiers under the Empire," *The Journal of Roman Studies*, Vol. 68 (1978).

Campbell, David. *Writing Security: United States Foreign Policy and the Politics of Identity*, Minneapolis: University of Minnesota, 1992.

Campbell, Leroy. *Mithraic Iconography and Ideology*, Leiden: Brill, 1968.

Carpenter, Edmund, Frederick Varley, Robert Flaherty. *Eskimo*, Toronto, University of Toronto, 1959.

Cassius Dio. *Roman History: The Reign of Augustus, trans.* Ian Scott-Kilvert, London: Penguin, 1987.

_____. *Roman History*, Vol. IX, Loeb Classical Library Edition, trans. Earnest Cary, Cambridge: Harvard, 1927.

_____. *Roman History*, Vol. VIII, Loeb Classical Library Edition, trans. Earnest Cary, Cambridge: Harvard, 1925.

Chakrabarti, Dilip K. "The Development of Archaeology in the Indian Subcontinent," *World Archaeology* 13, No. 3 (February 1982).

BIBLIOGRAPHY (Continued)

Chakrabarty, Dipesh. *Habitations of Modernity: Essays in the Wake of Subaltern Studies,* Chicago and London: University of Chicago, 2002.

Chakravarty, Gautam. *The Indian Mutiny and the British Imagination,* Cambridge: Cambridge University, 2005.

Chiarelli, Peter and **Patrick Michaelis,** "Winning the Peace: the Requirement for Full-Spectrum Operations," *Military Review,* (July-August 2005).

Marcus Tullius Cicero, *De Officiis,* trans. Walter Miller, Loeb Classical Library, Cambridge: Harvard, 1913.

Cohen, Shay J.D. "History and Historiography in Against Apion," *History and Theory,* Vol. 27 No. 4 (1988).

Cohn, Bernard. *Colonialism and Its Forms of Knowledge: the British in India,* Princeton: Princeton University, 1996

Connery, Christopher Leigh. *The Empire of the Text: Writing Authority in Early Imperial China,* New York: Rowman and Littlefield, 1998

Connolly, William E. "*Identity and Difference in Global Politics,*" *International/Intertextual Relations: Postmodern Readings of World Politics, eds.* James Der Derian and Michael Shapiro, Lexington, MA: Lexington Books, 1989.

Conrad, Joseph. "Heart of Darkness," *Great Short Works of Joseph Conrad,* New York: Harper and Row, 1967, p. 242.

Culler, Jonathon. *On Deconstruction: Theory and Criticism after Structuralism,* Ithaca, NY: Cornell Univ., 1982.

Dalrymple, William. *White Mughals: Love and Betrayal in Eighteenth Century India,* New Delhi: Viking, 2002.

Dankoff, Robert. *An Ottoman Mentality: The World of Evliya Celebi,* Leiden and Boston: Brill, 2004.

Davis, John. "History and the people without Europe," *Other Histories,* ed. Kirsten Hastrup, London and New York: Routledge, 1992.

BIBLIOGRAPHY (Continued)

De Certeau, Michel. *The Practice of Everyday Life*, trans. Steven Randall, Berkeley: University of California, 1984.

de Thevenot, Jean. *The Travels of Monsieur de Thevenot into the Levant*, London, Printed by H. Clark, for H. Faithorne, J. Adamson, C. Skegnes, and T. Newborough, 1687.

Declassified Key Judgments of the National Intelligence Estimate: "*Trends in Global Terrorism: Implications for the United States*," dated April 2006, accessed 7 Feb 2007 at http://www.dni.gov/press_releases/ Declassified_NIE_Key_Judgments.pdf

Delaney, David. "Making Nature/Marking Humans: Law as a Site of (Cultural) Production," *Annals of the Association of American Geographers*, Vol. 91, No. 3 (Sep 2001).

Deleuze, Gilles. *Repetition and Difference*, trans. Paul Patton, New York: Columbia, 1994.

Deleuze, Gilles and Felix Guattari. *A Thousand Plateaus: Capitalism and Schizophrenia*, trans. Brian Massumi, Minneapolis: University of Minnesota, 1987.

Depuydt, Leo. "The Date of Death of Jesus of Nazareth," *Journal of the American Oriental Society*, Vol. 122, No. 3. (Jul-Sep, 2002).

Der Derian, James. *Anti-Diplomacy: Spies, Terror, Speed, and War*, Cambridge: Blackwell, 1992.

Derrida, Jacques. *Of Grammatology*, trans. Gayatri Spivak, Baltimore: Johns Hopkins, 1976.

Doyle, Arthur Conan. "The Adventure of the Empty House," *The Complete Sherlock Holmes—Novels and Stories*, Vol. II, New Delhi: Classic Paperbacks, p. 218.

Doyle, Michael. *Empires*, Ithaca, NY and London: Cornell University, 1986.

Dresch, Paul. *Tribes, Government and History in Yemen*, Oxford: Clarendon, 1989.

Duff, Alexander. *The Indian Rebellion: Its Causes and Results in a Series of Letters*, New York: R. Carter, 1858.

Edwardes, Herbert and **Herman Merivale,** *Life of Sir Henry Lawrence,* London: Smith, Elder & Co., 1873.

Edwards, William. *Personal Adventures During the Indian Rebellion in Rohilcund, Futtehghur and Oude,* Allahabad (India): Legend Publications, 1974 (First published 1858).

Eftimiades, Nicholas. *Chinese Intelligence Operations,* Annapolis, MD: Naval Institute Press, 1994

Elam, Diane. *Feminism and Deconstruction,* New York and London: Routledge, 1994.

Evliya Efendi. *Narrative of Travels in Europe, Asia and Africa,* trans. Joseph van Hammer, London and New York: Johnson Reprint, 1968, (First Printing 1834).

Fadok, David. *John Boyd and John Warden: Air Power's Quest for Strategic Paralysis,* Maxwell AFB, AL: Air University Press, 1995.

Faroqhi, Suraiya. "Civilian Society and Political Power in the Ottoman Empire: A Report on Research in Collective Biography (1480-1830), *International Journal of Middle East Studies* Vol. 17, No. 1 (Feb 1995).

_____. "Social Mobility Among the Ottoman 'Ulema in the Late Sixteenth Century," *International Journal of Middle East Studies,* Vol. 4, No. 2 (Apr 1973).

_____. *Subjects of the Sultan: Culture and Everyday Life in the Ottoman Empire,* London and New York: I.B. Tauris, 2000.

_____. "The Tekki of Haci Bektas: Social Position and Economic Activities," *International Journal of Middle East Studies,* Vol. 7, No. 2 (April 1976).

Farrell, J.G. *The Siege of Krishnapur,* New York: New York Review Book, 2004.

Ferguson, Niall. *Empire: The Rise and Demise of the British World Order and the Lessons for Global Power,* London and New York: Basic Books, 2002.

_____. *Colossus: The Price of America's Empire*, New York: Penguin, 2004.

Finkel, Caroline. *Osman's Dream: The Story of the Ottoman Empire 1300-1923*, New York: Basic Books, 2005.

Ford, Simon. *The Situationist International: A User's Guide*, London: Black Dog, 2005.

Foucault, Michel. *The History of Sexuality Volume I, trans. Robert Hurley*, New York: Pantheon, 1978.

_____. *Power/Knowledge: Selected Interviews and Other Writings, 1972-1977*, ed. Colin Gordon, trans. Colin Gordon, Leo Marshall, John Mepham and Kate Soper, New Nork: Pantheon, 1980.

_____. *The Archaeology of Knowledge,* trans. A.M. Sheridan Smith, New York: Harper & Row, 1972.

_____. *The Order of Things: An Archaeology of the Human Sciences*, New York: Vintage, 1994.

_____. *Discipline and Punish: The Birth of the Prison*, trans. Alan Sheridan, New York: Vintage, 1991.

Freakley, Benjamin. *Infantry*, (March-April 2005).

Freitag, Sandria. "Crime in the Social Order of Colonial North India," *Modern Asian Studies*, Vol. 25, No. 2 (May, 1991).

Ganss, George, trans. *The Constitution of the Society of Jesus*, St. Louis: Institute of Jesuit Sources, 1970.

Garlick, Steve. "Distinctly Feminine: On the Relationship Between Men and Art,"*Berkeley Journal of Sociology*, 48 (2004).

Gardner, Alexander. *Soldier and Traveller: Memories of Alexander Gardner, Colonel of Artillery in the Service of Maharaja Ranjit Singh*, ed. Hugh Pearse, Jullundur City: Languages Department, Punjab, 1970 (First printing 1898).

Gardner, Jane F. *Being a Roman Citizen*, London and New York: Routledge, 1993.

BIBLIOGRAPHY (Continued)

Geertz, Clifford. "Local Knowledge: Fact and Law in Comparative Perspective," *Local Knowledge*, New York: Basic Books, 1983.

Gerber, Haim. *State, Society and Law in Islam: Ottoman Law in Comparative Perspective*, Albany, NY: State University of New York, 1994.

Gifford, Paul. "Some Recent Developments in African Christianity," *African Affairs*, Vol. 93, No. 373 (Oct 1994).

Gilsenan, Michael. *Recognizing Islam: Religion and Society in the Modern Middle East*, London and New York: I.B. Tauris, 2000.

Gocek, Fatma Muge and Marc David Baer. "Social Boundaries of Ottoman Women's Experiences," *Women in the Ottoman Empire: Middle Eastern Women in the Early Modern Era*, ed. Madeline Zilfi, Leiden, New York, Koln: Brill, 1997.

Goodwin, Godfrey. "The Dervish Architecture of Anatolia," *The Dervish Lodge: Architecture, Art and Sufism in Ottoman Turkey*, ed. Raymond Lifchez, Berkeley and Los Angeles: University of California, 1992.

Gordon, Stewart. *Marathas, Marauders, and State Formation*, Delhi: Oxford University, 1994.

Gowing, Alain. "Tacitus and the Client Kings," *Journal of the American Philological Association(1974-)*, Vol. 120, 1990.

Grubb, Judith Evans. *Women and the Law in the Roman Empire: A Sourcebook on Marriage, Divorce and Widowhood*, London and New York: Routledge, 2002.

Grunewald, Thomas. *Bandits in the Roman Empire: Myth and Reality*, trans, John Drinkwater, London and New York: Routledge, 1999.

Guastello, Stephen. *Chaos, Catastrophe and Human Affairs*, Mahwak, NJ: Lawrence Erlbaum, 1995.

Gubbins, M.R. *The Mutinies in Oudh*, Patna: Janaki Prakashan, 1978 (First published 1858).

Guha, Ranajit. *History at the Limit of World History*, New York: Columbia University, 2002.

BIBLIOGRAPHY (Continued)

Guha, Ranajit and **Gayatri Chakravarty Spivak.** eds. *Selected Subaltern Studies*, New York: Oxford University, 1988.

Haboush, JaHyun Kim. "Contesting Chinese Time, nationalizing Temporal Space: Temporal Inscription in Late Choson Korea," *Time, Temporality, and Imperial Transition: East Asia from Ming to Qing*, Ed. Lynn Strive, Honolulu: University of Hawaii and the Association for Asian Studies, 2005.

Hardt, Michael and Antonio Negri. *Empire*, Cambridge and London: Harvard University, 2000.

Harlan, Josiah. *Central Asia: Personal Narrative of Josiah Harlan, 1823-1841*, ed. Frank Ross, London: Luzac & Co., 1939.

Harland-Jacobs, Jessica. *Builders of Empire: Freemasons and British Imperialism, 1717-1927*, Chapel Hill, NC: University of North Carolina, 2007.

Hathaway, Jane. "The Military Household in Ottoman Egypt," *International Journal of Middle East Studies*, Vol. 27, No. 1 (Feb 1995).

Hattox, Ralph S. *Coffee and Coffeehouses: The Origins of a Social Beverage in the Medieval Near East*, Seattle: University of Washington, 1985.

Herodotus. *The Histories*, trans. A. D. Godley. Cambridge: Harvard University Press, 1920.

Heyd, Uriel. Review of Stanford Shaw, *Ottoman Egypt in the Eighteenth Century, Bulletin of the School of Oriental and African Studies*, Vol. 26, No. 1 (1963).

Hilton, Edward. *The Mutiny Records, Oudh and Lucknow (1856-57)*, Lahore: Panco Press, 1975.

Hobsbawm, E.J. *Bandits*, New York: Delacorte Press, 1969.

Hofstadter, Douglas. *Godel, Escher, Bach: an Eternal Golden Braid*, New York: Basic Books, 1999.

Hollevoet, Christel. "Wandering in the city flanerie to dérive and after: the cognitive mapping of urban space," *The Power of the City/The City of Power*, New York: Whitney Museum of American Art, 1992.

BIBLIOGRAPHY (Continued)

The Holy Bible, New International Version, Cambridge: Cambridge Univ., 1984.

Hutton, James. *Thugs and Dacoits of India*, Delhi: Gian, 1981 (First published 1857).

Imber, Colin. *Ebu's-su'ud: The Islamic Legal Tradition*, Stanford: Stanford University, 1997.

_____. *The Ottoman Empire, 1300-1650: The Structure of Power*, New York: Palgrave Macmillan, 2002.

Inden, Ronald. *Imagining India*, Bloomington, IN: Indiana University, 2000.

Irwin, Robert. *For Lust of Knowing: The Orientalists and Their Enemies*, London: Allen Lane, 2006.

Itzkowitz, Norman. *Ottoman Empire and Islamic Tradition*, Chicago and London: University of Chicago, 1972.

Jalali, Ali. "The Future of Afghanistan," *Parameters*, Spring 2006.

Jablonsky, David. "Time's Arrow, Time's Cycle: Metaphors for a Period of Transition," *Parameters*, (Winter 1997-1998), p. 4-27

Jameson, Fredric. *Postmodernism, or, the Cultural Logic of Late Capitalism.* Durham: Duke University, 1991.

Jasanoff, Maya. "Before and After Said," *London Review of Books*, 8 June 2006.

Josephus, Flavius. *The Works of Flavius Josephus.*, William Whiston, trans., Auburn and Buffalo: John E. Beardsley, 1895; available online at: *http://www.perseus. tufts.edu/cgi-bin/text?doc=Perseus%3Aabo%3 Atlg%2C0526%2C004&query=init*

Jung, Carl. *Memories, Dreams, Reflections*, New York: Vintage Books, 1965.

Kafadar, Cemal. "Self and Others: The Diary of a Dervish in Seventeenth Century Istanbul and First Person Narratives in Ottoman Literature," *Studia Islamica*, LXIX, 1969.

BIBLIOGRAPHY (Continued)

Karamustafa, Ahmet. "Introduction to Ottoman Cartography," and "Military, Administrative and Scholarly Maps and Plans," *The History of Cartography, Vol. 2 Book 1: Cartography in Tradional Islamic and South Asian Societies*, eds. J.B. Harley and David Woodward, Chicago: Univ. of Chicago, 1992.

Karsh, Efraim. *Islamic Imperialism: A History*, New Haven and London: Yale, 2006.

Kautilya, *The Arthashastra*, ed. and trans. L.N. Rangarajan, New Delhi: Penguin, 1992.

Kaye, Alan S. "The Etymology of 'Coffee': The Dark Brew," *Journal of the American Oriental Society*, Vol. 106, No. 3 (Jul-Sep 1996).

Kaye, John. *History of the Indian Mutiny of 1857-8*, Vol I., ed. George Malleson, Westport, CT: Greenwood Press, 1971 (First published 1897).

Kemp, Percy. "An Eighteenth-Century Turkish Intelligence Report," *International Journal of Middle East Studies*, Vol. 16, No. 4 (Nov 1984).

Kennedy, Dane. *The Highly Civilized Man: Richard Burton and the Victorian World*, Cambridge: Harvard University, 2005.

_____. "'Captain Burton's Oriental Muck Heap': The Book of the Thousand Nights and the Uses of Orientalism," *The Journal of British Studies*, Vol. 39, No. 3 (Jul 2000).

Kennedy, Paul. *The Rise and Fall of the Great Powers*, New York: Random House, 1987.

Khadduri, Majid. *War and Peace in the Law of Islam*, Baltimore: John Hopkins, 1955.

Kipling, Rudyard. *Kim*, London: Mcmillan, 1944.

_____. "The Man Who Would Be King," *Kipling: A Selection of His Stories and Poems*, Vol. II, ed. John Beecroft, Garden City, NY: Doubleday, 1956.

Kristeva, Julia. *Revolution in Poetics*, trans. Margaret Waller, New York: Columbia Univ., 1984.

Kuhn, Thomas. *The Structure of Scientific Revolutions, 3d* ed., Chicago and London: University of Chicago, 1996.

Kuhns, Woodrow. "Intelligence Failure: Forecasting and the Lessons of Epistemology," *Paradoxes of Strategic Intelligence*, ed. Richard Betts and Thomas Mahnken, London and Portland: Frank Cass, 2003.

Kunt, Metin Ibrahim. "Ethnic-Regional (Cins) Solidarity in the Seventeenth Century Ottoman Establishment," *International Journal of Middle East Studies*, Vol. 5, No. 3 (1974).

Laclau, Ernesto. "The Impossibility of Society," *Canadian Journal of Political and Social Theory*, Vol. 7.

Lalu, Pramesh. "The Grammar of Domination and the Subjection of Agency: Colonial Texts and Modes of Evidence," *History and Theory*, Vol. 39 No. 4 (Dec 2000).

Lambrick, H.T. "Editor's Introduction" in *Sindh, and the Races That Inhabit the Valley of the Indus*, by Richard Burton, Karachi: Oxford University, 1972.

Lane, Edward William. *The Modern Egyptians*, New York: E.P. Dutton, 1936.

Lang, Arthur Moffat. *Lahore to Lucknow: The Indian Mutiny Journal of Arthur Moffatt Lang*, ed. David Blomfield, London: Leo Cooper, 1992.

Lao-Tzu, *Te-Tao Ching*, trans. Robert Henricks, New York: Modern Library, 1993.

Lapidus, Ira M. "Sufism and Ottoman Islamic Society," *The Dervish Lodge: Architecture, Art and Sufism in Ottoman Turkey*, ed. Raymond Lifchez, Berkeley and Los Angeles: University of California, 1992.

Laplace, Pierre-Simon. *Philosophical Essay on Probabilities*, trans. Andrew Dale, New York: Springer-Verlag, (1819) 1995.

Lawrence, Henry. *Letters of Sir Henry Montgomery Lawrence (Selections from the correspondence of Sir Henry Montgomery Lawrence (1806-1857) during the Siege of Lucknow from March to July, 1857)*, ed. Sheo Bahadur Singh, New Delhi: Sagar Publications, 1978.

Lawrence, T.E. *Letters of T.E. Lawrence*, ed. David Garnett, New York: Doubleday, Doran & Co., 1939.

_____. *Seven Pillars of Wisdom: A Triumph*, Garden City, NY: Doubleday, Doran & Co., 1935.

_____. *T.E. Lawrence: Selected Letters*, ed. Malcolm Brown, New York and London: W.W. Norton and Company, 1989.

Leach, Eleanor Winsor. *The Rhetoric of Space: Literary and Artistic Representations of Landscape in Republican and Augustan Rome*, Princeton, NJ: Princeton Univ., 1988.

Lendon, J.E. *Empire of Honor: The Art of Government in the Roman World*, Oxford: Clarendon, 1997.

Lewis, Bernard. "Registers on Iran and Adharbayan in the Ottoman Defter-I Khaqani," *Studies in Classical Islam (7th-16th Centuries)*, London: Varorum Reprints, 1976.

Lifchez, Raymond. "The Lodges of Istanbul," and Klaus Krieser, "Dervish Living," *The Dervish Lodge: Architecture, Art and Sufism in Ottoman Turkey*, ed. Raymond Lifchez, Berkeley and Los Angeles: University of California, 1992.

Lindner, Rudi. *Nomads and Ottomans in Medieval Anatolia*, Bloomington, IN: Indiana University, 1983.

Lintott, Andrew. "What Was the 'Imperium Romanum,'" *Greece & Rome*, 2nd Ser. Vol. 28, No. 1, 1981.

Litowitz, Douglas. *Postmodern Philosophy of Law*, Lawrence, KS: University of Kansas, 1997.

Livy, *History of Rome*, Vol. 5, Everyman's Library, trans. Canon Roberts, New York: E.P. Dutton, 1912, 34:2.

Loescher, Michael, Chris Schroeder, Charles Thomas. *Proteus: Insights from 2020*, Washington, D.C.: 2000

Luce, Edward. "The Saffron Revolution," *Financial Times* (4 May 2002).

Luce, T.J.. "Ancient Views on the Cause of Bias in Historical Writing," *Classical Philology*, Vol. 84, No. 1(Jan 1989).

Lucian, *The True History, The Works of Lucian of Samosata*, Vol. II, trans. H.W. Fowler and F.G. Fowler, Oxford: Clarendon, 1905

Lunt, James. *Bokhara Burnes*, London: Faber and Faber, 1969.

Luttwak, Edward. *The Grand Strategy of the Roman Empire: From the First Century A.D. to the Third*, Baltimore and London: Johns Hopkins, 1976.

Lyon, David, ed. *Theorizing Surveillance: The Panopticon and Beyond*, Portland: Willan, 2006.

Lyotard, Jean-Francois. *The Postmodern Condition: A Report on Knowledge*, trans. Geoff Bennington and Brian Massumi, Minneapolis: University of Minnesota, (1979) 1993.

MacIntyre, Ben. *The Man Who Would Be King: The First American in Afghanistan*, New York: Farrar, Straus, Giroux, 2004.

MacMullen, Ramsay. *Enemies of the Roman Order: Treason, Unrest and Alienation in the Empire*, Cambridge: Harvard University Press, 1966.

_____. "Provincial Languages in the Roman Empire," *The American Journal of Philology*, Vol. 87, No. 1 (1966).

Maier, Charles. *Among Empires: American Ascendancy and Its Predecessors*, Cambridge and London: Harvard, 2006.

Mader, Gottfried. *Josephus and the Politics of Historiography: Apologetic and Impression Management in the Bellum Judaicum*, Leiden, Boston, Koln: Brill, 2000.

Mahmood, Tahir. "Interaction of Islam and Public Law in Independent India," *Perspectives on Islamic Law, Justice, and Society*, ed. R.S. Khare, Lanham, MD: Rowman and Littlefield, 1999.

Mandaville, Jon. "Usurious Piety: The Cash Waqf Controversy in the Ottoman Empire," *International Journal of Middle East Studies*, Vol. 10, No. 3 (Aug 1979).

Marin, Louis. *Utopics: Spatial Play*, trans. Robert Vollrath, New Jersey: Humanities Press, 1984.

Marx, Karl and Friedrich Engels. *The First Indian War of Independence, 1857-1859*, Moscow: Foreign Languages Publishing House, 1959.

Mattern, Susan. *Rome and the Enemy: Imperial Strategy in the Principate*, Berkeley: University of California, 1999.

McDonough, Thomas. "Situationist Space," *October*, No. 67 (Winter 1994).

McGinn, Thomas. *Prostitution, Sexuality and the Law in Ancient Rome*, New York and Oxford: Oxford University, 1998.

McKevitt, Gerald. *Brokers of Culture: Italian Jesuits in the American West 1848-1919*, Stanford: Stanford University Press, 2007.

McNaugher, Thomas. "The Real Meaning of Military Transformation: Rethinking the Revolution," *Foreign Affairs*, Vol. 86, No. 1 (Jan-Feb 2007), p. 140-147.

Menage, V.L. "Some Notes on the 'devshirme,'" *Bulletin of the Journal of Oriental and African Studies*, Vol. 29, No. 1 (1966).

Merivale, Charles. *A General History of Rome*, New York: Harper and Brothers, 1886.

Metcalf, Thomas. *Ideologies of the Raj*, Cambridge: Cambridge University, 1994.

Meyers, Jeffrey. "T.E. Lawrence in His Letters," *T.E. Lawrence: Soldier, Writer, Legend—New Essays*, ed. Jeffrey Meyers, London: Macmillan, 1989.

Michaels, Jim. "U.S. Advisors Find Joint Patrols with Iraqis Don't Go as Planned," *USA Today*, 5 Feb 2007.

Miller, Barnette. *Beyond the Sublime Porte*, New Haven: Yale, 1931.

BIBLIOGRAPHY (Continued)

Miller, Robert, ed. *The Complete Gospels*, San Francisco: HarperCollins, 1994.

Millward, James. "The Qing Formation, the Mongol Legacy and the 'End of History' in Early Modern Central Eurasia," *The Qing Formation in World Historical* Time, Cambridge and London: Harvard, 2004.

Mitchell, W.J.T. "Postcolonial Culture, Postimperial Criticism," *Transition*, 56 (1992).

Moir, Martin Ian. *A Study of the History and Organization of the Political and Secret Department of the East India Company, the Board of Control and the India Office 1784-1919* with a Summary *List of Records*, thesis in support of University of London Diploma in Archive Administration, August, 1996.

Moisi, Dominique. "The Clash of Emotions: Fear, Humiliation, Hope and the New World Order," *Foreign Affairs*, Vol. 86, No. 1 (Jan/Feb 2007).

Momigliano, Arnaldo. *Alien Wisdom: The Limits of Hellenization*, Cambridge: Cambridge University, 1971.

Momigliano, Arnaldo. "Tradition and the Classical Historian," *History and Theory* Vol. 11 No. 3 (1972).

Moreland, John. *Archaeology and Text*, London: Duckworth, 2001.

Motyl, Alexander J. "Why Empires Reemerge: Imperial Collapse and Imperial Revival in Comparative Perspective," *Comparative Politics*, Vol. 31, No. 2 (Jan 1999).

Mukherjee, Rudrangshu. " 'Satan Let Loose upon Earth': The Kanpur Massacres in India in the Revolt of 1857," *Past and Present*, No. 128 (Aug 1990).

Mukherjee, Upamanyo Pablo. *Crime and Empire: The Colony in Nineteenth-Century Fictions of Crime*, Oxford: Oxford University, 2003.

Necipoglu, Gulru. *Architecture, Ceremonial, and Power: The Topkapi Palace in the Fifteenth and Sixteenth Centuries*, Cambridge: MIT, 1991.

BIBLIOGRAPHY (Continued)

Nietzsche, Friedrich. *On the Genealogy of Morals*, trans. Walter Kaufmann and R.J. Holligndale, New York: Vintage Books, 1989.

National Archives of India, Home, Thagi and Dacaity, B 1. No. 16, 1890.

National Archives of India, Home, Thagi and Dacaity, B. 1, No. 8, 1868 [1858].

National Archives of India, Home, Thagi and Dacaity, B.1, No. 4, 1838.

"Arrested in Kathmandu: Does the new US embassy need a hijab?" *Nepali Times*, #368 (28 Sep 07 – 4 Oct 07); accessed 11 Oct 07 online at: *http://www.nepalitimes.com/issue/368/NepaliPan/14007.*

Nicolet, Claude. *Space, Geography, and Politics in the Early Roman Empire*, Ann Arbor: University of Michigan, 1991.

Oriental and India Office Collections, Mss. Eur., D1188.

Ortega y Gasset, Jose. *History as a System, and Other Essays Toward a Philosophy of History*, New York: Norton, 1961.

Parks, Fanny. *Begums, Thugs and White Mughals*, London: Sickle Moon, 2002 (originally published as *Wanderings of a Pilgrim in Search of the Picturesque*).

Peck, Graham. *Two Kinds of Time*, 2d Edition, Revised and Abridged, Boston: Houghton Mifflin, 1967.

Peirce, Leslie. *Morality Tales: Law and Gender in the Ottoman Court of Aintab*, Berkely, Los Angeles and London: University of California Press, 2003.

_____. *The Imperial Harem: Women and Sovereignty in the Ottoman Empire*, New York and Oxford: Oxford University, 1993.

_____. "Beyond Harem Walls," *Gendered Domains: Rethinking Public and Private in Women's History*, eds. Dorothy Helly and Susan Reverby, Ithaca and London: Cornell, 1992.

Pendall, David. "Persistent Surveillance and Its Implications for the Common Operating Picture," *Military Review*, Nov-Dec 2005, p. 41-50.

BIBLIOGRAPHY (Continued)

Perdue, Peter. "The Qing Empire in Eurasian Time and Space: Lessons from the Galdan Campaigns," *The Qing Formation in World Historical Time,* Cambridge and London: Harvard, 2004.

Phelan, John Leddy. "Authority and Flexibility in the Spanish Imperial Bureaucracy," *Administrators of Empire,* ed. Mark Burkholder, Brookfield, VT and Aldershot, UK: Ashgate, 1998.

Powell, Nancy. Testimony before the House International Relations Committee, "Policy in Afghanistan," *Congressional Quarterly,* 22 September 2005.

Price, David. "America the Ambivalent; Quietly Selling Anthropology to the CIA," *Anthropology Today,* December 2005, Vol. 21, No. 5, (p.1-2).

Purvis, Trevor and Alan Hunt. "Discourse, Ideology, Discourse, Ideology, Discourse, Ideology..." *The British Journal of Sociology,* Vol. 44, No.3 (Sep 1993).

Quaraishi, Salim al-Din. *Cry for Freedom: Proclamations of Muslim Revolutionaries of 1857,* Lahore: Sang-e-Meel Publications, 1997.

Raheja, Gloria Goodwin. "Caste, Colonialism and the Speech of the Colonized: Entextualization and Disciplinary Control in India, *American Ethnologist,* Vol. 23, No. 3 (Aug 1996).

Raj, Kapil. "Colonial Encounters and the Forging of New Knowledge and National Identities: Great Britain and India, 1760-1850," *Nature and Empire: Science and the Colonial Enterprise,* ed. Roy MacLeod, Osiris, Vol. 15, 2000.

Rajak, Tessa. *Josephus,* 2d ed., London: Geral Duckworth and Co., 2002.

Rajan, Balachandra. *Under Western Eyes: India from Milton to Macaulay,* Durham and London: Duke University, 1999.

Reclus, Elisee. *The Earth: A Descriptive History of the Phenomena of the Life of the Globe,* trans. B.B. Woodward, ed. Henry Woodward, New York: Harper and Brothers, 1872.

BIBLIOGRAPHY (Continued)

Reynolds, P.K. Baillie. "The Troops Quartered in the Castra Peregrinorum," *The Journal of Roman Studies*, Vol. 13 (1923).

Rice, Edward. *Captain Sir Richard Francis Burton: The Secret Agent Who Made the Pilgrimage to Mecca, Discovered the Kamasutra, and Brought the Arabian Nights to the West*, New York: Charles Scribner's Sons, 1990.

Richards, Thomas. *The Imperial Archive: Knowledge and the Fantasy of Empire*, London and New York: Verso, 1993.

Rives, J. "Human Sacrifice among Pagans and Christians," *The Journal of Roman Studies*, Vol. 85 (1995).

Roberts, Fred. *Letters Written During the Indian Mutiny*, New Delhi: Lal Publishers, 1979.

Rodriguez, Ileana, ed. *The Latin American Subaltern Studies Reader*, Durham and London: Duke University, 2001.

Rose, Jacqueline. *States of Fantasy*, New York: Oxford University Press, 1996.

Ross, Kristin. *The Emergence of Social Space: Rimbaud and the Paris Commune*, Minneapolis: University of Minnesota, 1988.

Roy, Parama. *Indian Traffic*, Berkely: University of California, 1998.

Rudich, Vasily. *Dissidence and Literature Under Nero: The Price of Rhetoricization*, London and New York, Routledge, 1997.

Russell, Ralph and Kurshidal Islam. *The Oxford India Ghalib: Life, Letters and Ghazals*, New Delhi: Oxford University, 2003.

Rutherford, Ian. "The Genealogy of the Boukoloi: How Greek Literature Appropriated an Egyptian Narrative-Motif," *The Journal of Hellenic Studies*, Vol. 120 (2000).

Sadler, Simon. *The Situationist City,* Cambridge: MIT, 1998.

Said, Edward. *Orientalism*, New York: Vintage, 1979.

Salway, Benet. "Sea and River Travel in Roman Itinerary Literature," *Space in the Roman World: Its Perception and Presentation*, eds. Richard Talbert and Kai Brodersen, Munster: Lit Verlag, 2004.

Scheuer, Michael. *Imperial Hubris: Why the West is Losing the War on Terror*, Washington, D.C.: Brassey's, 2004.

Schmidt, Alex and **Albert Jongman** et al. *Political Terrorism*, Amsterdam: Transaction Books, 1988.

Scholberg, Henry. *The Indian Literature of the Great Rebellion*, New Delhi: Promilla and Co., 1993.

Selden, Daniel. "*The Genre of Genre*," *The Search for the Ancient Novel*, ed. James Tatum, Baltimore: Johns Hopkins, 1994.

Sen, Sudpita. *Distant Sovereignty: National Imperialism and the Origins of British India*, New York and London: Routledge, 2002.

Shah, Idries. *The Pleasantries of the Incredible Mulla Nasrudin*, New York: E.P. Dutton, 1971.

Shah, Idries. *The Way of the Sufi*, New York: E.P. Dutton, 1970.

Shapiro, Michael. Violent Cartographies: *Mapping Cultures of War, Minneapolis and London*: University of Minnesota Press, 1997.

Shaw, Brent. "Bandits in the Roman Empire," *Past and Present*, No. 105 (Nov 1984).

Shaw, Stanford. "The Dynamics of Traditional Ottoman Society and Administration," *Ottoman Bureaucracy: Two Papers*, Bloomington, IN : Comparative Administrative Group, American Society for Public Administration, 1967.

_____. *History of the Ottoman Empire and Modern Turkey, Volume I: Empire of the Gazis: The Rise and Decline of the Ottoman Empire, 1280-1808*, Cambridge, London and New York: Cambridge, 1976.

Sheldon, Rose Mary. *Intelligence Activities in Ancient Rome: Trust in the Gods, but Verify*, New York: Frank Cass, 2005.

BIBLIOGRAPHY (Continued)

Sheridan, Greg. "A friendship to offer lasting dividends," *Sunday Telegraph* (Australia), 30 July 2006; "U.S., Britain in intelligence, defence deal," Indo-Asian News Service, 27 May 2006

Shinder, Joel. "Early Ototman Administration in the Wilderness: Some Limits on Comparison," *International Journal of Middle East Studies*, Vol. 9, No. 4 (Nov 1978).

Siegal, Jennifer. "Training Thieves: The Instruction of 'Efficient Intelligence Officers' in Pre-1914 Britain," *Intelligence and Statecraft: The Use and Limits of Intelligence in International Society*, eds. Peter Jackson and Jennifer Siegal, Westport, CT and London: Praeger, 2005.

Simonton, Dean. *Origins of Genius: Darwinian Perspectives on Creativity*, New York: Oxford University, 1999.

Singha, Radhika. "'Providential' Circumstances: The Thuggee Campaign of the 1830s and Legal Innovation," *Modern Asian Studies*, Vol. 27, No. 1 (Feb, 1993).

Sinnigen, William G. "Two Branches of the Late Roman Secret Service," *The American Journal of Philology*, Vol. 80, No. 3 (1959).

Sleeman, William. *Sleeman in Oudh: An Abridgement of W.H. Sleeman's A Journey Through the Kingdom of Oude in 1849-50*, ed. P.D. Reeves, Cambridge: Cambridge University, 1971.

Spear, Percival. "Bentinck and Education," *Cambridge Historical Journal*, Vol. 6, No. 1 (1938).

Spivak, Gayatri Chakravorty. *A Critique of Postcolonial Reason: Toward a Vanishing History of the Present*, Cambridge: Harvard, 1999.

_____. *Death of a Discipline*, New York: Columbia, 2003.

Staley, David. "A History of the Future," *History and Theory,* Theme Issue 42 (Dec 2002).

Stierlin, Henri. *The Roman Empire*, Koln and New York: Taschen, 1996.

Strabo. *Geography*, Vol. VIII, Loeb Classical Library, trans. Horace Leonard Jones, Cambridge: Harvard, 1932.

Sylvester, Christine. *Feminist International Relations: An Unfinished Journey*, Cambridge and New York: Cambridge University, 2002.

Tacitus. *The Annals and the Histories*, Modern Library Edition, trans. Alfred Church and William Brodribb, New York: Random House, 2003

Taylor, Meadows. *Confessions of a Thug*, New Delhi and Madras: Asian Educational Services, 1988 (First printed 1839).

_____. *The Story of My Life*, New Delhi: Asian Educational Service, 1986 (First published 1882).

Thomas, Troy. *Beneath the Surface: Intelligence Preparation of the Battlespace for Counterterrorism*, Washington, D.C.: Joint Military Intelligence College, 2004.

Thomson, Janice. *Mercenaries, Pirates, and Sovereigns*, Princeton: Princeton University, 1994.

Thornton, William. *New World Empire: Civil Islam, Terrorism and the Making of Neoglobalism*, New York and Oxford: Rowman and Littlefield, 2005.

Tschumi, Bernard. *Architecture and Disjunction*, Cambridge: MIT, 1996.

Tuan, Yi-Fu. *Topophilia: A Study of Environmental Perceptions, Attitudes and Values*, New York: Columbia, 1974.

Tufte, Edward. *The Cognitive Style of Power Point: Pitching Out Corrupts Within*, Cheshire, CT: Graphics Press, 2006

_____. *Envisioning Information*, Cheshire, CT: Graphics Press, 1990.

Turner, Scott. "Global Civil Society, Anarchy and Governance: assessing an emerging paradigm," *Journal of Peace Research*, Vol. 35, No. 1 (Jan 1998).

U.S. Army Field Manual 3-24, Counterinsurgency, Washington, D.C.: Headquarters, Department of the Army, 15 December 2006.

van Woerkens, Martine. *The Strangled Traveler: Colonial Imaginings and the Thugs of India*, trans. Catherine Tihanyi, Chicago: University of Chicago, 1995.

BIBLIOGRAPHY (Continued)

Velleius Paterculus, Roman History, Loeb Classical Library, trans. Frederick W. Shipley, Cambridge: Harvard, 1924, II:126:249.

Verma, Nirmal. "India and Europe: The Self and the Other," *Perceiving India: Insight and Inquiry*, ed. Geeti Sen, New Delhi, Newbury Park and London: Sage, 1993.

Verne, Jules. *Around the World in 80 Days*, trans. Michael Glencross, London: Penguin, 2004.

Virgil, *The Works of P. Virgilius Maro*, trans. Levi Hart and V.R. Osborn, New York: David McKay Company, 1952.

Virilio, Paul. *The Information Bomb*, trans. Chris Turner, London and New York: Verso, 2000.

_____. *A Landscape of Events*, trans. Julie Rose, Cambridge: MIT, 2000.

_____ and Sylvere Lotringer, *Pure War*, trans. Mark Polizzotti, New York: Semiotext(e), 1997.

Wagner, Kim. "The Deconstructed Stranglers: A Reassessment of Thuggee," *Modern Asian Studies*, Vol. 38, No. 4 (Oct, 2004).

Waltz, Kenneth. *Theory of International Politics*, Reading, MA: Addison-Wesley, 1979.

Watson, Alan. *Roman Law and Comparative Law*, Athens and London: University of Georgia, 1991.

Watson, Paul. "Democracy in the Balance," *Los Angeles Times*, 18 December 2006.

Weber, Max. *From Max Weber: Essays in Sociology*, eds. and trans. H.H. Gerth and C. Wright Mills, New York: Oxford University, 1946.

Webster, Graham. *Boudica: The British Revolt Against Rome* AD 60, Totowa, NJ: Rowman and Littlefield, 1978.

Westamacott Papers, Oriental and India Office Collections, Eur. MSS. C39.

BIBLIOGRAPHY (Continued)

Wheeler, John Archibald. *At Home in the Universe*, Woodbury, NY: American Institute of Physics, 1994.

White, Hayden. *The Content of the Form*, Baltimore and London: Johns Hopkins, 1987.

Widmer, Kingsley. "The Intellectual as Soldier," *T.E. Lawrence: Soldier, Writer, Legend—New Essays*, ed. Jeffrey Meyers, London: Macmillan, 1989.

Winichakul, Thongchai, *Siam Mapped: A History of the Geo-Body of a Nation, Honolulu:* University of Hawaii Press, 1994.

Winkler, Jack. "Lollianos and the Desperadoes," *The Journal of Hellenic Studies,* Vol. 100 (1980).

Winter, Michael. *Society and Religion in Early Modern Egypt: Studies in the Writing of 'Abd al-Wahhab al-Sha'rani*, New Brunswick and London: Transaction Books, 1982.

Wolf, Eric. *Europe and the People Without History*, Berkeley and Los Angeles: University of California, 1982.

Wolper, Ethel Sara. *Cities and Saints: Sufism and the Transformation of Urban Space in Medieval Anatolia*, University Park, PA: Pennsylvania State University, 2003.

Young, Paul. *The Nature of Information*, New York and London: Praeger, 1987.

Zilfi, Madeline C. "*The Kadizadelis: Discordant Revivalism in Seventeenth Century Istanbul*," Journal of Near Eastern Studies, Vol. 45, No. 4 (Oct 1986).

INDEX

A

Achilles Tatius 154,161
Afghanistan 2, 18, 20, 45, 56, 109, 111, 119, 123, 124, 129, 130, 142, 166
Agentes in Rebus 176
Appadurai, Arjun 17, 21
Archaeological Survey of India 107
Architecture 6, 10, 14, 31, 35, 37, 63, 66, 69, 75, 92, 94, 100, 193
Ayodhya 108

B

Babri Masjid 108
Bacon, Francis 4
Bagaudae 50
Banditry 50, 52
Barzakh 61, 64
Bellum Iustum 51
Bektashi 66
Bentham, Jeremy 6, 7
Borges, Jorge Luis 4, 24, 192
Boudica 173, 174, 175, 178, 179
Boukoloi 153, 154, 158, 166
Britannia 99, 108
Burnes, Alexander 130, 131
Burton, Richard 105, 127, 128, 129, 131, 196

C

Cairo 63, 147
Cassius Dio 50, 51, 111, 153, 154, 156, 159, 164, 174, 178, 179, 180
Catus Decianus 174, 177
China 142, 186, 188
Cohn, Bernard 8, 11
Conrad, Joseph 9
Cawnpore 120, 122
Chrono-politics 103, 107, 108, 111
Cunningham, Alexander 107

D

Debord, Guy 149, 151
Defter 77, 78, 79, 145, 148
Deleuze, Gilles 21, 33, 75, 84, 85, 98, 184
Delhi 6, 28, 30, 31, 34, 94, 107, 108, 113, 114, 117, 118, 120, 121, 131, 133
Derive 145, 148, 149

INDEX (Continued)

INDEX (Continued)

O

Octavian 51
OODA Loop 111
Orientalism 3, 105, 106, 126, 127
Osmanli 11
Oude 116

P

Panopticon 6, 7, 8, 9, 49, 68, 159
Peirce, Leslie 40, 56
Persistent Surveillance 8, 93
Pirates 33, 51, 52, 99
Pontius Pilate 47
Postmodernism 148, 156
PowerPoint 8, 76, 119, 162, 171
Psychogeography 148
Pynchon, Thomas 156

R

Rhizome 73, 74, 75, 79, 82, 83, 99
Rome 2, 12, 44, 47, 49, 54, 55, 56, 58, 59, 61, 66, 75, 82, 138, 139, 143, 161, 166, 173, 176, 178, 183

S

Said, Edward 3, 105, 106, 126
Scheuer, Michael 18
Schizophrenia 21, 22, 31, 75, 82, 99, 155
Sepoy Revolt 113
Seutonius Paulinus 176
Seyahatname 87, 147, 149
Shari'a 40, 41, 43, 44, 81, 169
Situationist 145, 148, 149, 150, 151
Speculatores 58
Sub-altern 8, 9, 144, 160, 186
Sleeman, William 29, 30, 31, 32, 33, 34, 116, 192
Spivak, Gayotri 22, 26, 102, 163
Star Wars 197
Sufi 64, 65, 66, 67, 68, 69, 81, 88, 146, 147, 151, 188, 192

INDEX (Continued)

ABOUT THE AUTHOR

Patrick Kelley is a U.S. Army Foreign Area Officer specializing in South Asia, a career path particularly suited to encouraging a distinctive interweaving of academic, intelligence and military issues. His academic background includes Masters' degrees in South Asian studies from the University of Michigan and in Security Studies from the University of Madras, as well as a year of study at the Defense Services Staff College in Tamil Nadu, India. Exploring unexpected connections has been a recurrent theme in his work, with one master's thesis on the relationship between archaeology and security affairs; and another on the application of ancient Indian political philosophy to modern South Asian international affairs—the latter becoming the first paper by an American student in fifty years to earn the *Lentaigne* award at the Indian Staff College. Kelley has served in a number of intelligence-related positions at the U.S. Pacific Command's Joint Intelligence Operations Center, punctuated by a tour as the senior strategic analyst at the Combined Forces Command—Afghanistan headquarters in Kabul. Following completion of the research fellowship which produced this book, he was assigned as the Chief, Office of Defense Cooperation, at the U.S. Embassy in Kathmandu, Nepal.

He can be contacted at: *patrick.arthur.kelley@us.army.mil.*

www.ingramcontent.com/pod-product-compliance
Lightning Source LLC
Chambersburg PA
CBHW081549280526
45788CB00011B/3418